Data-Driven DEI

Data-Driven DEI

The Tools and Metrics You Need
to Measure, Analyze, and Improve
Diversity, Equity, and Inclusion

DR. RANDAL PINKETT

WILEY

Published by John Wiley & Sons, Inc., Hoboken, New Jersey.
Published simultaneously in Canada.

For general information on our other products and services or for technical support, please contact our Customer Care Department within the United States at (800) 762-2974, outside the United States at (317) 572-3993 or fax (317) 572-4002.

Wiley publishes in a variety of print and electronic formats and by print-on-demand. Some material included with standard print versions of this book may not be included in e-books or in print-on-demand. If this book refers to media such as a CD or DVD that is not included in the version you purchased, you may download this material at **http://booksupport.wiley.com**. For more information about Wiley products, visit **www.wiley.com**.

Library of Congress Cataloging-in-Publication Data:

Names: Pinkett, Randal, author.
Title: Data-driven DEI : the tools and metrics you need to measure, analyze, and improve diversity, equity, and inclusion / Dr. Randal Pinkett.
Other titles: Data-driven diversity equity and inclusion
Description: First edition. | Hoboken, NJ : Wiley, [2023] | Includes index.
Identifiers: LCCN 2022053754 (print) | LCCN 2022053755 (ebook) | ISBN 9781119856870 (cloth) | ISBN 9781119856931 (adobe pdf) | ISBN 9781119856924 (epub)
Subjects: LCSH: Diversity in the workplace--Technological innovations. | Multiculturalism.
Classification: LCC HF5549.5.M5 P57 2023 (print) | LCC HF5549.5.M5 (ebook) | DDC 658.3008--dc23/eng/20221109
LC record available at https://lccn.loc.gov/2022053754
LC ebook record available at https://lccn.loc.gov/2022053755

COVER ART: © ZHENGSHUN TANG/GETTY IMAGES
COVER DESIGN: PAUL McCARTHY

SKY10041672_012023

To the entire BCT Family—past and present—without whom this book would not have been possible, and especially to my brother and business partner—colleague and college classmate:

Lawrence Hibbert

Data-Driven DEI is a direct result of the mission and vision we set out to accomplish when we began our social entrepreneurship journey more than three decades ago centered on the African philosophy of Ubuntu:

I am because we are!

Contents

Acknowledgments

*D*ata-Driven DEI has leveraged the contributions of countless individuals and organizations. First and foremost, I would like to sincerely thank all my colleagues at BCT Partners, including the executive leadership team, leadership team, DEI community of practice, and various lines of business that reflect our leading expertise in diversity, equity, inclusion, research, evaluation, analytics, learning, and beyond. Our mission at BCT Partners, to harness the power of diversity, insights, and innovation to transform lives, accelerate equity, and create lasting change, and our pioneering work that spans the globe in service to this mission, undergird everything captured within this book.

At BCT, I am enormously grateful to Lawrence Hibbert, president, for our partnership and his leadership; Peter York, principal and chief data scientist, for his input, reviews, and feedback; Damita Byrd, senior director of DEI, David Hunt, senior director of health equity, and Riikka Salonen, managing director of health equity, for their advice and assistance; Jaan Bernberg, for leading the development of the scorecards, dashboards, and mobile app mockups; Stacey Gatlin and Stephanie Snider, for helping coordinate the numerous moving parts; and Kate Jordan, Patricia Neuray, Tanisha Washington, Freida Hughes, and Amira Pinkett, for their support of the website. I would like to thank my colleagues at our joint venture partner, N-Touch Strategies, including Natasha Williams and Dr. Jenae Harrington, for their contributions to the research and development. I would also like to thank BCT's clients, who have been essential and instrumental to the growth of our data-driven DEI work and more, expressly Milton Anderson, managing partner at Korn Ferry and former executive vice president and chief administrative officer at RWJBarnabas Health; Leah Wallace, former senior vice president of workforce development and DEI at Citigroup; and Dennis Pullin, president and chief executive officer and Rhonda Jordan, executive vice president and chief human resources officer, at Virtua Health.

I am especially thankful to my mentors, Vincent R. Brown and Dr. Janet B. Reid, and our colleagues Patricia Melford, LaToya Everett, Pamela Ramsey, Angie Dodge, and Lena Ryals at VRBC and BRBS World; Steve Mahaley at Red Fern and Allison Mahaley at Red Fern and The Dialogue Company; Dr. Amanda Felkey at Lake Forest College; Ann Herrmann-Nedhi, Karim Nehdi, JT Thompkins, and Anne Griswold at Herrmann International; Julie O'Mara, Alan Richter, and Nene Molefi, authors of the Global Diversity, Equity & Inclusion Benchmarks (GDEIB), and Sudeep Mohandas at the Centre for Global Inclusion; Edward Boon at Promote International; Larry Mohl at Rali; Emily Aiken at IDI LLC; Lamont Robinson at RLC Diversity; Richard A. Kreuger and Mary Anne Casey at the University of Minnesota; Dr. Michael McAfee, Josh Kirschenbaum, Michael Hassid, and Jennifer Tran at PolicyLink; Gamiel Yafai at Diversity Marketplace; Jane Wesman and Andrea Stein at Jane Wesman Public Relations; and Sheilisa McNeal-Burgess.

Thank you also to the entire literary team at Wiley, including Richard Narramore, Deborah Schindlar, Dawn Kilgore, Michelle Hacker, Jeanenne Ray, Jozette Moses, Michelle Hacker, Gayathri Ganesan, Philo Antonie Mahendran, Jessica Filippo, and Kate Wimpsett. I am eternally indebted to Mike Campbell, former acquisitions editor at Wiley, for not only being the catalyst for this book but also for being a tremendous thought partner, prompting me to think deeply and critically about the book's framing, and helping strengthen its content by challenging my ideas in very positive and powerful ways. This acknowledgment is a minor gesture compared to your major role in bringing this book to fruition.

Last, but certainly not least, to the extent this book was a formidable undertaking, I am deeply appreciative of my entire family and village of friends, including my loving wife, Natasha, children, Amira, Jaz, Marquis, and Aniyah, and above all, God, with whom *all things* are possible, for the strength, the space, the stamina, and the support to see it to completion.

—Dr. Randal Pinkett
www.randalpinkett.com
www.bctpartners.com
www.datadrivendei.com

Introduction

DEI is a journey, not a destination.

DEI can be measured and managed.

When I first met Steve, he and his organization were in a very difficult situation. Steve had been long criticized for his lack of leadership, particularly with women and people of color, while he maintained that his management style was an effective one. His team was dysfunctional and lacked cohesion and trust. Moreover, while Steve's team bore some diversity, he was a member of the organization's senior leadership team, which bore little to no diversity. In stark comparison, their employee base and the communities surrounding their office locations reflected the full range of societal diversity. Like many organizations, while they had good intentions to improve diversity, equity, and inclusion (DEI), their efforts had largely failed due to a lack of acknowledgment and agreement about the issues they were facing, and the impact was severe. Employee engagement was low. They were losing people of color, particularly in middle management. They were under significant pressure from employees to diversify their senior ranks and create a more inclusive culture. Steve knew that he and his organization desperately needed help, and he lobbied to hire my firm, BCT Partners, to help his organization improve their DEI.

After engaging in several conversations with leaders about their mission and vision for DEI, our next step was to conduct several assessments: an implicit bias and cultural competence assessment for all leaders and managers, and a culture and climate assessment for the entire organization, including a survey, interviews, and focus groups. I vividly recall two pivotal moments in the early stages of this engagement.

The first pivotal moment was with Steve in a one-on-one coaching session where we discussed his implicit bias and cultural competence assessment results. He was stunned. Not only did the data clearly affirm his blind spots, particularly on matters relating to race/ethnicity and gender, but also his inability to navigate differences. *The data catalyzed a personal epiphany.* Thereafter, Steve was motivated to do the personal work of DEI, which is often the most challenging yet impactful, by undertaking a journey of personal learning, development, and growth. Today, he is seen as a more competent, credible, and capable colleague in the eyes of his peers (and a better person in the eyes of his friends and family) and has the tools, data, and metrics to know he is making progress.

The second pivotal moment was when my colleagues at BCT presented the results of the culture and climate assessment to the organization's senior leadership team. I could feel the tension in the room. We knew there was resistance to DEI in the senior ranks and, as a result, the assessment experienced significant delays. In fact, one of the reasons we administered the implicit bias and cultural competence assessments for leaders and managers was to meet people like Steve where they were in their DEI journey while opening a candid dialogue about their commitment to DEI (or lack thereof). This was a very data-driven organization that prided itself on science, evidence, and facts. They grilled our data science team about their sampling techniques and statistical analyses. They challenged them on their assessment methods and analytical models. They prompted them to probe deeper into their facts and their findings. By the time the tense meeting was over, the senior leadership team was convinced that they had issues, and they committed to undergoing change. *The data catalyzed an organizational commitment.* They were invigorated to do the organizational work of DEI, which they acknowledged would be a marathon not a sprint. We proceeded to work with them to develop and execute a DEI strategic plan that led to several DEI initiatives along with the key performance indicators (KPIs) to gauge progress, measure results, and demonstrate impact. Today, they have proudly been recognized as one of the top companies for their corporate diversity practices and among the top employers for women, people of color, veterans, working families, and members of the LGBTQIA+ community.

My experience with Steve and his organization speak to a very valuable lesson: *data matters to DEI.*

To be clear, data is not the end-all and be-all to DEI. It is not a panacea, nor do I intend to frame it in this way. The point of this book is that data, while not the entire DEI puzzle, is a very important piece.

W. Edwards Deming is frequently and incorrectly quoted with the famous phrase "If you can't measure it, you can't manage it." Ironically, Deming's full quote is, *"It is wrong to suppose that* if you can't measure it, you can't manage it." According to the W. Edwards Deming Institute, "Dr. Deming did very much believe in the value of using data to help improve the management of the organization. But he also knew that just measuring things and looking at data wasn't close to enough. There are many things that cannot be measured and still must be managed."[1] Fortunately, DEI is not one of those things, as you can measure it and manage it. There are several factors that contribute to a successful personal and organizational DEI journey, and data is one of them.

I liken data to the instrument panel on a plane. Long before there were instrument panels, people were able to fly planes. It was significantly harder without the instrument panel. Instrument panels have made the journey more efficient and effective at every step along the way. Similarly, improving DEI can be achieved without data, but it is significantly harder. Data makes the journey more efficient and effective at every step along the way.

It is also important to acknowledge that data has its own shortcomings and imperfections. It is not neutral. At different points throughout this book, I address the topics of "data bias" and "algorithmic bias"—those are how data carries and inherits its own assumptions and biases, as a reflection of human assumptions and biases. I will help you to recognize different kinds of data and algorithmic biases, and how to mitigate them leading to deeper understanding and greater impartiality along your *Data-Driven DEI* journey.

Societal Trends and DEI

Three societal trends speak to the growing importance of DEI:

1. **Diversity of People:** Diversity is growing across our globe including with respect to race and ethnicity. It is predicted that the world's middle-class population will

see a major influx from Asia, Latin America, and Africa by 2030, increasing the population to 4.9 billion, up from 1.8 billion in 2009.[2] This translates into growing diversity of talent, customers, and stakeholders as well.

2. **Diversity of Cultures:** Because of increased migration, there is a growing diversity of religion and language. The percentage of the U.S. population speaking a language other than English at home was 21% in 2013, a slight increase over 2010.[3] Moreover, the global population is estimated to grow by 32% by the year 2060 with Muslims expected to have grown by 70%, making it the fastest-growing religious group. The Pew Research Center estimates that in the second half of the twenty-first century, the number of Muslims will have surpassed the number of Christians.[4]

3. **Diversity of Thought:** Organizations increasingly recognize the value of diverse thinking and cognitive diversity as drivers for generating good ideas, building effective teams, mitigating blind spots, and fostering innovation. According to a study by the Boston Consulting Group, a 2014 survey of 1,500 executives, "breakthrough" innovators and leaders "cast a wide net for ideas."[5] The 2021 Readiness Gap survey of 1,500 companies showed that 75% of the companies considered innovation a top-three priority. This is an increase of 10 percentage points from 2020.[6] "In the race for new ideas, diversity of thinking is gaining prominence as a strategy to protect against groupthink and generate breakthrough insights," says Deloitte.[7]

This growing diversity will only continue to increase as time progresses. It undeniably makes our world a more beautiful place as we all benefit from experiencing different people, cultures, and ways of thinking. However, greater diversity can also lead to greater challenges and especially when our differences are not harnessed or managed productively. This reality is reflected throughout our global community.

Sadly, as our communities, schools, organizations, and society are becoming more diverse, certain segments of our society are becoming less civil, noticeably divided, and more exclusionary. Our society is increasingly comprised of what Turkish novelist, activist, and academic Elif Shafak calls "communities of the like-minded" who share the same values, beliefs, race/ethnicity, religion, socioeconomic status, political affiliation, and other identifiers. So many of us tend to surround ourselves and associate with people who are like us. To be clear, there is nothing wrong with being around people like you. This is a natural human phenomenon known by sociologists as homophily or an affinity bias. The challenge is that if we tend to be around people like us, we can become more prone to produce stereotypes and assumptions about those who are not like us, casting projections onto those outside of the communities of the like-minded to which we belong. The irony is that as our globe continues to experience increased diversity of people, cultures, and thought, we all seem to be driving deeper into our communities of the like-minded. This not only undermines the benefits of society's greatest asset—our cultural differences—but also further exacerbates society's greatest liability—our cultural ignorance. DEI represents a unique and unparalleled opportunity to break down the walls that can separate us in our personal lives, within our organizations, and throughout our society.

The Organizational Case for DEI

Arguments for the value of DEI to organizations have been made very clear. Some refer to this as "the business case" or "the organizational case" for DEI. The benefits from an organizational perspective are myriad and have to do with:

- *Winning the competition for talent.* Organizations that have a strong commitment to DEI are better positioned to recruit and retain skilled workers in today's marketplace.[8]
- *Strengthening customer orientation.* "[Customers] pay attention to how companies are speaking to them. As they spend more, they want more for themselves and from the brands they support," says Cheryl Grace, Nielsen's senior vice president of Community Alliances and Consumer Engagement and co-creator of Nielsen's 2019 Diverse Intelligence Series (DIS) Report.[9]
- *Increasing employee trust, retention, engagement, satisfaction, and performance.* There is strong evidence that diverse teams increase employee satisfaction and reduce conflicts between groups, improving collaboration and loyalty.[10,11,12]
- *Improving decision making and fostering innovation.* Research shows that while diverse teams take longer to achieve cohesiveness and make decisions, they make better decisions up to 87% of the time, as reported in *Forbes*, and "Diversity fosters innovation and creativity through a greater variety of problem-solving approaches, perspectives, and ideas."[13,14]
- *Enhancing the organization's image.* Incorporating a strong DEI agenda will improve your organization's image to employees as well as customers.[15,16]
- *Improving the financial bottom line.* Several studies by McKinsey have found that corporations that embrace gender and ethnic diversity on their leadership teams outperform their competition financially by as much as 25% and 36%, respectively.[17,18]

The Personal Case for DEI

By comparison to the organizational value for DEI, arguments pertaining to the personal case for DEI have not been as prominent or widely recognized. Moreover, at the end of the day, organizations do not change; people change. Or in the words of the Nigerian author, activist, and presenter of the TED Talk "The Danger of a Single Story," Chimamanda Ngozi Adichie, "Culture does not make people. People make culture."[19] In order for any organization to experience transformation, its people will have to undergo their own transformation. This explains why this book is centered first and foremost on you. When you change for the better, it benefits you, and the added benefit is that it also changes your organization for the better.

On a personal level, DEI can lead to a number of personal and professional benefits:

- *Enhanced personal growth.* A "growth mindset" believes you can always grow your skills and abilities through effort, application, and experience. Diverse relationships with people from different backgrounds and perspectives positively challenge you to move beyond your comfort zone into your growth zone and become a better person today than yesterday. They also lead to a richer human experience by exploring diverse cultures including music, art, food, religion, language, clothing, history, and more. If experience is the best teacher, diversity creates the best classroom!

- *Greater diversity of thought (cognitive diversity).* DEI enables you to tap into the diverse thinking of others to make better decisions, generate better ideas, improve problem solving, and foster greater innovation. "It's making sure you have little risk of being blindsided by something that a diverse team would have known about and would have identified as an opportunity or a risk. I think it brings far greater confidence to the decision making when you know you are being supported by people who have far more diverse points of view," says François Hudon of the Bank of Montreal.[20]

- *Improved health and wellness.* Research has found that "maintaining diverse relationships is just as important, if not more, than having a large number of relationships" and that "individuals with more diverse relationships had a lower risk of mortality and experienced less cognitive and physical decline."[21] This is a compelling personal argument alone.

- *Enriched learning and performance at school and work.* According to research at Princeton University, "Diversity of all kinds is generally associated with positive learning and performance outcomes. Not only do experiences with diversity improve one's cognitive skills and performance, it also improves attitudes about one's own intellectual self-confidence, attitudes toward the college experience, and shapes performance in the workplace."[22]

- *Mitigate biases and negative stereotypes.* The same Princeton study also found that "exposure to diversity can ameliorate negative stereotypes and biases people may have about people from different backgrounds and perspectives. In addition, increasing diversity in high-power positions can buffer underrepresented and stigmatized groups by providing in-group members as understanding and supportive role models."

- *Expanded network of relationships.* Researchers at Ohio State University and the University of Akron found that "workers with more diverse personal relationships were, not surprisingly, better at building a racially diverse network on the job. These individuals utilized this broader network to pursue extra tasks beyond their basic responsibilities and appeared to be more trusting of their supervisors. . . ."[23]

- *Increased range of opportunities.* "Diverse work teams are known to be better at assessing risks and gathering accurate facts, and companies with greater diversity in their leadership report higher innovation rates. It's a no-brainer that having a larger and more diverse professional network will lead to higher-performing teams and present a wider spectrum of opportunities, but if it all starts with increasing the diversity of your personal relationships this has to happen on your own time."[24]

- *More positive evaluations, earlier promotions, and higher compensation.* Research has found that individuals with relationships that are rich with opportunities to connect people that would otherwise be disconnected, "receive more positive evaluations, earlier promotions, and higher compensation."[25,26]
- *Expanded civic engagement and positive outcomes for others.* Lastly, the Princeton study, entitled, "Do Differences Make a Difference?" also found that, "increased exposure to diversity is positively associated with civic engagement" and that "individuals are more likely to perform activities and services in order to improve outcomes for others, and in doing so, they are making a difference in their homes, neighborhoods, workplaces, churches, and communities."

These are compelling arguments for DEI both personally and professionally. This suggests that while you do not have to have the most diverse, equitable, and inclusive relationships, you can significantly benefit from having diversity, equity, and inclusivity in your relationships. It also suggests that while you do not have to understand all cultures, you can significantly benefit from seeking understanding of different cultures. It all starts with improving your DEI, and that has to be something for which you are willing to commit time. *Data-Driven DEI* offers the blueprint.

What Is DEI?

Diversity is simply defined as the range of human differences. It is a fact, an attribute. Diversity is about representation. The inaugural work within the field was focused on the "D"—increasing diverse relationships and representation of people within organizations at all levels.

Very quickly it became clear that diversity alone was necessary but not sufficient to improve outcomes, and "D&I" arrived on the scene, adding inclusion to the paradigm. Inclusion is simply defined as involvement and empowerment. It is an action. As stated by Korn Ferry's Global Diversity and Inclusion Strategist Andrés Tapia, "Diversity is the mix, and inclusion is making the mix work." Similarly, I think of diversity as a fancy car, and inclusion as the car's engine. Just like the fancy car looks good, so does diversity. And just like the fancy car will get you nowhere without the engine, diversity will get you nowhere without inclusion. In fact, the importance of inclusion to improving outcomes became so widely acknowledged and understood that "I&D" began to take hold as an acronym of choice.

More recently, equity has not only entered the picture but also gained prominence. Equity is simply defined as fairness and equality in outcomes. It is a choice. Equity is also distinguished in its ability to play out very differently once it is applied to a specific industry, sector, or field. For example, the pursuit of health equity can be very different from the pursuit of equity in housing, education, financial services, or philanthropy. The field has generally and widely become recognized as "DEI" or "DE&I" or, more progressively, as "EDI," "ED&I," "EID," and "EI&D," to reflect the paramount importance of equity and inclusion more prominently to this work.

Two related terms have also emerged—justice and accessibility. Justice is defined as "dismantling barriers to resources and opportunities in society so that all individuals and communities can live a full and dignified life."[27] These barriers are essentially the "isms" in society: racism, classism, sexism, ageism, and so on. Justice, as well as the acronym "JEDI," has gained traction particularly among community, philanthropic, and civic organizations. Accessibility is defined as "the design, construction, development, and maintenance of facilities, information and communication technology, programs, and services so that all people, including people with disabilities, can fully and independently use them."[28] Accessibility has gained traction in various circles, thus spreading the acronyms "DEIA" and "IDEA." For example, in the United States, President Biden's Executive Order 14035 calls on the federal government to become "a model for diversity, equity, inclusion, and accessibility, where all employees are treated with dignity and respect."

For purposes of this book, I use DEI as a placeholder to refer to the entire field. This is not to indicate the relative importance of equity, inclusion, or diversity, and it is not to ignore the aspirations of justice or accessibility. The journey of *Data-Driven DEI* outlined in this book can be equally applied to all terms referenced above.

Arguably, the ultimate result of DEI is belonging (see Figure I.1). Belonging is simply defined as "feeling valued, heard, and accepted." It is an outcome. So many of us desire to feel a part of something greater than ourselves—to belong—and DEI provides a pathway to make that feeling a reality ("DEIB" and "DEI&B").

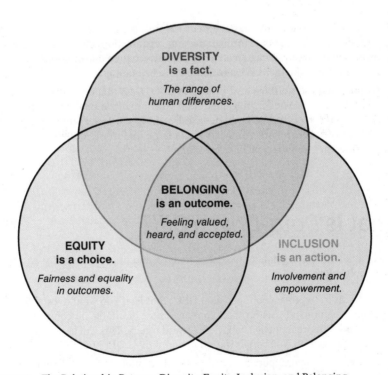

FIGURE I.1 The Relationship Between Diversity, Equity, Inclusion, and Belonging

What Is Data?

The simple definition of data is facts, figures, or information. The technical definition is a set of quantitative (information about frequency, likelihood, ratings, and more) or qualitative (contextual information and reasoning behind an answer) variables about one or more people. The types of data for DEI vary depending on personal and organizational cases.

Some personal examples are:

- **Personal preference data:** Data that characterizes your biases, temperament, personality, and behavior, and your unique style for thinking, communicating, resolving conflict, making decisions, and more. Understanding your preferences can help reveal your blind spots, foster greater self-awareness and awareness of others, and offer deeper insight into how your style can most effectively integrate with the styles of others.

- **Personal competence data:** Data that describes your knowledge, skills, attitudes, and attributes in specific areas such as cultural competence, inclusive leadership, conflict management, emotional intelligence, and beyond. Knowing your level of competence establishes a baseline upon which you can take steps to build your competence.

Some organizational examples are:

- **Personal behaviors and experiences data:** Data that captures the perceptions and perspectives of people throughout your organization. By understanding their lived experiences, you can create environments that enable everyone to be more engaged, feel more included, and sense more belonging.

- **Organizational policies and practices data:** Data that evaluates the practices and behaviors of your management and your organizational expectations, procedures, and regulations. By understanding how you fare against best practices and industry benchmarks, you can create fairer and more equitable policies and practices that lead to equal outcomes for all.

What Is *Data-Driven DEI*?

Data-Driven DEI is using data to measure, analyze, and improve diversity, equity, and inclusion. It is for you if:

- You want to improve your "personal DEI"; that is, if you want to establish more diverse relationships with others, produce more equitable outcomes for others, and exhibit more inclusive behaviors toward others. This can be independent of, or in concert with, your organization undertaking a DEI initiative.

- You are a manager, supervisor, leader, DEI champion, DEI council member, chief DEI officer, or other stakeholder who bears some responsibility for improving "organizational DEI"; that is, you want to expand your organization's diversity (representation), empower your organization's people, and increase their feelings of inclusion and belonging, strengthen your organization's culture and climate, and enhance your organization's policies and practices to be more equitable.

This book offers a data-driven approach to improving personal DEI and organizational DEI that can achieve measurable results.

A *Data-Driven DEI* initiative must meet the following five criteria:

1. Use data to perform an assessment that establishes a profile and baseline
2. Establish objectives with clearly defined goals
3. Leverage promising and proven practices based on research, science, and/or the experience of expert practitioners
4. Develop strategies with clearly defined measures
5. Use data to gauge progress, evaluate results, demonstrate impact and engender accountability

When these criteria are met, people and organizations alike can derive tremendous value from *Data-Driven DEI*:

- **Hindsight:** *Data-Driven DEI* helps you understand where you've been *(descriptive data)* and where you are *(diagnostic data)*—your "as is"—as you begin your DEI journey.
- **Foresight:** *Data-Driven DEI* illuminates what is possible for your future DEI journey—your "to be"—by identifying "what works" *(evaluative data)*: promising practices and proven practices that have produced results for others.
- **Insight:** *Data-Driven DEI* clarifies the most efficient, effective, and optimal strategies for your DEI journey. It offers recommendations *(prescriptive data)* and predictions *(predictive data)* that can inform your DEI journey and help close the gap between your current reality (your "as is") and your desired future (your "to be").
- **Oversight:** *Data-Driven DEI* enables you to establish clear objectives, goals, strategies, and measures, with metrics and key performance indicators (KPIs), to manage performance *(performance data)* and properly oversee your DEI journey.
- **Highlights:** *Data-Driven DEI* allows you to gauge progress *(outputs data)*, evaluate results *(outcomes data)*, and demonstrate impact. This captures and highlights your accomplishments, challenges, opportunities, and areas for improvement, and fosters continuous learning at every step along your DEI journey.

My Personal and Professional Passion for *Data-Driven DEI*

I have spent the past three decades as a DEI speaker, author, trainer, facilitator, strategist, and media commentator. I have worked with countless people and organizations across the globe on how to become more diverse, equitable, and inclusive. I am an

Intrinsic Inclusion™ certified facilitator, Herrmann Brain Dominance Instrument®
(HBDI®) certified practitioner, Intercultural Development Inventory® (IDI®) qualified administrator, High Performance Learning Journey® (HPLJ) champion, and an
official reference for the Global Diversity, Equity & Inclusion Benchmarks (GDEIB).
My formal education includes a BS in electrical engineering from Rutgers University
as an Academic All-America® Hall of Fame scholar-athlete, an MSc in computer science from Oxford University as a Rhodes Scholar, an MS in electrical engineering and
computer science from the Massachusetts Institute of Technology (MIT) School of
Engineering and MBA from the MIT Sloan School of Management as a participant
in the MIT Leaders for Global Operations (LGO) dual-degree program, and a PhD in
media arts and sciences from the Epistemology and Learning Group at the MIT Media
Laboratory. My doctoral dissertation focused on bridging the "digital divide" and asset-
based approaches to using technology and data for the benefit of disconnected, disadvantaged, and diverse communities. I see communities through the lens of their assets
and strengths and not their liabilities and deficiencies. My expertise therefore lies at
the intersection of DEI, technology, data, learning, and communities.

My company, BCT Partners (**www.bctpartners.com**), which I co-founded with
my Rutgers classmates including our president, Lawrence Hibbert, and Dr. Jeffrey
Robinson and Dallas Grundy, is a global, multi-disciplinary firm that delivers a full
range of research, training, consulting, technology, and data analytics services and
solutions. Our mission is to harness the power of diversity, insights, and innovation
to transform lives, accelerate equity, and create lasting change. DEI is who we are and
what we do:

- We help our clients compete in a diverse world by unlocking the power of DEI in
  the workforce, workplace, marketplace, and community.

- We are a leader in helping organizations make better decisions, improve outcomes, and amplify their impact toward a more equitable society.

- We possess a team of diverse DEI consultants, trainers, facilitators, coaches, and
  subject matter experts who offer thought leadership in areas such as unconscious
  bias, cultural humility, human resource development, change management,
  organizational development, cultural transformation, and beyond.

- We are a full-service DEI consultancy that combines best-in-class services such
  as assessment, strategy, training, coaching, facilitation, and performance management with cutting-edge research, neuroscience, behavioral science, social science, technology and data science including artificial intelligence (AI), machine
  learning (ML), natural language processing (NLP), and virtual reality (VR).

- We offer a growing suite of innovative solutions including Equitable Analytics™
  with Precision Modeling and the Equitable Impact Platform™ (EquIP™), that leverage predictive, prescriptive, and evaluative models to determine what causes a
  desired outcome for each segment of a population, equitably; *Through My Eyes*™
  VR, which is a series of immersions that foster human understanding and empathy; Intrinsic Inclusion™, which is grounded in diversity, neuroscience, and bias,
  to help individuals and teams disrupt unconscious biases and unlock improved
  decision making, communication, collaboration, innovation, and inclusivity; The
  Inclusion Habit™, a mobile-friendly behavior change platform replete with a
  library of Microcommitments that lead to specific inclusive behaviors and create

inclusive habits; and Rali, a comprehensive Change Experience Platform (CxP) built on a human-centered approach to behavior change—a comprehensive suite of communications, structured journeys, and interactive media capabilities that shape culture for initiatives that matter.

We have been recognized by *Forbes* as one of America's Best Management Consulting Firms, Ernst & Young as EY Entrepreneur of the Year, *Manage HR Magazine* as a Top 10 Firm for Diversity & Inclusion, the *Black Enterprise* BE100s list of America's largest Black-owned businesses, and the *Inc. 5000* list of the fastest-growing private companies in America. We are also a proud platinum-level sponsor of the Global Diversity, Equity & Inclusion Benchmarks (GDEIB).

What distinguishes me and BCT is how we fully integrate research, science, technology, and data to accelerate DEI. This book brings together my personal experiences and that of my colleagues at BCT to describe how you and your organization can do the same.

The Journey Ahead: The Five-Step Cycle of *Data-Driven DEI*

The five-step cycle of *Data-Driven DEI* is shown in Figure I.2. Throughout this book, I will refer very often to your "*Data-Driven DEI* journey" or, more simply, your "DEI journey." I am specifically referring to these steps of *Data-Driven DEI*. They equally apply to people and organizations with nuances that will be highlighted along the way.

This book walks you through each step according to two tracks: a personal DEI track that outlines how you can measure, analyze, and improve your DEI, and an organizational DEI track that outlines how you can help your organization to do the same. Anyone seeking personal improvements to DEI, from individual contributors to executives, can benefit from the personal DEI track. Managers, supervisors, executives, and DEI champions and leaders responsible for improving DEI for themselves and their organization can benefit from both tracks. This book is organized into the following steps, whereas each step encompasses both tracks (with the exception of Step 1, which is broken up into separate parts for each track):

- **Step 0: DEI Incentives**—The journey begins with a foundational Step 0: DEI Incentives. In this foundational step you must get honest with yourself for the personal DEI journey, and honest about your organization's true aims for its DEI journey. This step will require self-reflection and introspection to identify intrinsic factors driving your pursuit of DEI. You will ask yourself the deeper questions such as "why do I even care?" or "why should I spend my time trying to improve DEI?" You must also examine the extrinsic factors that are driving the pursuit of DEI, such as improved performance evaluations and increased compensation for people and improved employee engagement or increased profitability for organizations. Ultimately you will develop a DEI mission and vision in this step. You will only need to perform Step 0 once to embark upon a *Data-Driven DEI* journey. The next five steps represent a never-ending, continuous cycle as you grow in your DEI journey.

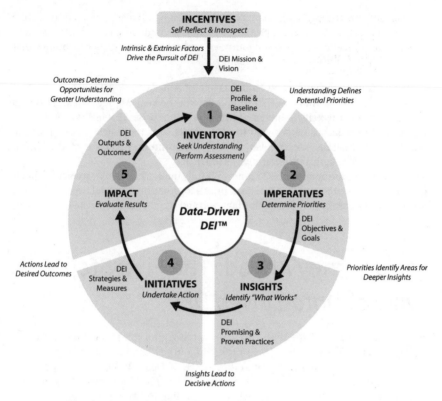

FIGURE I.2 The Five-Step Cycle of *Data-Driven DEI*™

- **Step 1: DEI Inventory for People**—In this step you will compile the data necessary to establish a profile and baseline of your personal DEI preferences and competences. You will gather diagnostic data to help clearly define your current position or your "as is."

- **Step 1: DEI Inventory for Organizations**—As a part of this step you will compile the data necessary to establish a profile and baseline of your organization's people, policies, practices, and performance ("the 4 P's"). You will gather diagnostic data to help clearly define your organization's current position or its "as is." Step 1 for people and organizations calls for deeper understanding because it will help define potential priorities.

- **Step 2: DEI Imperatives**—At this juncture, you will determine priorities that are reflected by clearly defined objectives with associated and measurable goals or metrics. The range of objectives may vary dramatically from appreciating differences personally to managing conflict organizationally and far beyond. Establishing these imperatives—or your "to be"—will identify areas for deeper insights.

- **Step 3: DEI Insights**—During this step you will identify "what works"—such as promising and proven practices based on research, science, and the experience of expert practitioners—to avoid reinventing the wheel and optimizing the journey. These insights will lead to decisive actions.

- **Step 4: DEI Initiatives**—Here you will determine which DEI strategies, that is, activities and actions, are best for you to take. You will also determine which quantifiable measures are best for you and/or your organization to gauge progress. These actions will lead to desired outcomes.

- **Step 5: DEI Impact**—Finally, you will evaluate your results including outputs to gauge progress and outcomes to measure impact. Your outcomes will determine opportunities for greater understanding. By the time you arrive at Step 5, you will have the necessary ingredients to produce a dynamic and comprehensive personal DEI strategic plan for you and/or an organizational DEI strategic plan that is driven by data, defined via measures, metrics, and key performance indicators (KPIs), and designed to meet your needs. It will be replete with objectives, goals, strategies, and measures to gauge progress, evaluate results, demonstrate impact and engender accountability. You will then rinse and repeat the five-step cycle of *Data-Driven DEI* over and over again from Step 5 back to Step 1 by reassessing your baseline and reestablishing a new profile, because DEI is a journey and not a destination.

- **Conclusion**—A vision for the future of *Data-Driven DEI*.

To assist in your DEI journey, visit **www.datadrivendei.com** to find additional information and various resources including an extensive and comprehensive list, or menu, of personal and organizational DEI measures, metrics, and key performance indicators (KPIs), promising and proven practices, and case studies, as well as downloadable templates for developing a personal DEI strategic plan, called the Crawl-Walk-Run Personal Action Plan, and an organizational DEI strategic plan.

Prepare yourself for the journey that lies ahead to move beyond your comfort zone into your growth zone. The work of DEI is not about seeking places of comfort, but rather about getting comfortable in places of discomfort. Get comfortable with being uncomfortable. Also know that discomfort and growth must coexist. You cannot have one without the other. I think of strengthening DEI like strengthening a muscle. For a muscle to get stronger, it must experience discomfort. *Data-Driven DEI* is about strengthening your DEI muscle while leveraging data to achieve faster and better outcomes. Much as data has dramatically improved how athletes improve their outcomes on the playing field, data can dramatically improve how you improve your personal and organizational outcomes in life and at work. So, if you find yourself experiencing any discomfort along your journey, I encourage you to lean into the discomfort because that means you are strengthening your DEI muscle and growing into a better person today than yesterday. I firmly believe that is time very well spent, and I trust you will agree.

STEP 0

DEI Incentives—Self-Reflect and Introspect

Get comfortable with being uncomfortable.

Organizations don't change. People change.

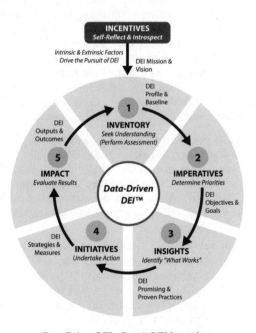

Data-Driven DEI—Step 0: DEI Incentives

Your journey begins with the foundational **Step 0: DEI Incentives**, which calls for self-reflection and introspection. The basic definition of an incentive is something that motivates or drives a person to do something or behave in a certain way. By the end of this step, you will identify the DEI incentives that motivate or drive the pursuit of DEI for you and/or your organization.

I begin this chapter by introducing a framework—dimensions of personal transformation—that sets the stage for understanding, exploring, and identifying your personal DEI incentives. This first half of the **Step 0: DEI Incentives** culminates with the development of a personal DEI mission and vision. The second half of **Step 0: DEI Incentives** expands upon the dimensions of personal transformation to introduce dimensions of organizational transformation. This similarly sets the stage to clarify your organizational DEI incentives and culminates with the development of an organizational DEI mission and vision. The reason it is important to understand these concepts at the onset of our journey is because I will reference or build upon them throughout the book.

Dimensions of Personal Transformation

The dimensions of personal transformation can help you to understand all of the things that make you . . . you. More specifically, I am referring to your personal identity, mission, vision, beliefs, values, preferences, competences and, ultimately, behaviors.

To explain the dimensions of personal transformation, I use the analogy of an iceberg in Figure 0.1. Much as an iceberg is comprised of what is visible (above the waterline), and invisible (below the water line), you are comprised of aspects that are largely visible to other people and aspects that are largely invisible to other people. Whereas 90% of an iceberg lies below the waterline, much of what makes you who you are is unseen and not directly observable. These are the internal dimensions of personal transformation, which can be found at the bottom of the figure:

- *Identity* defines who you are; it grounds you like an anchor. It is the story you tell yourself about yourself. It represents the personal characteristics you hold dearest and would not want to give up. Said differently, this dimension speaks to how you identify with respect to race, ethnicity, gender, sexual orientation, religion, marital status, parental status, physical ability, organizational classification, and more. For example, you could identify as a Latina, female, heterosexual, Christian, wife, mother, able-bodied, social worker.

- *Mission* or *purpose* defines where you're going and your reason for being; they guide you like a compass. Mission and purpose represent what you are meant to accomplish and what you are called to do with your life. For example, your purpose could be to educate students, maximize their potential, and prepare them to be responsible adults who make a positive difference in the world. Author Mark Twain once said, "The two most important days of your life are the day you were born and the day you find out why."

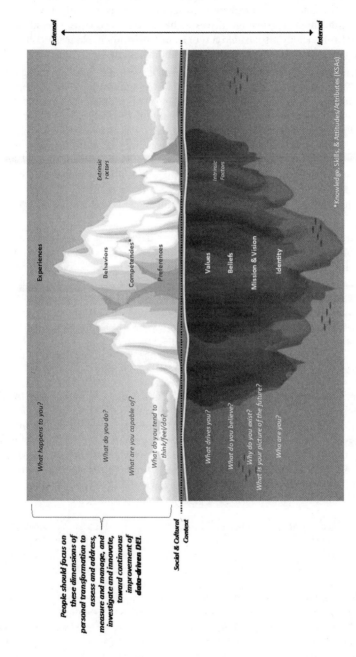

Internal

External

*Knowledge, Skills, & Attributes/Attitudes (KSAs)

Intrinsic Factors

Extrinsic Factors

Experiences

Behaviors

Competencies*

Preferences

Values

Beliefs

Mission & Vision

Identity

What happens to you?

What do you do?

What are you capable of?

What do you tend to think/feel/do?

What drives you?

What do you believe?

Why do you exist?
What is your picture of the future?

Who are you?

People should focus on these dimensions of personal transformation to assess and address, measure and manage, and investigate and innovate, toward continuous improvement of data-driven DEI.

Social & Cultural Context

FIGURE 0.1 Dimensions of Personal Transformation

- *Vision* describes where you ultimately see yourself; the picture you paint of your future. For example, you could envision yourself as a bridge builder between cultural communities that would otherwise be disconnected or you could envision yourself as a socially responsible corporate executive and inclusive servant-leader who upholds the ideals of people, planet, and prosperity.

- *Beliefs* are ideas you hold to be true. Experiences naturally generate thoughts and ideas. When we build up enough experiences in support of (or in contradiction to) a thought, those thoughts become beliefs. Two people could experience the same events that lead to the same thoughts, but it is their beliefs that can lead them to dramatically different actions and outcomes. For example, imagine that two people review the same resume of a new majority candidate in accounting. If one person believes that new majorities are as capable in accounting as any other group while the other believes that new majorities are incapable in accounting when compared to other groups, it could lead to dramatically different actions and outcomes. An example of an empowering belief is that a more diverse, equitable, and inclusive world is a better world.

- *Values* are the sum of beliefs—basic and fundamental practices about what is desirable, worthwhile, and important to you—that define what drives you. Values also define how you desire to conduct yourself while fulfilling your mission along the path to achieving your vision. For example, love, service, honesty, integrity, kindness, fairness, and equity are values. Two closely related concepts are wants and needs. *Wants* are desires, something unnecessary but desired or items that increase the quality of living. *Needs* are necessities; things that are thought to be a necessity or essential items required for life. For example, you may want to treat people more fairly at your place of employment, but you may need to perform well there to earn a living and support yourself and family.

Personal identity, mission, vision, beliefs, and values represent the internal dimensions and foundational underpinnings of personal transformation. According to evangelical leader and former head of Youth for Christ and World Vision International Dr. Ted Engstrom, "The secret of life is to know who you are [identity] and where you are going [purpose]" (I would humbly add to also know what you believe, value, want, and need). As you will see later in this step, these *personal intrinsic factors*, that are all found below the waterline, may motivate you to pursue DEI. What is found above the waterline are the external dimensions of personal transformation:

- A *preference* is something you tend to think, feel, and do; a particular tendency, trend, inclination, feeling, opinion, or predisposition toward or away from something or someone. A preference is also a bias that can lead to a blind spot. It can direct your attention to one area and cause you to completely miss or overlook something in another area. For example, imagine you have a high preference for creative thinking over logical thinking. Your natural inclination allows you to easily generate creative ideas, but it also causes you to have a blind spot for identifying the logical steps of a plan to execute the ideas. By raising awareness of your preferences, you can mitigate your blind spots. In this example, you can mitigate your blind spot for logical thinking by being more deliberately engaged during planning activities. The objective of personal transformation is therefore not to change preferences, but rather, to shift, stretch, flex, or expand into areas outside of your preferences and mitigate blind spots

- A *competence* is the ability to do something properly and successfully—a combination of practical and theoretical *knowledge* (the things you know), cognitive *skills* (the things you can do), and *attitudes/attributes* (inherent characteristics often expressed through the things you think, do, and feel) (KSAs). The objective of personal transformation is therefore to improve and increase competence. For example, if you have low intercultural competence that causes you to miss differences, judge differences, or de-emphasize differences, then you would benefit from increased intercultural competence that enables you to more deeply comprehend differences or to bridge differences.

- *Behaviors* are how you act and conduct yourself, especially toward others. Behaviors are your actions or reactions to your surrounding environment. They are an outward and observable expression of your identity, mission, vision, beliefs, values, preferences, and competences. A related concept is *personality*, which is defined as individual differences in patterns of thinking, feeling, and behaving. In other words, your personality reflects your preferences, competences, and behaviors.

As shown in Figure 0.1, your preferences and competences are learned and developed over years through your life's *experiences*, which also shape your behaviors. Moreover, there are also other *personal extrinsic factors* such as social pressure, peer pressure, compensation, bonuses, performance evaluations, awards, recognitions, and other external dynamics beyond your control that may influence how you behave, the competences you develop, and even what you prefer to think, feel, and do.

Lastly, if you look closely at Figure 0.1, you also see a dotted line right at the waterline between the internal and the external dimensions. This dotted line represents the *social and cultural context*, including relationships, norms, and standards, that can also play an important role in your personal transformation. For example, the people who are a part of your inner circle, including people in your household, such as family and loved ones, or your colleagues at your place of employment, can have a positive, negative, or neutral influence on you. If they believe a more diverse, equitable, and inclusive world is a better world, they can be encouraging and reinforcing of your DEI journey. If they do not harbor this belief, they can be discouraging and detrimental to your DEI journey. Or, they may not have any effect on your DEI journey. In this regard, the dotted line is like a permeable filter that can shape or reshape your internal and external dimensions of personal transformation.

What Are Your Personal DEI Incentives?

Personal intrinsic incentives motivate a person to do something out of their own self-interest or desires, without any outside pressure or promised reward. By taking the time to conduct self-reflection and introspection on your personal intrinsic factors such as identity, mission, vision, beliefs, values, wants, and needs, you can best paint the picture of your personal intrinsic incentives for DEI. For example, let's assume that you identify as a white man whose religious beliefs that all people should be treated with dignity and respect lead you to value fairness, and that your mission is to serve others, while your vision is to become a school principal in a multicultural district. If you have had limited exposure to differences, then you are likely to have a personal intrinsic incentive for DEI. This may lead you to raise awareness of your preferences and biases and to build your competence to mitigate those biases to become a more inclusive educator and leader. Alternatively, let's assume that you identify as an Asian American woman whose cultural beliefs and values are centered on collectivism, family recognition through achievement, and humility, and that your mission is to honor your family, while your vision is to become a nonprofit executive director who demonstrates excellence as a servant-leader. If you are working in a community that is rapidly becoming more diverse, yet you have a limited understanding of other cultures, then you are likely to have a personal intrinsic incentive for DEI. This may lead you to build your knowledge of cross-cultural differences and increase your intercultural competence as a way to more effectively understand, navigate, and bridge differences within the community.

Personal extrinsic incentives are rewards such as an increase in pay for achieving a certain result; or avoiding punishments such as disciplinary action or criticism as a result of not doing something; or seeking favor with peers. As a part of your process of self-reflection and introspection, you should also consider personal extrinsic factors such as compensation, bonuses, performance evaluations, awards, recognitions, and the like, that may lead to personal extrinsic incentives to pursue DEI. For example, if, on your performance evaluation, you are being evaluated for how well you develop people, then you may be motivated to raise your awareness of your communication preferences, develop stronger competences in interpersonal communication, and adapt your behaviors when communicating with others in order to achieve a high-performance rating. The performance evaluation is a personal extrinsic factor that led to a personal extrinsic incentive. The reason you are motivated to improve your communication preferences, competences, and behaviors is because it is included in the performance evaluation.

Consider these questions as you go through your personal reflection and introspection process:

- Do your personal values align with the principles of DEI?
- Do your personal beliefs reflect the personal case for DEI?
- What is your incentive for personal DEI?
- What causes you to be committed to personal DEI?
- Is there a specific want and/or need that motivates your pursuit of personal DEI?
- What is your ultimate objective for personal DEI?

Taking the time to answers to these questions will not only clarify what motivates you to pursue personal DEI, but it will also set the stage for you to craft the key takeaways from **Step 0: DEI Incentives**: a personal DEI mission, vision, and aims.

Crafting a Personal DEI Mission and Vision

One of the final deliverables of this inaugural step is to craft a **personal DEI mission and vision statement**. In his book *First Things First*, Stephen Covey refers to developing a mission and vision statement as "connecting with your own unique purpose and the profound satisfaction that comes from fulfilling it."[1] A personal DEI mission and vision statement aligns your personal mission and vision with the objectives of diversity, equity, and inclusion.

Do not confuse your personal DEI mission and vision with your personal mission and vision discussed earlier. Here, as the name implies, your personal DEI mission and vision are specific to your DEI journey. Your personal DEI mission and vision answer the following DEI-specific questions:

DEI Mission:	*What is the purpose for your DEI journey?*
	Why are you pursuing DEI?
DEI Vision:	*What is the destination for your DEI journey?*
	What kind of environment do you hope to create for others?

The following is my personal DEI mission and vision:

- **Dr. Pinkett's Personal DEI Mission:** To deeply understand the experiences of people who are different than me, to personalize individuals and mitigate the impact of my biases, to be an ally in equal partnership with those less privileged than me, and to treat people the way they want to be treated.

- **Dr. Pinkett's Personal DEI Vision:** I will have authentic, culturally diverse, and global relationships. I will bridge differences and be a bridge between communities of the like-minded; I will behave inclusively toward others and be an inclusive servant-leader; and I will dismantle personal, interpersonal, institutional, and systemic barriers to help create environments that produce equitable outcomes for all.

When combined, a personal DEI mission and vision address two overarching questions, respectively: *What is the reason for your DEI journey? What is the destination for your DEI journey?* The considerations outlined in the preceding sections—identity, mission, vision, beliefs, values, wants, and needs—should ultimately lead you to identify a burning and all-embracing DEI mission and vision that inspire you to set out on your DEI journey. In doing so, always keep in mind that the journey alone is far more important than the destination. You do not have to reach the destination to be "successful." Success is found in the journey itself as it is ongoing and never-ending.

Establishing Personal DEI Aims

The final deliverable of this inaugural step is to establish one or more **personal DEI aims** that, as the name implies, point you in the right direction for your DEI journey. By establishing aims, you have a general sense of direction and understanding of the areas to explore for your DEI journey. For example, you will have a general sense of whether you are ultimately seeking to become a better spouse or significant other because you recently entered a new relationship; or a better co-worker because you recently joined a new team; or to better understand cultural differences because you've relocated internationally; or to become a more inclusive leader because you find yourself in a new managerial or supervisory position. Each scenario points you to—*aims* you toward—different areas to explore for your DEI journey.

For example, based on internal factors stemming from your religious beliefs and personal values, your aim could be to "treat people fairly." Based on external factors such as your desire to achieve a high rating on your performance evaluation at work, your aim could be to "work effectively with people of different cultural backgrounds." Or, due to a combination of both factors and your role as a manager or supervisor, to "be an inclusive leader who personalizes individuals, treats people and groups fairly, and leverages the thinking of diverse groups," could be your aim. Or you may harbor these same internal and external factors and, after performing some self-reflection and introspection, you realize that you sit in a position of privilege and unearned advantage. To help those who may have less privilege, your aim could be to "eliminate barriers and be an ally in equal partnership with women throughout my division" or to "eliminate barriers to racism and be an antiracist in equal partnership with people of color throughout my division." These are all reasonable and appropriate DEI aims. Table 0.1 summarizes twelve examples of personal DEI aims. As you can see, DEI aims do not have to be complicated.

As you craft your personal DEI aims, you are not limited to one of the items listed in Table 0.1. I encourage you to combine several on the list and to look beyond the list to make your aims as personal and relevant as possible.

The preceding discussion has focused on transforming you or, more broadly, transforming people. People are the fundamental building block of relationships, families, neighborhoods, communities, and society. People are also the fundamental building block of organizations. As we now shift from personal DEI to organizational DEI, it is important to note that organizations do not change, people change. It is only by transforming people that you can transform an organization. Just as it is of paramount importance for individual people like you to identify their personal incentives and motivations for pursuing DEI, the people who comprise an organization must do the same for its pursuit of DEI. Next, I expand upon the dimensions of personal transformation and personal DEI incentives, to explore the dimensions of organizational transformation and organizational DEI incentives. This will similarly culminate in an organizational DEI mission, vision, and aims that will be carried into **Step 1: DEI Inventory**.

TABLE 0.1   Examples of Personal DEI Aims

Personal DEI Aims	
Diversity: The Range of Human Differences *(A Fact)*	
1. Appreciate differences	Learn more about people who are different from me.
2. Recognize my biases	Become more self-aware of my biases.
Inclusion: Involvement and Empowerment *(An Action)*	
3. Mitigate bias	Treat people fairly.
4. Navigate differences	Work effectively with people of different cultural backgrounds.
5. Be inclusive	Be an inclusive leader who personalizes individuals, treats people and groups fairly, and leverages the thinking of diverse groups.
6. Resolve conflict	Work with others to resolve conflict.
Equity: Fairness and Equity in Outcomes *(A Choice)*	
7. Be a mentor	Develop the women on my team.
8. Be a sponsor	Advocate for people of color in my department.
9. Be an ally	Eliminate barriers and be an ally in equal partnership with women throughout my division.
10. Be an antiracist	Dismantle barriers to racism and be an antiracist in equal partnership with people of color throughout my division.
11. Improve performance	Improve my job performance evaluation.
12. Increase compensation	Increase my compensation.

Dimensions of Organizational Transformation

To explain the dimensions of organizational transformation, I use the analogy of an iceberg once again to frame our understanding of what makes an organization . . . an organization. Much as an iceberg is comprised of what is visible (above the water-line) and invisible (below the water line), organizations are also comprised of aspects that are largely visible and discernable to other people (external) and aspects that are largely invisible to other people and not discernable (internal). Whereas 90% of an iceberg lies below the waterline, much of what governs an organization is unseen and not directly observable. All of what can be found below the waterline are internal factors of organizational transformation in Figure 0.2.

- *Mission or Purpose* is the reason why the organization exists; the foundation for everything the organization ultimately does. For example, BCT's mission is "to harness the power of diversity, insights, and innovation to transform lives, accelerate equity, and create lasting change."

- *Vision* is what your organization is seeking to achieve; the picture of the future the organization seeks to create. For example, BCT's vision is "to transform individuals, institutions, and society to become more equitable. We are leading the way in bringing sustainable and scalable social impact so its effects are felt for generations to come."

- *Beliefs* are principles that govern the organization: its philosophy. For example, at BCT we believe that "A more diverse, equitable, and inclusive world is a better world."

- *Values* are the sum of beliefs; basic and fundamental practices about what is desirable, worthwhile, and important to your organization. Values are how the organization expects the people who work for it to act, while fulfilling the mission, along the path toward achieving the vision. For example, love, service, honesty, integrity, kindness, fairness, and equity are values. BCT's values are Ubuntu (an African philosophy meaning, "I am because we are"), passionate, multidisciplinary problem solvers, courageously candid, catalysts for change, DEI champions, and pursuers of excellence. Two closely related concepts are wants and needs. *Wants* are a desire: something unnecessary but desired or items that increase organizational sustainability and growth. *Needs* are a necessity: something thought to be a necessity or essential items required for organizational sustainability and growth. For example, your organization may need people to be treated more fairly, and your organization may need to be competitive in the marketplace to remain in existence.

In *The Fifth Discipline*, organizational development expert Peter Senge refers to organizational mission, vision, and values—as "governing ideas." Senge argues that great organizations have a larger sense of purpose and seek to contribute to the world in some unique way, to add a distinctive source of value. As you see in the next section, organizational mission, vision, beliefs, and values represent organizational *internal factors* that are all found below the waterline and may motivate your organization to pursue DEI. What is found above the waterline are the external dimensions of organizational transformation:

- *People:* The personal behaviors, engagement, and lived experiences of people within the *organizational culture and climate* as reflected by their personal perceptions and perspectives of the organization. For example, people who experience an organizational culture and climate of psychological safety, where they can openly engage without fear of negative consequences, are more likely to show their true selves, speak candidly, disagree, foster innovation, question others, and admit mistakes. This can lead to high-performing teams and innovation.

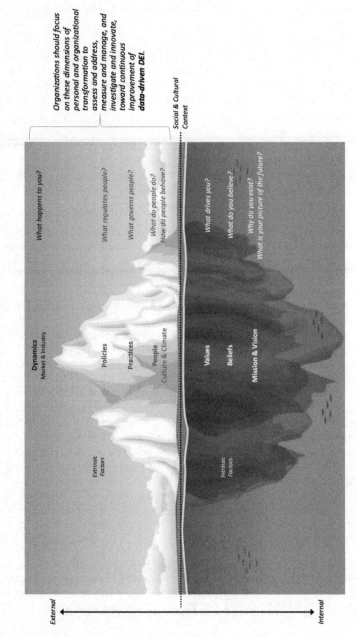

External

*Organizations should focus on these dimensions of personal and organizational transformation to assess and address, measure and manage, and investigate and innovate, toward continuous improvement of **data-driven DEI**.*

Social & Cultural Context

Dynamics
Market & Industry

What happens to you?

Policies

What regulates people?

Practices

What governs people?

People
Culture & Climate

What do people do?
How do people behave?

Values

What drives you?

Beliefs

What do you believe?

Mission & Vision

Why do you exist?
What is your picture of the future?

Extrinsic Factors

Intrinsic Factors

Internal

FIGURE 0.2   Dimensions of Organizational Transformation

11

Conversely, in an organizational culture and climate of psychological distress, where open engagement is discouraged and negative consequences abound, people are far less likely to exhibit those same behaviors. This can lead to dysfunctional teams and stagnation.

- *Management Practices:* The specific actions and procedures performed by management to govern staff and practice organizational leadership. Examples include the presence or absence of commitment to DEI, coaching, mentorship, sponsorship, allyship, and diversity-related compliance handling. How these practices are performed by different managers, and how employees experience these practices, can vary dramatically.

- *Organizational Policies:* The documented policies, regulations, and expectations that govern the organizational functionality. Examples include recruitment, hiring, retention, promotions, compensation, discipline, discrimination, harassment, bullying, and terminations. Even when organization policies are standardized throughout an organization, how they are executed and enforced can vary dramatically for different demographic groups.

As shown in Figure 0.2, organizations are constantly navigating and being subjected to *market and industry* dynamics such as competition, new entrants, economic conditions including recessions, supply chain disruptions, and more. Moreover, there are also other *organizational extrinsic factors* that organizations face such as social conditions including social unrest, health conditions including pandemics, geopolitical developments including wars, environmental developments including natural disasters, human tragedies such as mass shootings, and so on, public perceptions and public pressure to respond to these events, and even rewards such as awards, recognitions, and positive publicity. These external dynamics, which are often beyond the organization's control, may influence people's behavior, management's practices, and the organization's policies.

Lastly, if you look closely at Figure 0.2, you also see a dotted line right at the waterline between the internal and the external dimensions. This dotted line represents the *social and cultural context* including relationships, norms, and standards, that can also play an important role in your organizational transformation. For example, if your organizational culture is team oriented, it likely reflects more harmonious relationships that could have a positive effect on your DEI journey. By comparison, if your organizational culture is highly competitive, it could have the opposite—negative— effect. In this regard, the dotted line is like a permeable filter that can shape or reshape your internal and external dimensions of organizational transformation.

Dimensions of Personal and Organizational Transformation

Figure 0.3 depicts the dimensions of personal transformation on the left-hand side and the dimensions of organizational transformation on the right-hand side.

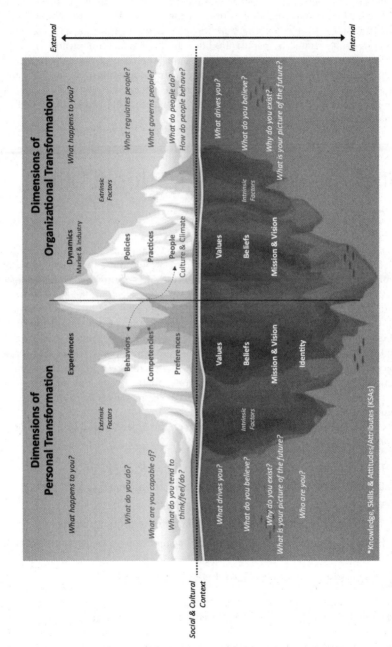

FIGURE 0.3 Dimensions of Personal and Organizational Transformation

By juxtaposing the two, you can clearly see their interrelationships. What inextricably links the personal and organizational dimensions is people (notice the curved and dashed line connecting "behaviors" on the left-hand side and "people" on the right-hand side). People are the building blocks of organizations. Therefore, the behaviors demonstrated by people are both the final visible dimension of personal transformation (i.e., the topmost part above the waterline of the personal iceberg) and the first visible dimension of organizational transformation (i.e., the bottommost part above the waterline of the organizational iceberg). Stated simply, changing organizations begins with changing people, and changing people is ultimately reflected in changing their behaviors.

What Are Your Organizational DEI Incentives?

Organizational intrinsic incentives are those that motivate an organization to do something out of their own self-interest or desires, without any outside pressure or promised reward. Here in **Step 0: DEI Incentives**, just as the determination of personal DEI incentives calls for self-reflection and introspection, the same is true for determining organizational DEI incentives. It is only after careful consideration and deep thought around the organizational intrinsic factors of mission, vision, beliefs, and values, that you and your organization's leaders can determine their organizational intrinsic incentives to pursue DEI. You and your organization's leaders must also consider organizational extrinsic factors, such as market and industry dynamics; social, economic, and environmental conditions; public perceptions, public pressure, rewards, and recognitions, that may create extrinsic incentives for your organization to pursue DEI.

Consider these questions as you go through the reflection and introspection process for your organization:

- Do your organizational values align with the principles of DEI?
- Do your organizational beliefs reflect the organizational case for DEI?
- What is your incentive for organizational DEI?
- What causes your organization to be committed to organizational DEI?
- Is there a specific want and/or need that motivates your pursuit of organizational DEI?
- What is your ultimate objective for organizational DEI?

Setting aside time to wrestle with these questions will yield two valuable benefits. First, it will clearly illuminate and communicate what motivates your organization to pursue DEI. Second, the answers provide the necessary inputs to craft the final pieces of the **Step 0: DEI Incentives** puzzle, namely, an organizational DEI mission, vision, and aims.

Crafting an Organizational DEI Mission and Vision

One of the final deliverables of this inaugural step is to craft an **organizational DEI mission and vision statement**. Your organizational DEI mission and vision statement align your organizational mission and vision with the objectives of diversity, equity, and inclusion. Per the discussion earlier in this step, do not confuse your organizational DEI mission and vision with your organizational mission and vision discussed earlier. Here, as the name implies, your organizational DEI mission and vision are specific to your DEI journey and answer the following DEI-specific questions:

DEI Mission:	*What is the purpose for your organization's DEI journey?*
	Why is your organization pursuing DEI?
DEI Vision:	*What is the destination for your organization's DEI journey?*
	Who does your organization strive to become?
	What kind of environment does your organization hope to create?

Ongig, a company that transforms visuals and text to attract top-tier talent and diversity, offers seven characteristics of an exceptional DEI mission and vision statement:[2]

1. **Inclusive language.** Exemplar DEI mission and vision statements use inclusive language. What this means is that it is close to bias-free, race-neutral, and gender-neutral and does not have exclusionary words such as "he/she" (instead of "they") or "the disabled (instead of "people with disabilities").

2. **Highly readable.** An effective DEI mission and vision statement is, like any quality writing, highly readable. What's that mean? It means it's written in plain language.

3. **Building community.** The best DEI mission and vision statements include stakeholders other than just your employees.

4. **Examples of underrepresented groups.** Inclusive DEI mission and vision statements mention specific underrepresented groups like "gender, race, culture, and sexual orientation." Some other core groups to consider are family status, religion, ethnicity, national origin, physical disability, veteran status, or age.

5. **Mention that all levels should be diverse.** A good DEI mission and vision statement for organizations focuses on all levels of employees/associates/colleagues.

6. **Mention DEI initiatives ("pillars") if you have them.** If you have such DEI pillars such as inclusive hiring, mandatory unconscious bias training, employee resource groups (ERGs), building equity-driven products, and delivering equity-driven services, consider mentioning it in your DEI mission statement.

7. **Diversity of thoughts and ideas count, too.** Many DEI initiatives focus purely on being inclusive of underrepresented groups, which is vital, but diversity of thoughts/ideas is also key.

Here are five examples of awesome organizational DEI mission and vision statements from different organizational contexts:

1. American Red Cross (Nonprofit)

   Our DEI Mission:

   The American Red Cross will consistently deliver its products, goods, and services in a culturally competent manner.

   Our DEI Vision:

   The American Red Cross aspires to be an organization fully committed to diversity, equity, and inclusion by creating and maintaining a diverse, high-performing workforce of employees and volunteers who reflect all communities we serve; by cultivating a collaborative, inclusive and respectful work environment that empowers all contributors; and by leveraging diverse partnerships—all of which helps to ensure culturally competent service delivery supported by effective community leadership and engagement.

2. University of California, Davis (Academic)

   Our vision is to develop and nurture a community where everyone can reach their full potential in the Medical Microbiology and Immunology Department, UC Davis. We provide resources that promote equal access and opportunity for all people in order to achieve a prosperous society, and we advocate for policies that promote diversity and inclusion in the UC workforce. Our goal is to empower all members of our community in order to remove barriers throughout our campus caused by social injustice, inequality, and racial trauma. We are committed to engaging the voices of our community to promote equality and compassion for all.

3. Johnson & Johnson (Corporate)

   Our Vision: Be yourself, change the world.

   Our vision at Johnson & Johnson, is for every person to use their unique experiences and backgrounds, together—to spark solutions that create a better, healthier world.

   Our Mission: Make diversity and inclusion how we work every day.

   Our mission is to make diversity & inclusion our way of doing business. We will advance our culture of belonging where open hearts and minds combine to unleash the potential of the brilliant mix of people, in every corner of Johnson & Johnson.

4. The Ford Foundation (Philanthropic)

Diversity, equity, and inclusion are core to our mission and to who we are as a foundation. To address the challenges of a complex—and increasingly diverse—world, we need to make sure every person has a voice and a seat at the table. While we strive to build a future grounded in justice, we know tackling inequality around the globe begins at home. We are committed to not only creating a diverse team where everyone feels represented and respected but also embedding these values across our work and philanthropy at large.

5. United States of America (Government)

Federal Government-wide DEIA Vision Statement:

The federal government will advance and embed Diversity, Equity, Inclusion, and Accessibility (DEIA) throughout its workforce.

Federal Government-wide DEIA Mission Statement:

Across the federal government, agencies will work collaboratively to drive innovation and organizational outcomes, draw from the full diversity of the nation, and position the federal government to serve as a model employer that values and promotes equity for all Americans.

When combined, organizational DEI mission and vision address two overarching questions, respectively: *What is the reason for the DEI journey? What is the destination for the DEI journey?* The considerations outlined in the previous section—mission, vision, beliefs, values, wants, and needs—should ultimately illuminate a DEI mission and vision that govern your organization's ongoing and never-ending DEI journey.

When we work with our clients at BCT, the DEI mission and vision are typically two parts of an even broader **Organizational DEI Framework** or **Organizational DEI Charter**, which is comprised of some or all of the following:

DEI Statement of Commitment:	*What is your promise?*
	What can people expect from you?
DEI Mission:	*What is the purpose for your DEI journey?*
	Why are you pursuing DEI?
DEI Vision:	*What is the destination for your DEI journey?*
	Who do you strive to become?
	What kind of environment do you hope to create?
DEI Values:	*What do you believe?*
DEI Definitions:	*How do you define diversity, equity and inclusion?*

The organizational DEI framework or charter sets the stage for all things DEI. It reshapes and redefines your organization through the lens of DEI and makes clear where you stand, what you stand for, and how DEI is defined and understood. We typically work with our clients to establish a DEI Council/Committee/Task Force/ Steering Committee—a diverse and inclusive body representing different functions, levels, roles, identities, and responsibilities throughout the organization—to develop the DEI framework or charter in partnership with the organization's executive leadership. Based on Appreciative Inquiry (AI), a strengths-based, positive approach to organizational change and strategic innovation, the DEI Council should work intensively, not only to develop the organizational DEI framework or charter, but also a three- to five-year organizational DEI strategic plan. This could be accomplished at a retreat or during meetings that are spaced out over several months. The latter will be explored briefly in **Step 2: DEI Imperatives** and more fully in **Step 4: DEI Initiatives.** For purposes of *Data-Driven DEI*, the DEI mission and vision represent two of three essential components to begin your journey. The third and final component is to establish DEI aims.

Establishing Organizational DEI Aims

The final deliverable of this inaugural step is to establish one or more **organizational DEI aims** that, as the name implies, point you in the right direction for your DEI journey. By establishing organizational DEI aims, you at least have a general sense of direction and understanding of the areas to explore for your organization's DEI journey. For example, you will have a general sense of whether you are ultimately seeking to increase diversity (representation) at all levels; or to strengthen a culture of employee engagement, inclusion, and belonging; or to mitigate bias in human resources (HR) policies and practices to improve equitable outcomes for women; or to dismantle institutional and structural barriers to racism and improve equitable outcomes for people of color. Each scenario points you to—*aims* you toward—different areas to explore for your DEI journey. Table 0.2 summarizes 12 examples of organizational DEI aims. As you can see, DEI aims do not have to be complicated.

Figure 0.4 illustrates how personal DEI aims can also directly relate to organizational DEI aims. This mapping may be helpful if you are an employee, manager, supervisor, or executive seeking to align your personal DEI agenda with your organization's DEI agenda.

DEI Aims vs. DEI Objectives

Here in **Step 0: DEI Incentives**, I specifically distinguish DEI "aims" from "objectives" as they are closely related but distinctly different. DEI aims are preliminary and broad DEI objectives. DEI objectives will be established during **Step 2: DEI Imperatives**, which is, of course, after you have completed **Step 1: DEI Inventory** and performed a DEI assessment. The reason why establishing DEI objectives is deferred until then is because *it is always best to finalize DEI objectives* after *you have performed a*

TABLE 0.2   **Examples of Organizational DEI Aims**

Organizational DEI Aims	
Diversity: The Range of Human Differences *(A Fact)*	
1. Increase diversity (representation)	Increase diversity (representation) at all levels
2. Increase awareness of diversity and/or biases in people	Increase awareness of bias and understanding of different cultures
Inclusion: Involvement and Empowerment *(An Action)*	
3. Mitigate the impact of bias on people	Mitigate the impact of bias on interpersonal relationships
4. Improve communication, teamwork, collaboration, and/or innovation	Improve teamwork and collaboration leading to greater innovation
5. Increase engagement, inclusion, and/or belonging	Strengthen a culture of employee engagement, inclusion, and belonging.
6. Manage conflict	Manage intercultural conflict
Equity: Fairness and Equity in Outcomes *(A Choice)*	
7. Foster development	Foster the professional development of women
8. Promote advancement	Promote the advancement of people of color
9. Eliminate barriers and/or improve equity in policies and practices	Mitigate bias in human resources (HR) policies and practices and improve equitable outcomes for persons with disabilities
10. Dismantle racism	Dismantle personal, interpersonal, institutional and systemic barriers to racism and improve equitable outcomes for Black talent
11. Improve productivity	Improve employee productivity
12. Increase profitability	Increase net income (or net assets or retained earnings)

DEI assessment. Oftentimes, "you don't know what you don't know," and an assessment can lead to new and/or unanticipated understandings that refine or completely reshape your aims into objectives. However, DEI aims to not only set initial direction but also aid you in choosing the personal DEI core preferences and competences that will comprise the focus of your DEI journey, as well as scaffold you in selecting the right instrument for your DEI assessment, which will be discussed in the next **Step 1: DEI Inventory**.

Personal DEI Aims		Organizational DEI Aims
Diversity		**Diversity**
Appreciate differences	← 1 →	Increase diversity (representation)
Recognize differences and/or biases	← 2 →	Increase awareness of diversity and/or bias
Inclusion		**Inclusion**
Mitigate the impact of biases	← 3 →	Mitigate the impact of bias
Navigate and bridge differences	← 4 →	Improve teamwork and innovation
Be inclusive	← 5 →	Increase engagement and inclusion
Resolve conflict	← 6 →	Manage conflict
Equity		**Equity**
Be a mentor	← 7 →	Foster development
Be a sponsor	← 8 →	Promote advancement
Be an ally	← 9 →	Eliminate barriers
Be an antiracist	←10→	Dismantle racism
Improve performance	←11→	Improve productivity
Increase compensation	←12→	Increase profitability

FIGURE 0.4 Mapping Personal DEI Aims to Organizational DEI Aims

Comprehensive Personal and Organizational DEI Assessment Framework

In the next **Step 1: DEI Inventory**, you will explore a deeper understanding of you and/or your organization: Where are you currently in your DEI journey? How do you compare to other people or organizations? What are your strengths and limitations? The answers to these and other questions can be found by performing an assessment, which is the basis for the next step and represents the first and most important step of the *Data-Driven DEI* five-step cycle.

All BCT's DEI assessments are conducted through the lens of our "4 P's" comprehensive personal and organizational DEI assessment framework shown in Figure 0.5. Our approach uses data to assess people, practices, policies, and performance through the lens of DEI. The aforementioned "Dimensions of Personal and Organizational Transformation" define our 4 P's comprehensive DEI assessment framework. In fact, to clearly see the close interrelationship between the dimensions and the framework, I encourage you to look back at Figure 0.3: Dimensions of Personal and Organizational Transformation and compare it to Figure 0.5: BCT's DEI Assessment Framework. Both figures capture almost the exact same information, with the exact same words, only in a different format! The only subtle differences are that the personal and organizational DEI mission visions have been added to the personal and organizational foundation, respectively, and a fourth "P" of

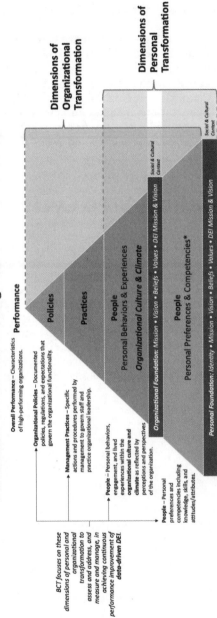

FIGURE 0.5 BCT's Comprehensive Personal and Organizational DEI Assessment Framework: The 4 P's of People, Practices, Policies, and Performance

21

performance has been added to the mix. Whereas the dimensions were presented in Figure 0.3 as an iceberg to visually depict internal (below the waterline) and external (above the waterline) dynamics, the framework is presented in Figure 0.5 as a pyramid to depict the dimensions as building blocks for comprehensive assessment and understanding.

The 4 P's comprehensive DEI assessment framework is driven by two overarching approaches. As a result, the next step—**Step 1: DEI Inventory**—is broken up into two parts representing the personal and organizational tracks. The first part, **Step 1: DEI Inventory for People**, outlines an approach to *personal DEI assessment* (i.e., for you to assess your preferences and competences). The second part, **Step 1: DEI Inventory for Organizations**, outlines an approach to *organizational DEI assessment* (i.e., for your organization to assess its people behaviors and experiences, management practices, organizational policies, and overall performance).

Entering the Five-Step Cycle of *Data-Driven DEI*

Now that you have determined your DEI incentives and unearthed the motivations that drive you and/or your organization to pursue DEI, you are ready to enter the five-step cycle of *Data-Driven DEI*. The remaining steps are part of an ongoing and never-ending cycle of continuous learning toward improving DEI. Determining a new or different DEI mission or vision would, of course, necessitate revisiting this **Step 0: DEI Incentives**. However, once you have a firm sense of what motivates you and/or your organization to pursue DEI (incentives), your DEI purpose (mission), desired future (vision), and a general sense of direction (aims), then it is into the cycle you go!

STEP 1

DEI Inventory for People—Seek Understanding

If you can't measure it, it will be harder to manage it.

If you don't assess it, it will be more difficult to address it.

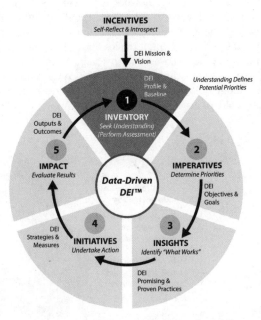

Data-Driven DEI—Step 1: DEI Inventory for People

A DEI inventory for people—a **personal DEI assessment**—collects data from you, typically in the form of a questionnaire, survey, or form and, in doing so, delivers two valuable outputs:

1. A *profile*—a report containing data and a descriptive representation of you based on the assessment's area(s) of focus. The profile summarizes insights, findings, and/or recommendations specific to you and your personal DEI journey.

2. A *baseline*—a starting data point and/or reference data point to gauge progress along your personal DEI journey. The baseline provides the means to evaluate your learning, development, and growth.

A personal DEI assessment helps you understand where you are personally and determine where you want to go. **Step 1: DEI Inventory** is the most important step of the *Data-Driven DEI* five-step cycle because your DEI strategic plan will only be as good as your DEI assessment. As you will see in our final **Step 5: DEI Impact,** it is often by re-administering the same personal DEI assessment you identify here in **Step 1: DEI Inventory** that you evaluate results.

Personal DEI Assessment Framework

This step outlines how you can perform your own personal DEI assessment along the two lines of **BCT's Personal DEI Assessment Framework** shown in Figure 1.1: *preferences* and *competences*. This framework represents a subset of BCT's Comprehensive DEI Assessment Framework: The 4 P's of People, Practices, Policies, and Performance previously shown in Figure 0.5 that is focused on people only. I begin by explaining the difference between preferences and competences as these concepts will undergird everything that is covered in this step and the remainder of this book. After explaining how to assess your preferences and competences, I provide a list of personal DEI assessment tools you can employ and how to select the right one for you based on your personal DEI aims.

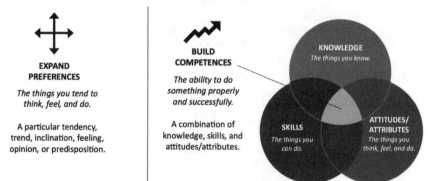

EXPAND PREFERENCES

The things you tend to think, feel, and do.

A particular tendency, trend, inclination, feeling, opinion, or predisposition.

BUILD COMPETENCES

The ability to do something properly and successfully.

A combination of knowledge, skills, and attitudes/attributes.

KNOWLEDGE
The things you know.

SKILLS
The things you can do.

ATTITUDES/ ATTRIBUTES
The things you think, feel, and do.

FIGURE 1.1 BCT's Personal DEI Assessment Framework

Understanding Preferences and Competences

To perform your own personal DEI assessment, you need to understand preferences and competences and how they differ.

Preferences

Preferences are the things you tend to think, feel, and do. A preference is a particular tendency, trend, inclination, feeling, opinion, or predisposition toward or away from something or someone. The characteristics of a preference are:

- **Learned**—Your preferences are learned and develop over years through your life's experiences. Through nature (innate and intrinsic factors), and nurture (environmental and extrinsic factors) you begin to make choices. According to Herrmann Global, the company that administers the Herrmann Brain Dominance Instrument® (HBDI®), "Preferences grow during our developmental years and well into our 20s and beyond as we experience continued brain development, learn different subjects in school, develop areas of interest, experience initial work activities and make career choices. Our preferences will 'settle in' and remain stable if our life situation and career remains stable . . . they can change when a significant life change occurs such as a major career shift, family changes or value-shifting life experiences."[1]

- **Measurable**—Preferences can be measured using an assessment tool or instrument that locates your preferences along a scale or a series of scales that create a map.

- **Neutral**—There is no good or bad, better or worse, or right or wrong, when it comes to preferences. They are neutral. For example, if you prefer water with lemon, and your friend prefers water without lemon, neither of you is right or wrong, just different. However, a preference is also a bias that can lead to a blind spot. A preference can direct your attention to one area and cause you to completely miss or overlook something in another area. For example, if you prefer logical thinking (i.e., left brain) over creative thinking (i.e., right brain), you may need to take deliberate steps to stretch and exercise creative thinking during a brainstorming session. Otherwise, you may have a blind spot for ideas or opportunities that could be generated. Alternatively, if you prefer abstract thinking (i.e., upper brain) over concrete thinking (i.e., lower brain), you may have to flex into the latter when called upon to develop an execution plan that requires concrete and specific action steps. Otherwise, you may have a blind spot that causes you to produce an incomplete or ineffective execution plan. So, while a preference is neither negative nor positive, it can lead to a negative outcome if it causes you to overlook or miss something important.

As it relates to improving your personal DEI, the objective is therefore not to change preferences, but rather, to shift, stretch, flex, or expand into areas outside of your preferences and mitigate blind spots. Examples of preferences that directly relate to DEI are biases, leadership style, personality, communication style, temperament, cognitive style, cross-cultural dimensions, conflict style, and cognitive or thinking style, to name a few. A more complete list is provided later in this step in the section "A List of Personal DEI Assessment Tools."

Competences

A competence is the ability to do something properly and successfully. It is a combination of practical and theoretical *knowledge*, cognitive *skills*, and *attitudes/attributes* (KSAs):

- **Knowledge**—Knowledge is the things you know. It includes awareness and information including facts, definitions, terminology, procedures, theories, concepts, and models. For example, knowing that a microaffirmation is a small, subtle behavior that sends the message that you value others, and being able to cite examples of common microaffirmations, represent knowledge.

- **Skills**—Skills are the things you can do. Skills are usually learned through the transfer of knowledge. A person acquires the knowledge on how to perform a skill and then begins to physically demonstrate the skill. For example, during a course in microaffirmations you may learn that one of the best ways to affirm others is by responding constructively to different points of view, that is, showing that you understand someone else's perspective, with whom you disagree, before you offer a different point of view. However, if you never put what you have learned into practice it remains something you know (i.e., knowledge) but not something you do (i.e., a skill). Once you regularly and instinctively find yourself affirming others by responding constructively to different points of view, your knowledge has translated into a skill.

- **Attitudes/Attributes**—Attitudes/attributes are inherent characteristics often expressed through the things you think, do, and feel. A person's attitude or feeling about the skill will determine their motivation for applying that skill and excelling in it. In other words, just because you *can* do something does not mean you *actually* do it. If you have a negative attitude/attribute regarding how people should be treated, then even if you possess the skill of affirming others, it is unlikely you will exercise it when dealing with others. By comparison, if you have a positive attitude/attribute regarding how people should be treated, you are far more likely to develop and demonstrate the skill of affirming others when dealing with them.

In combining knowledge, skills, and attitudes/attributes, the characteristics of a competence are C.O.M.P.T.:

- **C**onnected, relatable, and relevant to your personal or professional environment or other life experiences
- **O**bservable and visible to you and others
- **M**easurable using an assessment tool or instrument that locates you on a developmental continuum

- **P**erformance-based and demonstrable as evidenced by the proper and successful accomplishment of tasks, assignments, exercises, activities, and the like
- **T**ransferable and can be used in a variety of different contexts

For example, affirming others is connected to your personal and professional environment, easily observed by you and others, measurable using a self-assessment or third-party assessment, based on your performance and success in creating environments where others feel affirmed, and can be transferred to a variety of different contexts including parenting children, working with colleagues, coaching athletes, mentoring co-workers, leading teams, and much more.

You can always acquire more knowledge, develop more skills, and cultivate more positive attitudes/attributes. *As it relates to improving your personal DEI, the objective is therefore to improve and increase your competences.* Examples of competences that directly relate to DEI are affirming others, allyship, antiracism, cultural competence, conflict resolution, and dialogue, to name a few. A more complete list is provided later in this step in the section "A List of Personal DEI Assessment Tools."

Preferences vs. Competences

You can have a high preference for something (i.e., you love to cook) but low competence (i.e., your meals are not tasty), and you can have a low preference for something (i.e., you dread reconciling your bank account) but high competence (i.e., you maintain impeccable bank records). A preference for a given activity and the competence required to perform that activity are not the same thing. A good way to distinguish between the two is that your preferences generally reflect your *nature*, the things you are inclined to do, while your competences reflect your *nurture*, the things you are able to do. You can develop competence in any area; however, it may require more energy and motivation in an area of low preference.

Conducting a Personal DEI Assessment

A comprehensive approach to personal DEI assessment is to assess both preferences and competences. Per BCT's Personal DEI Assessment Framework shown in Figure 1.1, our approach to personal DEI assessment includes:

- **People: Personal Preferences**—We assess personal preferences using a range of assessment tools such as the Implicit Association Test (IAT), Herrmann Brain Dominance Instrument® (HBDI®), Intercultural Conflict Style Inventory® (ICS®), and more.
- **People: Personal Competences**—We assess personal competences including knowledge, skills, and attitudes/attributes (KSAs) using a range of assessment tools such as the Intrinsic Inclusion Inventory™ (I3™), Intercultural Development Inventory® (IDI®), and more.

Understanding your preferences in a particular area raises your awareness and can mitigate your blind spots. Knowing your level of competence alerts you to areas of strength and areas for improvement. Assessing both preferences and competences empowers you to increase your competences in areas of low preference and, in doing so, enhance your ability to shift and expand beyond your preferences when needed. Your preferences should never be used as an excuse for negative behavior, but rather, an explanation of behavior that can translate greater awareness into greater empowerment. For example, if you have a preference for people who are like you and someone brings to your attention that you were unintentionally dismissive of an idea from someone different from you, then that represents an opportunity to learn (and apologize). Said differently, even in situations where you have a positive intent, your preferences can cause you to have a negative impact. You must own your intent *and* your impact.

In the sections that follow, I walk you through how to assess your personal preferences and your competences.

Assessing Your Preferences

I begin by explaining how to assess your preferences against a *preference scale*, which measures one-dimensional preferences, and then I explain how to assess your preferences against a *preference map*, which measures multidimensional preferences.

Understanding a Preference Scale
Figure 1.2 provides a basic example of a one-dimensional preference scale.

Left preference scale #1 and right preference scale #2 could represent any two opposing preferences, such as water with lemon and water without lemon; introversion vs. extroversion; thinking vs. feeling, logical thinking (i.e., left brain) and creative thinking (i.e., right brain); or abstract thinking (i.e., upper brain) and concrete thinking (i.e., lower brain), and those preferences could be measured anywhere between a "strong preference" for preference scale #1 on the far left and "strong preference" for preference scale #2 on the far right. For example, imagine that this scale measured your preference for water with lemon (preference scale #1) and water without lemon (preference scale #2). If you had a slight preference for water without lemon, the preference scale would appear as shown in Figure 1.3 with your measure of "slight preference" showing on the scale. You can easily imagine that the same preference scale shown in Figure 1.4 could also represent a "slight preference" for introversion over extroversion, or creative thinking over logical thinking, or other preferences pertaining to DEI.

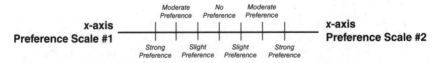

FIGURE 1.2   Basic Example of One-Dimensional Preference Scale (*x*-axis)

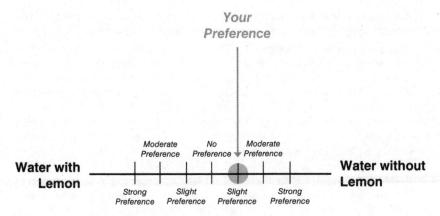

FIGURE 1.3   Basic Example of a One-Dimensional Preference Scale (*x*-axis) with a Measure

Along these lines, a one-dimensional personal DEI assessment will locate you between two different preferences scales such as your preference for Black people compared to white people; your association of men and women with science and the arts; your preference for young people compared to the elderly; or your preference for physically abled people compared to physically disabled people, for example.

As a specific example of a preference scale, I will use unconscious bias and implicit bias and an associated assessment tool, the Implicit Association Test (IAT). These work extremely well for illustrative purposes because, as mentioned earlier, a preference is literally a bias. I begin with a brief primer on unconscious bias, followed by background information and an overview of the IAT as an example of a tool that uses different preference scales to assess your biases.

Example of a Preference: Unconscious Bias   Our understanding of unconscious bias has changed radically over time. In the past, we regarded our biases as aberrant, conscious, and intentional. Today, research suggests that human biases are normal, unconscious, and largely unintentional. This science of unconscious bias draws upon multiple disciplines such as biology, neuroscience, and cognitive science (cognitive bias), sociology (social cognitive theory), biology, and psychology (categories and implicit bias). From this growing body of work, here are some basics you should understand about the science of your brain and the science of bias:

- *Bias Begins in the Brain*—Humans face a problem: Our brains are exposed to more information at any one moment in time than we are capable of processing. Scientists estimate that, at any given moment, our brains are exposed to as many as 11 million pieces of information, but our brains can only functionally deal with about 40 things at a time. Consequently, our brains develop preferences— mental shortcuts about other people or groups—that save time and *usually* yield reliable results but do not *always* yield reliable results. Therein lies our biases. Human biases have evolved out of these preferences, shortcuts, and brain processes, whereas 95% of mental processes are unconscious; only 5% are conscious.

According to Dr. Sondra Thiederman, "Unconscious Bias is a labor-saving device. It enables you to form an opinion without having to dig up the facts."[2]

- *Bias is a Defense Mechanism*—The human brain basically contains two different operating systems as shown in Figure 1.4. Daniel Kahneman, a Nobel Prize–winning economist, has described these systems in his book entitled *Thinking, Fast and Slow*.[3] The first of these systems, the "Thinking Fast" system, is located in the amygdala, which is also referred to as the "primitive brain" because it is governed by survival instincts.[4] The amygdala is the oldest part of the human brain and controls our "fight or flight" impulses. It receives direct input from all sensory organs, enabling it to respond rapidly to immediate threats in advance of more elaborative cognitive processing. It plays a central role in arousal, attentiveness, and triggering the flight-or-fight response, reacting to social threats in the same way it reacts to physical ones. The brain therefore acts as a prediction machine that is wired for threat identification. Unconscious bias, then, is the immediate, reflexive, defensive reaction to people that we regard as being not like us or "other." Our biases are triggered by the things we can see or hear. Seeing these people or pictures of these people immediately puts our brains on alert for possible danger. Moreover, our biases are most likely to be activated when four key conditions are present: stress, time constraints, multi-tasking, and the need for closure.

- *Bias Can Be "Outsmarted"*—The second of these brain systems, the "Thinking Slow" system, is located in the prefrontal cortex, which is also referred to as the "executive brain" because it contains our higher-order reasoning and logic skills (see Figure 1.4).[13] In effect, this system allows us to "outsmart our brains" by taking the time to think about whether the "other" truly represents a threat to us. For example, when we think of people as individuals instead of as members of collective social or cultural groups ("individuation"), our brains can turn off the alarm signal from the amygdala and consciously override our unconscious biases.

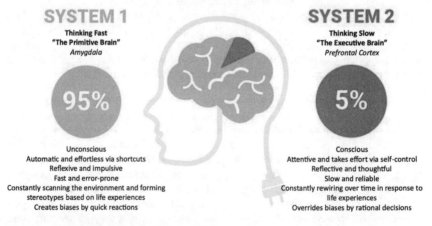

YOUR BRAIN AT WORK

SYSTEM 1
Thinking Fast
"The Primitive Brain"
Amygdala

95%

Unconscious
Automatic and effortless via shortcuts
Reflexive and impulsive
Fast and error-prone
Constantly scanning the environment and forming
stereotypes based on life experiences
Creates biases by quick reactions

SYSTEM 2
Thinking Slow
"The Executive Brain"
Prefrontal Cortex

5%

Conscious
Attentive and takes effort via self-control
Reflective and thoughtful
Slow and reliable
Constantly rewiring over time in response to
life experiences
Overrides biases by rational decisions

FIGURE 1.4 Neuroscience of the Brain and Bias

Just as our preferences are learned, our biases are learned. You may have a bias or a preference for certain races/ethnicities, genders, ages, religions, nationalities, and so on. Oftentimes our biases reflect our personal identity and the people who surround us. We all have biases. To be biased is to be human. Like all preferences, a bias is neither good nor bad; better nor worse; right nor wrong. And because our biases are learned they can be unlearned. Among the best ways to mitigate bias are to raise your awareness of your biases from the unconscious to the conscious realm, slow down, be objective when making decisions, and, above all, interact with people different than you. Enter the Implicit Association Test (IAT), which measures unconscious and implicit bias.

Example of a Preference Scale: Unconscious Bias and the Implicit Association Test (IAT)   According to the *Proceedings of the National Academy of Sciences of the United States of America (PNAS)*, "Harvard University experimental social psychologist Dr. Mahzarin Banaji is on the frontlines of the 'implicit revolution,' a paradigm shift in psychology that, since the 1980s, has been reconceiving the relationship between unconscious and conscious mental processes. Banaji and her colleague Dr. Anthony Greenwald [at the University of Washington] applied the concept to social psychology via the intertwined concepts of attitude, belief, and identity."[5] Banaji and Greenwald are co-authors of the seminal book *Blindspot: Hidden Biases of Good People*. "In 1995, the duo defined implicit social cognition, introduced the term 'implicit bias,' and foreshadowed the Implicit Association Test (IAT) to detect and measure automatic, unintentional biases. The IAT and other methods have enabled Banaji and her colleagues to uncover hidden biases in the form of attitudes and beliefs (stereotypes) of gender, race/ethnicity, age, sexuality, and other common social group identifiers."

The Implicit Association Test (IAT) "measures attitudes and beliefs that people may be unwilling or unable to report," according to Project Implicit, a nonprofit organization and international collaborative of researchers who are interested in unconscious bias.[6] Project Implicit was founded in 1998 by Drs. Greenwald and Banaji and Dr. Brian Nosek at the University of Virginia. The mission of Project Implicit is to educate the public about bias and to provide a "virtual laboratory" for collecting data on the internet. Project Implicit scientists produce high-impact research that forms the basis of our scientific knowledge about bias and disparities.[7] "The IAT measures the strength of associations between concepts (e.g., black people, gay people) and evaluations (e.g., good, bad) or stereotypes (e.g., athletic, clumsy). The main idea is that making a response is easier when closely related items share the same response key. We would say that one has an implicit preference for straight people relative to gay people if they are faster to complete the task when Straight People + Good / Gay People + Bad are paired together compared to when Gay People + Good / Straight People + Bad are paired together."

The IAT is available at no cost and can be taken by visiting: **implicit .harvard.edu/implicit/takeatest.html**. Multiple IATs are available including the following (preference scale in parenthesis as worded by Project Implicit):

- Native American IAT (Native-White American)
- Gender-Career IAT (family and females/career and males)

- Weight IAT (fat/thin)
- Sexuality IAT (Gay-Straight People)
- Weapons IAT (weapons/harmless objects)
- Gender-Science IAT (liberal arts and females/science and males)
- Race IAT (Black-White)
- Religion IAT (familiarity with religious terms from various world religions)
- Asian IAT (Asian-European American)
- Transgender IAT (transgender people/cisgender people)
- Arab-Muslim IAT (Arab Muslim/Other People)
- Skin-tone IAT (light skin/dark skin people)
- Disability IAT (physically disabled/physically abled people)
- Presidents IAT (popularity of current U.S. president)
- Age IAT (young/old People)

We use these tests quite extensively in our DEI and unconscious bias training at BCT. I've taken most of them, and they are not for the faint of heart! Be prepared for your results, which may be sobering and surprising.

Figure 1.5 shows an example of the report generated by the Black-White IAT.

If this were your IAT report, it would suggest that you have a slight automatic preference for white people when compared to Black people. (Note: As you can see from the results of IAT research by Project Implicit summarized in Figure 1.5, 17% of people across all racial/ethnic backgrounds have a slight automatic preference for white people over Black people.) These results would not mean you are a good or a bad person or that you necessarily treat white people better than Black people. The results would mean that you are human—we all have unconscious biases—and, because unconscious bias is a preference, it may be reflected in your behaviors in ways that you are unaware and are unintentional. Therefore, if you were interviewing a Black person for an employment position, it would be important and incumbent upon you to take deliberate steps to mitigate your racial bias to ensure fairness.

The value of a preference scale is that it allows you to see where your preferences lie along the scale and, when combined with research like that from the IAT, how you compare to others. Additionally, preference scales can be combined to create a preference map that provides even deeper insights and understandings.

From Preference Scales to Preference Maps
The prior examples have depicted one-dimensional preference scales along the x-axis (from left to right). To help explain the difference between a preference scale and a preference map, I will offer some additional examples of one-dimensional preference scales, only these will be depicted along the y-axis (from top to bottom).

A second basic example of a one-dimensional preference scale (along the y-axis) is shown in Figure 1.6. In identical fashion to the previous example, top preference scale #3 and bottom preference scale #4 could represent any two opposing preferences and those preferences could be measured anywhere between a "strong preference" for preference scale #3 at the top and "strong preference" for preference scale #4 at the

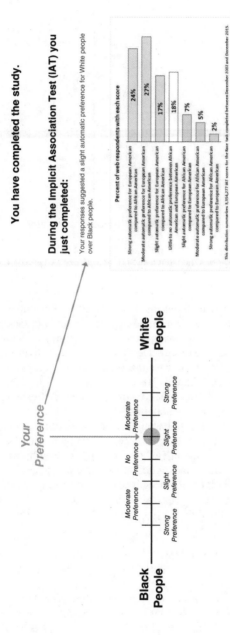

You have completed the study.

During the Implicit Association Test (IAT) you just completed:

Your responses suggested a slight automatic preference for White people over Black people.

Your Preference

Black People

Strong Preference · Moderate Preference · Slight Preference · No Preference · Slight Preference · Moderate Preference · Strong Preference

White People

Percent of web respondents with each score

Strong automatic preference for European American compared to African American — 24%

Moderate automatic preference for European American compared to African American — 27%

Slight automatic preference for European American compared to African American — 17%

Little to no automatic preference between African American and European American — 18%

Slight automatic preference for African American compared to European American — 7%

Moderate automatic preference for African American compared to European American — 5%

Strong automatic preference for African American compared to European American — 2%

This distribution summarizes 3,314,277 IAT scores for the Race task completed between December 2002 and December 2015.

FIGURE 1.5   Example of a One-Dimensional Preference Scale Using the Implicit Association Test (IAT)

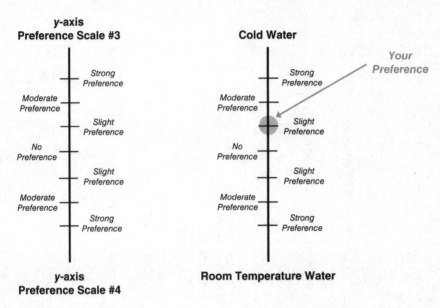

FIGURE 1.6 Basic Example of a One-Dimensional Preference Scale (*y*-axis) and with a Measure

bottom. If you had a slight preference for cold water when compared to room tem-perature water, the preference scale would appear as shown in Figure 1.6 with your measure of "slight preference" showing on the scale. Again, you should be able to eas-ily imagine that the same preference scale shown in Figure 1.6 could also represent a "slight preference" for thinking over feeling, or abstract thinking over concrete think-ing, or other preferences pertaining to DEI.

Figure 1.7 shows an example of the report generated by Gender-Science IAT and depicted along the *y*-axis (from top to bottom).

If this were your IAT report, it would suggest that you have a slight automatic preference for associating men with science and women with liberal arts. (Note: As you can see from the results of IAT research by Project Implicit summarized in Figure 1.7, 18% of men and women who have completed the IAT have a slight auto-matic preference for associating men with science and women with liberal arts.) In other words, if you were interviewing a woman for a scientific employment position, it would be important and incumbent upon you to take deliberate steps to mitigate your gender bias to ensure fairness.

Understanding a Preference Map   A preference map is a multidimensional land-scape that locates you between several different preference scales. A basic example of a two-dimensional preference map (a combined *x*-axis and *y*-axis) is shown in Figure 1.8.

As you can see, Figure 1.8 combines two one-dimensional preference scales into a two-dimensional preference map. For example, if preference scale #1 represented a preference for water with lemon and preference scale #2 represented a preference for water without lemon, while preference scale #3 represented a preference for cold water and preference scale #4 represented a preference for room temperature water, then Figure 1.8 would suggest that you have a slight preference for cold water with lemon.

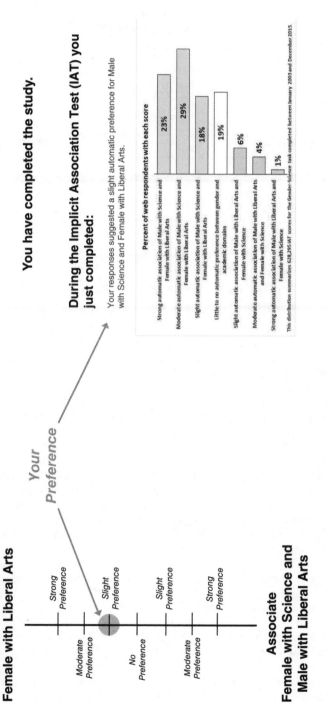

You have completed the study.

During the Implicit Association Test (IAT) you just completed:

Your responses suggested a slight automatic preference for Male with Science and Female with Liberal Arts.

Percent of web respondents with each score

Strong automatic association of Male with Science and Female with Liberal Arts	23%
Moderate automatic association of Male with Science and Female with Liberal Arts	29%
Slight automatic association of Male with Science and Female with Liberal Arts	18%
Little to no automatic preference between gender and academic domains	19%
Slight automatic association of Male with Liberal Arts and Female with Science	6%
Moderate automatic association of Male with Liberal Arts and Female with Science	4%
Strong automatic association of Male with Liberal Arts and Female with Science	1%

This distribution summarizes 628,295 IAT scores for the Gender-Science task completed between January 2003 and December 2015.

Your Preference

Associate Male with Science and Female with Liberal Arts

Strong Preference

Moderate Preference

Slight Preference

No Preference

Slight Preference

Moderate Preference

Strong Preference

Associate Female with Science and Male with Liberal Arts

FIGURE 1.7   Example of a One-Dimensional Preference Scale Using the IAT

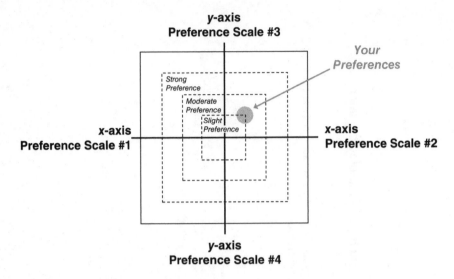

FIGURE 1.8 Example of a Two-Dimensional Preference Map

Example of a Preference Map: Race IAT and Gender-Science IAT In similar fashion to Figure 1.8, Figure 1.9 combines the previous examples of the one-dimensional Race IAT and the one-dimensional Gender-Science IAT into a two-dimension Race and Gender-Science preference map.

If these were your results from the IAT, it would suggest that you have a slight automatic preference for white people and a slight automatic association of men with science. In other words, if you were interviewing a Black woman for a scientific employment position, it would be important and incumbent upon you to take deliberate steps to mitigate both your racial bias and your gender bias to ensure fairness. We will revisit these and other strategies in **Step 3: DEI Insights** and **Step 4: DEI Initiatives**. Moreover, jumping slightly ahead to **Step 2: DEI Imperatives**, which calls for you to develop personal DEI objectives and goals, based on these assessment results your personal DEI objective could be to mitigate your racial and gender biases to ensure fairness, and your personal DEI goal could be to improve your scores on a diverse 360° assessment (explained later in this step) with people of different races and genders in scientific positions.

One of the values of a preference map is that it allows you to easily and visually see interrelationships among your preferences, which mirror the DEI concept of *intersectionality*—that is, how different aspects of a person combine and create overlapping identities, experiences, privileges, and advantages/disadvantages. Intersectionality reflects the complex nature of our human experience and how people identify. Preference maps reflect the complex nature of our preferences against those identifiers and other salient dimensions of the human experience.

For example, I identify as Black, male, Christian, heterosexual, and able-bodied, from among other identifiers. To understand my lived experiences is to understand how each of these identifiers has affected my lived experiences. Along the same lines,

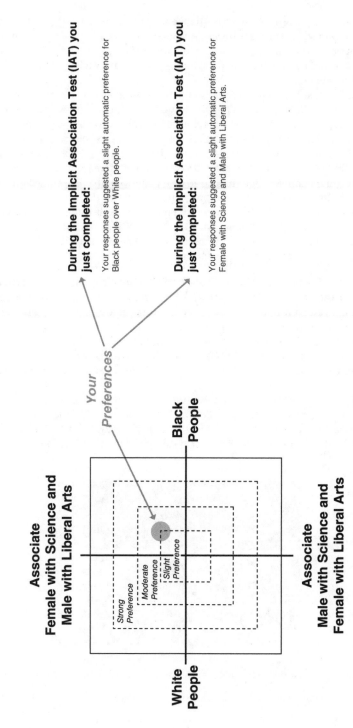

During the Implicit Association Test (IAT) you just completed:

Your responses suggested a slight automatic preference for Black people over White people.

During the Implicit Association Test (IAT) you just completed:

Your responses suggested a slight automatic preference for Female with Science and Male with Liberal Arts.

Your Preferences

**Associate
Female with Science and
Male with Liberal Arts**

Black People

Strong Preference

Moderate Preference

Slight Preference

White People

**Associate
Male with Science and
Female with Liberal Arts**

FIGURE 1.9 Example of a Two-Dimensional Preference Map Using the IAT

much as the previous example assessed preferences, or biases, along the lines of race/ethnicity and gender, it also offered a way of providing overlapping and layered insights to preferences, or biases, at the intersection of race/ethnicity and gender. These results can be extraordinarily valuable to understanding yourself and understanding how you may interact with others.

The IAT is used to assess people against a one-dimensional preference scale. I have employed it here to explain one-dimensional preference scales and as a building block to explain two-dimensional preference maps. However, Project Implicit does not provide IAT results as preference maps, only preference scales. I presented combined Race IAT and Gender-Science IAT results for illustrative purposes as a means to explain preference maps. To help make the concept of preference maps even clearer, my next and final example will introduce an assessment tool that is specifically geared toward generating a two-dimensional preference map: The Herrmann Brain Dominance Instrument® (HBDI®). This is another good example because HBDI®, and the Whole Brain® Thinking model upon which it is based, are both rooted in cognitive science and characterize thinking preferences and cognitive diversity, which can be universally understood and applied to anyone.

Example of a Preference Map: Whole Brain® Thinking and the Herrmann Brain Dominance Instrument® (HBDI®)   According to the theories of brain specialization and lateralization, interconnected networks across different regions of the brain preside over different types of thinking (see Figure 1.10). People are said to prefer certain types of thinking over others, which is reflected in the way we communicate, what motivates us, what we learn, what we pay attention to, and more. This ultimately impacts our behaviors and how we interact at home, at work, and in the world.

Ned Herrmann, whose journey is captured in his book *The Creative Brain*, was the head of management education at General Electric in the 1970s and 1980s, leading GE's renowned Crotonville, New York, corporate university.[8,9] His background was in physics; he was also an accomplished opera singer, painter, and sculptor. This gave

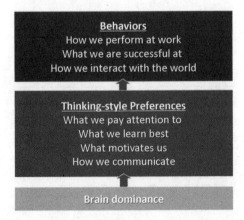

FIGURE 1.10   The Impact of Whole Brain® Thinking: Dominance, Preferences, and Behaviors

him an appreciation of different styles of creativity. During the late 1970s he led the efforts to update GE's management training programs to make them more reflective of individual differences in learning and thinking style preferences, based on the ground-breaking work of Roger Walcott Sperry. Herrmann's research with GE employees was shaped by Sperry's work illustrating the different processing specialties of key areas in the brain for logical/rational thought vs. intuitive/creative thinking. Herrmann also drew insight from Paul MacLean's work understanding distinctions between the cerebral cortex and limbic systems of the brain in abstract/theoretical vs. concrete/realistic thinking, respectively. This ultimately resulted in the Whole Brain® Model with four quadrants, one for each cognitive system, which is described in Table 1.1 and depicted in Figure 1.11.

Buying a car provides a good example of how Whole Brain® thinking works as shown in Table 1.2.

The Herrmann Brain Dominance Instrument® assessment, or HBDI® survey, is comprised of 120 questions that measure thinking preferences based on the Whole Brain® model. Over 2 million HBDI® assessments have been completed worldwide, and the HBDI® has shown strong repeated evidence of validity in psychometric research, including very good test-retest reliability and internal consistency. Face validity is extraordinarily high at over 95%. The HBDI® Profile or assessment report represents a two-dimensional preference map and provides the following key information about you (see Figure 1.12a):

TABLE 1.1   Ned Herrmann's Four-Quadrant Whole Brain® Model

Whole-Brain® Model	
A (Blue)	**D** (Yellow)
Analytical	**Experimental**
Upper-left quadrant	*Upper-right quadrant*
Purpose • Fact • What	**Possibilities • Future • Why**
A person with a preference for activities that involve logic, analysis, fact-finding, and quantitative reasoning.	An original and holistic person motivated by novelty, possibility, variety, oddities, and incongruities (not structure), with a preference for matters requiring intuition, integration, and synthesis.
B (Green)	**C** (Red)
Practical	**Relational**
Lower-left quadrant	*Lower-right quadrant*
Process • Form • When	**People • Feeling • Who**
An action-oriented person with a preference for activities that involve organization, sequencing, planning, and detail.	A sensitive and feeling-based people-reader and mood-minder with a preference for activities reflecting interpersonal, kinesthetic, and emotional significance.

Source: N. Herrmann, *The Creative Brain* (Lake Lure, NC: Ned Herrmann/Brain Books, 1989).

 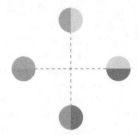 

Research on specific functional regions of the brain . . .

. . . synthesized into four key interconnected cognitive modes . . .

. . . and adapted as a holistic framework & common language for organizational application

FIGURE 1.11 Ned Herrmann's Four-Quadrant Whole Brain® Model
Source: **https://www.thinkherrmann.com/whole-brain-thinking**.

TABLE 1.2 Example of How the Whole Brain® Model Works When Buying a Car

A (Blue) Analytical	D (Yellow) Experimental
• Ease of maintenance • Wants to know how it works • Likes power and precision handling • Wants to see data and statistics on performance • Looks at energy efficiency • Looks at cost of vehicle, trade-in value • Comparison shopping with other vehicles	• More willing to experiment and take some risks • First-model buyer; early innovator • Looks at the aesthetic qualities: sportiness, color, form, and cutting-edge qualities • Wants it to fit the dream, personal image, and long-range plans
B (Green) Practical	C (Red) Relational
• Interested in safety features and durability • Considers the practicality of size, number of doors, storage space, and stain-resistant materials • Examines features such as interior trunk/gas unlock • Looks at maintenance requirements • Has done research and knows what they want	• Will buy based on a friend's recommendation • Feel and comfort of the vehicle is important and user-friendliness of controls • Wants to love the car • Impacted by friendliness of sales and service organization • Knows it's the right choice

HBDI®

	A	B	C	D
Preference Code	1	2	1	1
Profile Scores	73	61	68	79
Under Pressure	58	82	82	58

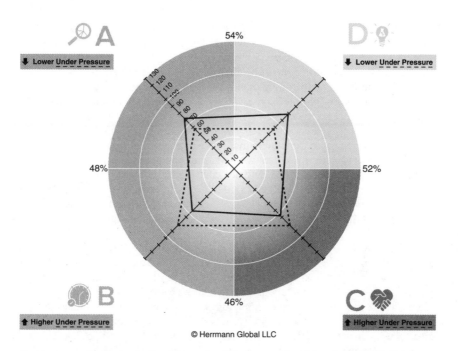

© Herrmann Global LLC

FIGURE 1.12A Example of a Two-Dimensional Preference Map Using the HBDI® Profile

- **Preference Code:** A classification of your overall preference score in each quadrant of the Whole Brain® model. You will have a score here between 1 and 3. A score of 1 indicates a primary or high preference and relates to a score between 67 and 189 and above. A score of 2 indicates a secondary or intermediate preference and relates to a score between 34 and 66. A score of 3 indicates a tertiary or low preference and relates to a score of between 0 and 33.
- **Profile Scores:** Your profile scores for each quadrant under normal circumstances, ranging from 0 to 189. The higher the score for a quadrant the higher the degree of preference for that thinking style.

- **Under Pressure:** Your profile scores for each quadrant under pressure, ranging from 0 to 189. The higher the score for a quadrant the higher the degree of preference for that thinking style under pressure.
- **Percentages:** The percentages at the top and bottom show how much you prefer the cerebral mode of thinking (abstract and theoretical) vs. the limbic mode of thinking (realistic and concrete). The percentages to the left and right show how much you prefer to think (with the rational analytical and practical) versus the intuitive mode of thinking (experimental and interpersonal).
- **Kite-Shaped Figures:** The kite-shaped figure with a solid line visually depicts the four thinking preference profile scores under normal circumstances. The kite-shaped figure with a dashed line visually depicts the four thinking preference profile scores under pressure.

If Figure 1.12a represented your HBDI® report, you would also have a slight thinking preference for cerebral (abstract and theoretical) thinking (54%) and right mode (experimental and interpersonal) thinking (52%). Under normal circumstances, you would have a "triple dominant profile" of "1211" reflecting three primary and high thinking preferences (three preference codes of 1, namely, an "analytical" profile score of 73, "relational" profile score of 68, and "experimental" profile score of 79) and one secondary and intermediate thinking preference (one preference code of 2, namely, a "practical" profile score of 61). In other words, under normal circumstances, you may have a blind spot for matters that relate to practical thinking such as organizing, planning, and attention to details. Once again, jumping slightly ahead to **Step 2: DEI Imperatives**, if your personal DEI objective is to stretch and expand your thinking preference into the "practical" quadrant, then your personal DEI goal could be to complete a diverse 360° assessment (explained later in this chapter) now and one year later to see if family, friends, or colleagues have observed greater intentionality toward organizing, planning, and paying attention to details.

Under pressure, your preferences would generally shift away from experimental thinking (profile score decreases from 79 to 58) and analytical thinking (profile score decreases from 73 to 58) and shift toward practical thinking (profile score increases from 61 to 82) and relational thinking (profile score increases from 68 to 82). Figure 1.12b shows the preference tilt for your general score and your under pressure score—it visually depicts how your preferences shift when operating under normal circumstances to operating under pressure. As you can more clearly see in Figure 1.12b, because your preference tilt under pressure is toward practical thinking (the lower left quadrant) such as organizing and planning, and relational thinking (the lower right quadrant) such as matters related to interpersonal relationships and intuition, you could therefore have a blind spot for experimental thinking (the upper right quadrant) such as synthesizing and conceptualizing ideas, and analytical thinking (the upper left quadrant) such as matters requiring logic and ration.

Once again, the value of a preference map like the HBDI® individual report is that it not only deepens your understanding of yourself, but that you can also generate an HBDI® pair report that compares your profile with another person, and an HBDI® team report that analyzes a group of people. This can lead to more productive communication, meetings, team building, innovation, and more. To take the HBDI® inventory and debrief your results, you must engage an HBDI® Certified Practitioner, which includes several professionals at BCT Partners.

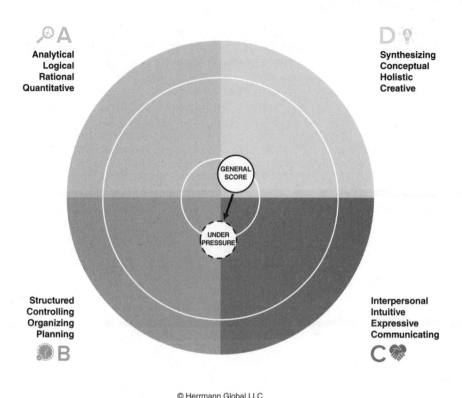

© Herrmann Global LLC

FIGURE 1.12B   Example of a Two-Dimensional Preference Map Using the HBDI® Profile (General Score and Under Pressure)

To learn more about how you or your organization can leverage the Herrmann Brain Dominance Instrument® (HBDI®), please contact our team at BCT Partners at: **info@bctpartners.com** and connect with one of our HBDI® Certified Practitioners.

While the preceding examples depicted two-dimensional preference maps, preference maps can be multidimensional and depict any number of preferences using several axes and various shapes, sizes, colors, numbers, and more, on the map. Next, I will explain how to assess your competences against a continuum, which is relatively easier to explain.

Assessing Your Competences

Competence is measured by locating where you are along a developmental continuum. Unlike a preference assessment such as the IAT or HBDI®, which evaluates your tendencies to do certain things, a competence assessment evaluates your capacity or ability to do certain things as evidenced by your knowledge, skills, and attitudes/attributes (KSAs). For example, I have evidence to suggest I have a high degree of competence for public speaking. I have studied great public speakers (knowledge). I have honed my abilities as a keynote speaker, trainer, and facilitator over the past 30 years (skills). I have certain innate characteristics or gifts, such as the ability to rhyme and use alliteration (natural attributes) that I have further developed through regular practice and rehearsals (nurtured attributes), combined with the empowering belief (attitude) that I can be a great public speaker through continuous self-improvement. In a given week, I can deliver up to 10 speeches or seminars to audiences ranging from 10 people to 10,000 people, and I consistently receive positive evaluation marks with invitations to return and speak at events again. If I were to measure my competence for public speaking, I would likely score on the higher end of the continuum. By comparison, I have a low degree of competence as a vocalist. I cannot sing or, stated differently, I could not carry a tune if it had a handle! I don't have the knowledge, skills, or attributes of a great singer and if I were to measure my competence for singing, I would likely score at the bottom of the continuum. Assessing your competences requires finding a tool or instrument that can locate you on a developmental continuum by measuring your level or degree of competence in the specific area(s) you seek to evaluate.

Understanding a Competence Continuum

A competence continuum is an easy concept to understand and requires less explanation than a preference scale or map. Figure 1.13 shows a basic example of a linear competence continuum comprised of three levels from Level #1 to Level #3.

For example, imagine that Figure 1.13 depicts a continuum for public speaking or singing competence ranging from beginner (Level #1) to intermediate (Level #2) to advanced (Level #3). A competence assessment would evaluate your knowledge, skills, and attitudes/attributes (KSAs) for public speaking or singing and locate you on the continuum. Assuming you were assessed at the intermediate level (Level #2), you could then pursue ways to increase your competence to the advanced level (i.e., move up to continuum to Level #3) by increasing your knowledge, improving your skills, and/or enhancing your attitudes/attributes (KSAs) related to public speaking or singing.

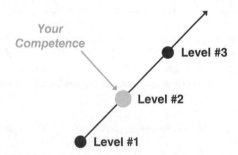

FIGURE 1.13 Basic Example of a Linear Competence Continuum

To explain a competence continuum, I will use inclusive behaviors and the Intrinsic Inclusion Inventory™ (I3™), as my first example. Inclusive behaviors naturally extend our previous discussion about unconscious and implicit bias and are a common and effective measure of DEI for people (and organizations).

Example of a Competence Continuum: Intrinsic Inclusion™ and the Intrinsic Inclusion Inventory™ (I3™)   Whether it's conscious, unconscious, or implicit—to be biased is to be human. Despite this reality, some humans behave more naturally inclusively than others. Their internal motivation and drive to connect with others who are different from them is natural, intentional, and impactful. They practice key behaviors that disrupt bias and create inclusion. Based on the research outlined in their book, *Intrinsic Inclusion: Rebooting Your Biased Brain*, Dr. Janet B. Reid and Vincent R. Brown refer to this phenomenon as Intrinsic Inclusion™. They define the following five characteristics of people with an intrinsically inclusive mindset:[10]

1. **Naturally Seek People Who are Like and Unlike Themselves**—seek to build relationships with those who are like and unlike themselves with the same amount of enthusiasm. This includes relationships with other people both personally and professionally.

2. **Naturally Curious**—They have a natural curiosity and seek to gain a deeper understanding of people from cultures and with lived experiences that differ from their own.

3. **Not Afraid of Others Who are Different**—They have less unjustified fear and negative stereotyping of those who are different. Therefore, they often build highly effective, diverse, and inclusive teams.

4. **Learn from Mistakes**—They know they might make mistakes in dealing with those who are different, but that doesn't deter them from pursuing relationships. They readily acknowledge and learn from a mistake and act to rectify the situation.

5. **DEI Champions**—They consistently deliver to their organizations the advantages of DEI, such as increased employee engagement, innovations, better problem solving, lower turnover, and bottom-line benefits, while also appreciating and uplifting the importance of people.

Intrinsic Inclusion™ lies at the intersection of diversity, neuroscience, and bias.[11] Just as our individuality develops in dimensions—internal traits (primary), external experiences (secondary), and on-the-job classifications (organizational)—so does our unique set of biases. Bias is an automatic reaction to both inherent and learned preferences such as food, music, and status. Curious and adventurous personality types are intrinsically more inclusive when outside the social group to which they psychologically identify (i.e., their "in-group") and may pause their reflexive and automatic responses to act more reflectively and deliberately. Most people are unaware of instinctive preferences—unconscious and implicit biases—and may not recognize bias as a factor in their behavior. The good news is this: We can learn to disrupt automatic thoughts and consider new information. This is the basis of a concept known as "neuroplasticity" or the ability of our brain to form, organize, and reorganize synaptic connections. Empirical data strongly indicates we can grow new neural pathways for greater neural flexibility and cognitive function including behaviors that disrupt our biases.

Based on their research to identify ways to prevent our preconceptions from hijacking our thoughts and determining our judgment, Dr. Russell Fazio of The Ohio State University and Dr. Michael Olson of the University of Tennessee found that "motivation and opportunity can be determinants of spontaneous behavior." Their theory, known as the M.O.D.E. model (**M**otivation and **O**pportunity can be the **De**terminants for Spontaneous Behavior), gives us a methodology for gaining control over our thought processes and their outcomes, as shown in Figure 1.14.

Dr. Fazio refers to M.O.D.E. as a "gating mechanism." With enough motivation (i.e., any incentive that causes a person to stop and think about outcomes such as concern for safety, sticking to a budget, avoiding embarrassment, or important new information) and the opportunity (i.e., people having the resources to think clearly and consciously, meaning they aren't tired, in a hurry, feeling stereotyped, or distressed in other ways), our brains can shut the gate on, or interrupt, an automatically activated attitude. This allows new ideas to inform deliberate, better-informed decisions and actions. With motivation and opportunity, people can develop a mindset of curiosity and intrinsic inclusion and embrace what Dr. Reid and Brown have popularized as "The Power of the Pause"—a deliberate pause that has power to stop automatic reactions, allowing our brain to consider biases and new information, and then to control decisions. Dr. Reid and Brown have identified the following four behaviors—or "inclusion accelerators"—that can cultivate the Power of the Pause, upend patterned thinking, and may reboot our biased brain (see Figure 1.15):

1. **Shared Trust** occurs when a significant relationship forms between people different from each other that allows them to be vulnerable. It has three components:

    1. Enables learning and growth
    2. Equally shared among all parties
    3. Shared definition and framework

2. **Respectful Empathy** occurs when a person embodies the perspectives and feelings of another and chooses to bond with them. It is not sympathy. Respectful empathy has three components:

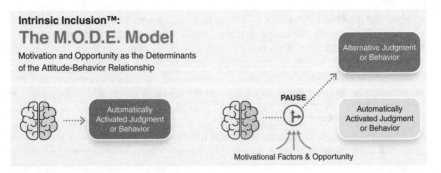

Intrinsic Inclusion™:
The M.O.D.E. Model
Motivation and Opportunity as the Determinants
of the Attitude-Behavior Relationship

Alternative Judgment or Behavior

PAUSE

Automatically Activated Judgment or Behavior

Automatically Activated Judgment or Behavior

Motivational Factors & Opportunity

FIGURE 1.14 The M.O.D.E. Model (**M**otivation and **O**pportunity Can Be the **De**terminants for Spontaneous Behavior) of Intrinsic Inclusion™

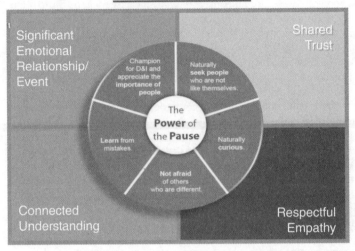

INTRINSIC INCLUSION™

FIGURE 1.15 The Five Characteristics and Four Inclusion-Accelerating Behaviors of Intrinsic Inclusion™

1. Cognitive empathy: intuitively knowing how another thinks
2. Emotional empathy: understanding how another feels
3. Compassionate empathy: wanting to connect with and understand another deeply

3. **Significant Emotional Relationship/Event** occurs when people who are different from one another develop deep respect, become close, and are concerned for one another. It has three components:

   1. Life-altering impact
   2. Emotional connection
   3. Meaningful and enduring

4. **Connected Understanding** occurs when two or more people understand and appreciate how others different from themselves prefer to communicate and process information. It has three components:

   1. Mutual respect and understanding
   2. Communicating in ways that ensure all voices are heard equally
   3. Heightened attentiveness to the styles of others

Biases will always exist, but in changing how you think, feel, and act, these four inclusion-accelerating behaviors can also change your personal and professional relationships and performance. By seeking experiences and opportunities to demonstrate these behaviors, you will lead a more intrinsically inclusive existence. Intrinsic Inclusion™ powerfully illuminates how individuals and teams can disrupt unconscious biases—unlocking improved decision making, communication, collaboration, innovation, inclusion, and belonging.

Dr. Reid, Vincent Brown, LaToya Everett, Patricia Melford, John Grooms, and BCT's Peter York, Dr. Miriam Sarwana, Dr. Astrid Hendricks, Phylicia Thompson, Dr. Lisa Kulka, E'Driana Berry and I conceptualized and developed the Intrinsic Inclusion Inventory™ (I3™). It is a statistically valid and reliable psychometric instrument that measures the competence or ability of people and organizations to be intrinsically inclusive by assigning a score or index to each of the seven different roles that inform the inclusion accelerators.

For example, looking slightly ahead to **Step 2: DEI Imperatives** once again, if your personal DEI objective is to improve your competence with demonstrating inclusive behaviors, then your personal DEI goal could be to complete the I3™ assessment six months apart and increase your score from one level to the next.

I3™ offers individual and group reports, which deepen your understanding of yourself and others such as colleagues, coworkers, and close friends and family. This can help you to become more effective in leading and working with others more inclusively, optimizing teams, and improving organizational performance.

To learn more about how you or your organization can leverage the Intrinsic Inclusion Inventory™ (I3™), please visit: **www.intrinsicinclusion.com** or contact our team at BCT Partners at: **info@bctpartners.com** and connect with one of our Intrinsic Inclusion™ Certified Facilitators.

Next, I will use intercultural competence and the Intercultural Development Inventory® (IDI®) as another example of a competence continuum. As its name implies, intercultural competence is not only a competence but also a concept that can be universally applied across multiple cultures and cultural contexts.

Example of a Competence Continuum: Intercultural Competence and the Intercultural Development Inventory® (IDI®) According to IDI, LLC, intercultural competence is defined as "the capability to shift cultural perspective and appropriately adapt behavior to cultural differences and commonalities. Intercultural competence has been identified as a critical capability in a number of studies focusing on overseas effectiveness of international sojourners, international business adaptation and job performance, international student adjustment, international transfer of technology and information, international study abroad, and inter-ethnic relations within nations."[12]

The Intercultural Development Continuum™ (IDC™) describes orientations toward cultural difference and commonality that are arrayed along a continuum from the "monocultural mindsets" of Denial and Polarization through the transitional orientation of Minimization to the "intercultural or global mindsets" of Acceptance and Adaptation. The capability of deeply shifting cultural perspective and bridging behavior across cultural differences is most fully achieved when one maintains an Adaptation perspective. This continuum is adapted from the Developmental Model of Intercultural Sensitivity originally proposed by Milton Bennett and includes the following five orientations:

1. **Denial**—An orientation that recognizes more observable cultural differences (e.g., food), but may not notice deeper cultural difference (e.g., conflict resolution styles) and may avoid or withdraw from such differences.

2. **Polarization**—An orientation that views cultural difference in terms of "us" and "them." This ranges from:
   - Defense—a more uncritical view toward one's own cultural values and practices coupled with an overly critical view toward other cultural values and practices, to
   - Reversal—an overly critical orientation toward one's own cultural values and practices and an uncritical view toward other cultural values and practices.

3. **Minimization**—An orientation that highlights cultural commonality and universal values and principles that may also mask deeper recognition and appreciation of cultural differences.

4. **Acceptance**—An orientation that recognizes and appreciates patterns of cultural difference and commonality in one's own and other cultures.

5. **Adaptation**—An orientation that can shift cultural perspective and change behavior in culturally appropriate and authentic ways.

Dr. Mitchell R. Hammer, president of IDI, LLC, conducted the cutting-edge research that resulted in the Intercultural Development Inventory® (IDI®).[13,14] The IDI® measures how a person or a group of people tends to think and feel about cultural difference stemming from any aspect of diversity, human identity, and cultural difference. It assesses the core mindset regarding diversity and cultural difference and determines your level of intercultural competence along the IDC™. It is a statistically valid and reliable psychometric instrument that measures one's current degree of intercultural sensitivity and intercultural competence affects or "shows up" in your interactions (e.g., cross-cultural communication) with other people.

Figure 1.16 provides an example of an IDI® report, which provides the following key information:

- **Perceived Orientation (PO):** A measure of how you rate yourself in terms of your own capability to adapt to cultural differences along the developmental continuum.

- **Developmental Orientation (DO):** Your primary orientation or how you are more likely to experience cultural differences and similarities. This is a more accurate measure of how you experience and adapt to cultural differences and similarities. This is also how others likely experience you.

- **Orientation Gap:** This reflects the difference between your Perceived Orientation and the Developmental Orientation. Your Perceived Orientation score may be higher than the Developmental Orientation score or vice versa. This indicates that you may be overestimating or underestimating your level of intercultural competence.

If this were your IDI® report, based on your development orientation (DO) score of 124.26, your primary orientation toward cultural differences would be within

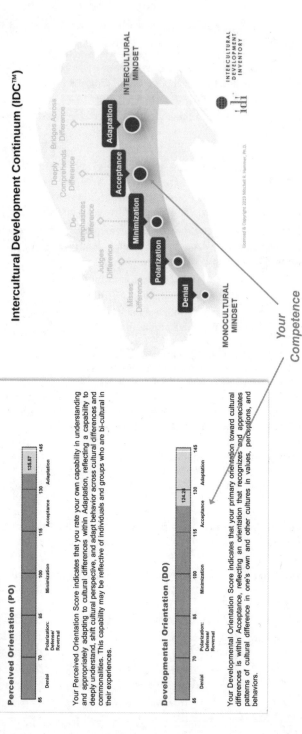

FIGURE 1.16   Example of a Competence Continuum Using the IDI®

"Acceptance," reflecting an orientation that recognizes and appreciates patterns of cultural difference in your own culture and other cultures in values, perceptions, and behaviors. Once again, looking ahead to **Step 2: DEI Imperatives,** if your personal DEI objective is to improve your intercultural competence and ability to navigate difference, then your personal DEI goal could be to increase your IDI® score from Level 3: Minimization to Level 4: Acceptance in one year.

The IDI® also offers individual and group reports. This can help you to become more effective in leading, working in, and succeeding in an increasingly diverse domestic and global workplace and marketplace, and enable your team to do the same. To take the IDI® assessment and debrief your results, you must engage an IDI® Qualified Administrator, which includes several professionals at BCT Partners.

To learn more about how you or your organization can leverage the Intercultural Development Inventory® (IDI®), please contact our team at BCT Partners at **info@bctpartners.com** and connect with one of our IDI® Qualified Administrators.

As a final example of a competence continuum, I will use antiracism and the Antiracist Style Indicator (ASI), which measure antiracist competence.

Example of a Competence Continuum: Antiracism and the Antiracist Style Indicator (ASI)

"Being an antiracist involves making intentional and conscious decisions to support policies, practices and procedures that promote racial equity in housing patterns, criminal justice system, wealth distribution, education, healthcare, and voting rights. Being an antiracist is also a dynamic process that plays out in your everyday life in your attitudes and beliefs. Beyond working to dismantle systemic racism, being an antiracist involves how you express yourself as a racial person and how you interact within a multiracial society with others who do not share your same racial identity," according to Deborah L. Plummer, author of the Antiracist Style Indicator (ASI).

"Rooted in Gestalt psychology principles and family systems theory, the 70 items of the Antiracist Style Indicator (ASI) reflect the attitudes, knowledge and skills [KSAs] for being an effective antiracist." The ASI assigns a score in each of three categories— Underfunctioning, Functioning, Overfunctioning—that represent the degree to which these characteristics show up in your lifestyle. Underfunctioning and Overfunctioning both represent lower levels of competence while Functioning represents the highest level of competence as shown in Figure 1.17. "Functioning antiracists are effective disrupters and eradicators of racism who turn us and them into we. They recognize and understand the structures that shape and maintain racism. They understand racial dynamics and treat associated tensions as challenges to be mastered with education and learning and work to stay updated on contemporary scholarship," says Plummer, "The ASI does not predict success or failure in being an antiracist. As a self-assessment tool, it is designed to help you focus on specific aspects of your personality, behavior, skills, and knowledge as areas of strength and weaknesses. You can make your own interpretations about your scores and determine choices for your growth areas. It is an ipsative measure rather than a norm-based assessment, meaning your score only applies to you and you can take it again over time to see if your scores change and improve."[15]

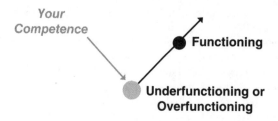

FIGURE 1.17   Example of a Competence Continuum Using the Antiracist Style Indicator (ASI)

Assessing Your Preferences and Competences

As mentioned previously, the value of personal DEI assessments like the IAT, HBDI®, ASI, I3™, IDI®, and the like, is the ability to generate a profile that fosters understanding and delivers insights, and to establish a baseline from which to establish personal DEI objectives and goals, which is the basis for **Step 2: DEI Imperatives**. I strongly recommend that you assess both your preferences and your competences to engender a comprehensive personal DEI journey and to empower yourself with insights into your blind spots, areas of strength, and areas for improvement.

Once you know your preferences, you can establish objectives to shift, stretch, flex, or expand into areas of low preference. Once you know the level at which your competence is assessed, you can more easily begin to chart a path for where you aspire to be and, of equal importance, where you can realistically be in a certain amount of time. Although it is possible, it is less likely that you will skip over several levels of a competence continuum in a short period of time. So, your short-term to medium-term personal DEI objectives and goals should necessarily be centered on what it will take to get from one level to the next. When you assess both preferences and competences, you can also focus certain efforts on increasing competence in areas of low preference, thereby further enhancing your ability to stretch and expand when needed. Assessing your preferences and competences helps paint a complete picture.

Leveraging Diverse 360° Assessments   An excellent tool to include in your personal DEI assessment is a 360° assessment. A 360° assessment typically combines a self-assessment with assessments from other people representing three levels of hierarchy: (1) a lower level (subordinate) such as direct reports, (2) a peer level such as colleagues, and (3) a higher level (super-ordinate) such as a manager or supervisor. Its named is derived from obtaining comprehensive feedback across all three angles and perspectives. I am a big fan of 360° assessments for several reasons.

First, 360° assessments are great because they can assess both preferences and competences including those centered on emotional intelligence. You essentially get a "two-for-one" benefit by taking one assessment to cover both preferences and competences. Second, they go wide and deep. They assess a wide range of competences at the same time, such as leadership, communication, productivity, teamwork, and development of others. They also provide deep feedback in each of these areas by allowing you to compare your self-assessment to the assessments of others, which can offer interesting comparisons between your perspective on your strengths and areas for improvement and the assessments of others. Third, they can often be administered anonymously, thus increasing the likelihood of honesty and transparency. Finally, they can be easily combined with other assessments. I recommend combining a 360° assessment with more focused and specialized assessments such as the IAT, HBDI®, ASI, I3™, IDI®, and the like.

At BCT, we put a DEI spin on 360° assessments. In place of, or in addition to, seeking feedback from a subordinate, peer, and super-ordinate, we recommend seeking feedback from colleagues who are different from you with respect to race/ethnicity, gender, age, physical ability, gender identity, sexual orientation, religion, national origin, languages spoken, and beyond. We refer to this as a *diverse 360° assessment.*

To perform a diverse 360° assessment, you can use a formal 360° assessment tool like the ones highlighted in the next section, or you may opt for a less formal approach: You could easily develop your own survey or questionnaire in the areas of greatest interest to you for others to complete (moreover, several of the formal 360° assessment tools allow you to add your own questions) or you could simply arrange a day/time to meet with each person you have selected to be a part of your 360° assessment, elicit their feedback verbally, and take notes. My point here is that a diverse 360° assessment can be a simple, powerful, and invaluable way to conduct a personal DEI assessment. You will be amazed at the insights you can glean from others when you seek diverse perspectives on how well you function in diverse settings.

As you will see later, for objectives that may be seemingly difficult to measure such as being an ally or an antiracist, a diverse 360° assessment will serve you well as a tool for measuring progress and evaluating results. Moreover, it is also an excellent fail-safe for personal DEI assessment. If you have trouble determining or deciding the right personal DEI assessment for you, then you can always rely on a diverse 360° personal assessment to meet your needs.

A List of Personal DEI Assessment Tools

You are now fully versed in the differences between assessing personal preferences and assessing personal competence. A list of personal DEI assessments of preferences and competences can be found in Table 1.3 with the following headings:

- **Name of Assessment Tool**—The name of the assessment tool.
- **What Does It Measure?**—A summary of what the assessment tool proclaims to measure.
- **When Should You Use It?**—A short synopsis of the circumstances under which you should consider using this assessment tool.

TABLE 1.3 List of Personal DEI and Related Assessments

Name of Assessment Tool	What Does It Measure?	When Should You Use It?	Valid? Reli-able?	Individual & Team Report? (Individual/ Team) Is There a Cost? (Free/Fee/Both) Is a Certified Practitioner Required? (Required/ Not Required/ Optional)?
Personal Preferences				
Implicit Association Test (IAT)	Implicit bias	Designed to measure beliefs and attitudes that individuals may be unwilling or unable to report. The IAT measures strengths of associations between concepts, evaluations, and stereotypes. **implicit.harvard.edu.**	Not Valid Not Reli-able	Individual Fee Not Required
Hermann Brain Dominance Instru-ment (HBDI®)	Thinking pref-erences	Thinking styles assessment tool used to identify one's preferred approach to emotional, analytical, structural, and strategic thinking. **thinkherrmann.com**	Valid Reliable	Individual & Team Fee Required
Intercultural Conflict Style® (ICS®) Inventory	Intercultural conflict style	Assesses culturally learned approaches for communicating information and resolving conflict in four styles: discussion, engagement, accommodation, and dynamic. **icsinventory.com**	Valid Reliable	Individual & Team Fee Required
Cultural Values Profile	Cultural values	Assesses 10 cultural values that differ greatly between nationalities, ethnicities, religions, age groups, and other demographic classes of people. Measures individual preferences that influence approaches to life, school, and work. **culturalq.com**	Valid Reliable	Individual & Team Fee Not Required

Assessment	Type	Description	Validity/Reliability	Availability	Fee	Certification
Myers-Briggs Type Indicator® (MBTI®)	Personality	Personality assessment designed to identify natural preferences in how one directs and receives energy, how one takes in information, how one decides and comes to conclusions, and how one approaches the outside world. **themyersbriggs.com**	Valid Reliable	Individual & Team	Fee	Not Required
Alternatives to MBTI® (Type-Finder®, Type Explorer®, Jung Typology Test™, and Personality Style Instrument)	Personality	Personality assessments designed to identify natural preferences using the 16 personality types referenced in the Myers-Briggs Type Indicator. **www.typefinder.com** **www.16personalities.com** **www.humanmetrics.com** **kilmanndiagnostics.com**	Valid Reliable	Individual & Team	Varies	Not Required
Keirsey Temperament Sorter (KTS)	Temperament	Designed to help one understand self and others by classifying four personality types across four scales of behavior: artisan, guardian, idealist, rational. **www.keirsey.com**	Valid Reliable	Individual (Free & Fee) Team (Fee)		Optional
DiSC Assessment	Personality	Assessment used to determine personality type and behavior style by ranking four areas of behavior: dominance, influence, steadiness, conscientiousness. **www.discprofile.com**	Not valid Reliable	Individual & Team	Fee	Not Required
Birkman Colors	Personality and behavior	Designed to help one understand self and others measured by four benchmarks: usual behaviors, interests, needs, and stress behaviors. **birkman.com**	Valid Reliable	Individual & Team	Fee	Optional
Hogan Assessments (talent development)	Personality and Performance	Assessment tools that cultivate strategic self-awareness so employees, leaders, and your organization will all reach their highest potential. **www.hoganassessments.com/talent-development/**	Valid Reliable	Individual & Team	Fee	Required

(Continued)

TABLE 1.3 (Continued)

Name of Assessment Tool	What Does It Measure?	Description	Valid? Reliable?	Individual & Team Report? (Individual/Team) Is There a Cost? (Free/Fee/Both) Is a Certified Practitioner Required? (Required/Not Required/Optional)?
Thomas-Kilmann Conflict Mode Instrument (TKI®)	Conflict mode	Assessment tool that helps individuals understand how different conflict styles affect personal and group dynamics using five conflict-management modes: competing, collaborating, compromising, avoiding, and accommodating. **kilmanndiagnostics.com**	Valid Reliable	Individual & Team Fee Not Required
Hartman Value Profile (HVP)	Thinking style	Critical thinking assessment measuring an individual's problem-solving strengths, problem-solving struggles, and the ability to avoid blind spots related to situational bias. **www.valuepartnersconsulting.com**	Valid Reliable	Individual Fee Required
SOCIAL STYLES™ Assessment	Acting, thinking, and making decisions	Designed to measure how one displays behavior patterns categorized in four styles: driving, expressive, amiable, and analytical. **www.tracom.com**	Valid Reliable	Individual & Team Fee Optional
Insights Discovery	Preferred behaviors, strengths, and challenges	Based on four colors, insights discovery helps individuals learn more about their preferred behaviors, the strengths they bring, and the challenges they're likely to face. **www.insights.com**	Valid Reliable	Individual & Team Fee Not Required

Personal Competences

Intrinsic Inclusion Inventory™ (I3™)	Inclusive behaviors	Measures the competence or ability of people and organizations to be intrinsically inclusive according to the following four behaviors ("inclusion accelerators"): Shared Trust, Respectful Empathy, Significant Emotional Relationship/Event, and Connected Understanding. These behaviors can cultivate the Power of the Pause, upend patterned thinking, and reboot our biased brain. **www.intrinsicinclusion.com**	Valid Reliable	Individual & Team Fee Not Required
Intercultural Development Inventory® (IDI®)	Intercultural competence	Assessment tool used to assess the capability to shift cultural perspectives and appropriately adapt behavior to culture differences and commonalities. **idiinventory.com**	Valid Reliable	Individual & Group Fee Not Required
Antiracist Style Indicator (ASI)	Efficacy to dismantle racism	Designed to measure an individual's orientation toward racist behavior. **asi.dlplummer.com**	Not Valid Not Reliable	Individual Fee Not Required
Internalized Racism Inventory (IRI)	Attitudes and behaviors toward racism	Designed to assess discriminatory interests, values, attitudes, and behaviors based on race, ethnicity, or national origin. **www.culturalbridgestojustice.org**	Not Valid Not Reliable	Individual Fee Not Required
Internalized Sexism Inventory (ISI)	Attitudes and behaviors toward sexism	Designed to assess discriminatory interests, values, attitudes, and behaviors based on sex and gender. **culturalbridgestojustice.org**	Not Valid Not Reliable	Individual Fee Not required
The White Privilege Test (WPT) (26)	Awareness of white privilege	Tool used to assess the presence of privilege based on common interactions. **monitorracism.eu**	Not Valid Not Reliable	Individual Fee Not Required

(Continued)

TABLE 1.3 (Continued)

Name of Assessment Tool	What Does It Measure?	Description	Valid? Reliable?	Individual & Team Report? (Individual/ Team) / Is There a Cost? (Free/Fee/Both) / Is a Certified Practitioner Required? (Required/ Not Required/ Optional)?
The White Privilege Test (WPT) (30)	Awareness of white privilege	Designed to explore the presence of white privilege and used to build racial consciousness as a personal and professional development exercise. **www.theantiracisteducator.com**	Not Valid Not Reliable	Individual Fee Not Required
The White and Male Privilege Test (WMPT) (46)	Awareness of white and male privilege	Tool used to assess the presence of white privilege and male privilege based on common interactions. **www.nationalseedproject.org**	Not Valid Not Reliable	Individual Fee Not required
Intercultural Awareness Profiler (IAP)	Intercultural awareness	A diagnostic questionnaire designed to assess the personal orientation of choices that an individual makes when resolving intercultural business issues. **www3.thtconsulting.com/tools/intercultural-awareness-profiler/**	Valid Reliable	Individual Fee Not Required
Intercultural Competence Profiler (ICP) – Self Assessment and Observers' (360°)	Intercultural competence	A developmental tool that measures an individual's competence in dealing with cultural differences in a bias-free manner, providing immediate insights on the competence to Recognize, Respect, Reconcile, and Realize cultural differences (4R). **www3.thtconsulting.com/tools/intercultural-competence-profiler-icp/**	Valid Reliable	Individual Fee Not Required

Name	Category	Description	Validity/Reliability	Individual/Team	Fee	Required
The Passions, Awareness, Skills, and Knowledge Inventory (PASK)	Self-efficacy to discuss differences	Assessment tool used to measure an individual's current strengths as well as areas of improvement with intention to promote cultural humility and dialogue about differences. **sparqtools.org/areyoureadytotalk-instructions/**	Not Valid, Not Reliable	Individual	Fee	Not Required
CliftonStrengths	Talent	Talent assessment designed to identify an individual's top five, innate strengths that fall under the domains of strategic thinking, relationship building, influencing, and executing. **www.gallup.com/cliftonstrengths**	Valid, Reliable	Individual & Team	Fee	Not Required
StandOut Strengths Assessment	Traits and talents	Work-focused talent assessment designed to identify an individual's top two strength roles using a series of situational judgment scenarios. **marcusbuckingham.com**	Valid, Reliable	Individual & Team	Fee	Not Required
Inclusive Leader Self-Assessment (ILSA)	Inclusive leadership	Reflection and learning tool used to measure characteristics of inclusive leadership and where an individual falls on the Inclusive Leadership Continuum: aware, unaware, active, advocate. **inclusiveleaderassessment.com**	Unknown	Individual	Fee	Not required
360° Inclusive Leader Assessment	Inclusive leadership	Gathers feedback and self-assessment results in specific goals supporting the ability to be visible, effective change agents. **wmfdp.com/customized-solutions/**	Unknown	Individual	Fee	Unknown
Life Styles Inventory™ (LSI) [includes 360°]	Thinking and behavior	Designed for managers, leaders, students, and those in professional and technical roles, the LSI empowers people to actualize their potential and contribute to the success of their organization. **humansynergistics.com**	Valid, Reliable	Individual	Fee	Not Required
STAR 360	Leadership	Survey tool that utilizes nine executive leader competences to measure an individual's proficiency in critical leadership skills. **www.star360feedback.com**	Not Valid, Not Reliable	Individual	Fee	Not Required

(Continued)

TABLE 1.3 (Continued)

Name of Assessment Tool	What Does It Measure?	Description	Valid? Reliable?	Individual & Team Report? (Individual/Team) Is There a Cost? (Free/Fee/Both) Is a Certified Practitioner Required? (Required/Not Required/Optional?)
CheckPoint 360®	Leadership	Leadership assessment tool designed to help managers identify and prioritize development opportunities and leadership skill-building. **assessmentleaders.com**	Valid Reliable	Individual Fee Not Required
SpiderGap (360°)	Performance	Feedback tool that identifies priorities for professional development using customized questionnaires and templates based on organizational goals. **www.spidergap.com**	Not Valid Not Reliable	Individual Fee Not Required
SurveySparrow (360°)	Performance	Designed to assess strengths, areas of improvement, blind spots, and hidden strengths to promote personal and professional development. **www.surveysparrow.com**	Not Valid Not Reliable	Individual Fee Not Required
Culture Amp (360°)	Effectiveness	Employee engagement, performance, and development tools—all in one intuitive platform—including Individual Effectiveness 360, Manager Effectiveness 180, Leadership Effectiveness 360, and Team Effectiveness assessments. **www.cultureamp.com**	Unknown	Individual & Team Fee Not Required

Name	Measures	Description	Validity		
VIA Survey of Character Strength	Traits	Survey tool designed to assess an individual's character strengths using 24 predetermined traits. **www.viacharacter.org**	Valid Reliable	Individual	Fee Not Required
Global Leadership Survey (GLS)	Leadership	Assessment tool for understanding leadership styles designed around four dimensions—values, action, ideas, and people. **www.globaldiversityservices.com**	Valid Reliable	Individual	Fee Not Required
Personal Preferences and Competences					
Cultural Intelligence (CQ) Pro Assessment	Cultural values and cultural intelligence (CQ)	Assesses cultural values—10 cultural values that differ greatly between nationalities, ethnicities, religions, age groups, and other demographic classes of people—and cultural intelligence (CQ)—a skill set that predicts effectiveness in diverse situations by measuring capabilities in four distinct areas: CQ Drive, CQ Knowledge, CQ Strategy, and CQ Action. **culturalq.com**	Unknown	Individual	Fee Not Required
360 Inclusive Leadership Compass (ILC)	Inclusive leadership effectiveness	A multi-rater feedback tool that measures Inclusive Leadership effectiveness and identifies everyday actions to support behavioral change across the areas of self (embrace), others (empower), team (embed), and organization (enable). **inclusiveleaershipcompass.com**	Valid Reliable	Individual & Team	Fee Not Required
Emotional Quotient Inventory (EQ-I 2.0)	Emotional intelligence	The Emotional Quotient Inventory 2.0 (EQ-i 2.0) measures an individual's emotional intelligence including five areas of emotional and social functioning. It also provides a deeper understanding of how the results affect a participant's workplace performance (conflict resolution, change management, teamwork, decision making, and more). **www.eiconsortium.org**	Valid Reliable	Individual & Team	Fee Not Required

(Continued)

TABLE 1.3 (Continued)

Name of Assessment Tool	What Does It Measure?	Description	Valid? Reliable?	Individual & Team Report? (Individual/Team) Is There a Cost? (Free/Fee/Both) Is a Certified Practitioner Required? (Required/Not Required/Optional?)
Emotional Quotient Inventory 360 (EQ-360)	Emotional intelligence	Using the same model as the EQ-i 2.0, the EQ-360 allows leaders to receive feedback from peers, managers, direct reports, and others on how they leverage their emotional intelligence. **www.eiconsortium.org**	Valid Reliable	Individual Fee Not Required
Six Seconds Emotional Intelligence Assessment (SEI®)	Emotional intelligence	The Six Seconds Emotional Intelligence Assessment (SEI®) is a complete solution for EQ measurement and development that equips people with a framework for putting emotional intelligence into action. **www.6seconds.org**	Valid Reliable	Individual & Team Fee Not Required
Six Seconds Emotional Intelligence Assessment (SEI®) 360	Emotional intelligence	Using the same model as the SEI®, the SEI® 360 is an in-depth, multi-rater feedback tool that provides clear, valuable feedback in a framework for action. **www.6seconds.org**	Valid Reliable	Individual Fee Not Required
Global Diversity Survey (GDS)	Interpersonal and self-awareness	Utilizes the head (insight), heart (inclusion), and hands (adaptation) model to assess awareness of and understanding of self, others, and the world. **www.globaldiversityservices.com**	Not Valid Not Reliable	Individual Fee Not Required

Global Gender Intelligence Assessment (GGIA)	Gender intelligence	Assessment and understanding of the cognitive, emotional, and behavioral aspects of gender. **www.globaldiversityservices.com**	Not Valid Not Reliable	Individual Fee Not Required
AEIOU Single-Rater	Negotiation and conflict management	Assesses communication behaviors during conflict, as well as the ability to negotiate when conflict arises. The assessment measures on five scores: Attacking, Evading, Informing, Opening, and Uniting (AEIOU). **www.globaldiversityservices.com**	Not Valid Not Reliable	Individual Fee Not Required
AEIOU Multi-Rater	Negotiation and conflict management	Using the same model as the AEIOU Single-Rater, the AEIOU Multi-Rater includes feedback from up to five people (360°). **www.globaldiversityservices.com**	Not Valid Not Reliable	Individual Fee Not Required
The Energy Leadership™ Index (ELI)	Perception and approach to work and life	Assesses the way a person views the world, and turns it into something tangible—a metric that you can see and feel and even reevaluate in the future. **www.energyleadership.com/assessment**	Valid Reliable	Individual Fee Required

To learn more about Intrinsic Inclusion™, reference the book *Intrinsic Inclusion: Rebooting Your Bias Brain* by Dr. Janet Reid and Vincent Brown (Cincinnati, OH: New Phoenix Publishing, 2021).

To learn more about emotional intelligence, reference the book *Bar-On Emotional Quotient Inventory, Technical Manual (A Measure of Emotional Intelligence)*, by Dr. Reuven Bar-On (Toronto: Multi-Health Systems, 2000).

- **Validity**—The extent to which the assessment tool measures what it was designed to measure ("valid"). This may include both *construct validity*, the extent to which the assessment tool measures a theoretical phenomenon that is not easily observed, and *face validity*, the extent to which users and professionals feel confident, superficially and subjectively, that the assessment tool delivers on its promise.

- **Reliability**—The extent to which the assessment tool repeatedly and consistently measures what it was designed to measure ("reliable"). Most widely used assessment tools have undergone a process of confirming validity and reliability. This information is made publicly available and describes the methods and evidence used to support the validity and reliability of the assessment tool as well as appropriate and inappropriate uses of the assessment tool.

- **Individual and Team Report**—Does the vendor offer reports for individuals only ("individual only")? Individual and aggregated reports for teams ("individual & team")?

- **Is There a Cost?**—Is the assessment available at no cost ("free"), or is the assessment only available at a cost ("fee"), or is the individual assessment available at no cost while the team assessment is available at a cost ("both" free and fee).

- **Is a Certified Practitioner Required?**—In order to take the assessment and/or access the report, are you required to work through a certified practitioner or qualified administrator or other approved third-party? Yes ("required"), no ("not required"), or is a certified practitioner available but not required ("optional")?

Once again, while certain personal DEI journeys may only require an assessment of your preferences or competences, I strongly recommend that you assess both your preferences and your competences to paint a complete picture of your DEI profile and baseline.

Choosing the Right Personal DEI Assessment Tool for You

Now it is time to choose the right tools for your personal DEI assessment that align with your personal DEI aims.

Your personal DEI aims will naturally suggest whether you will need to assess your preferences or your preferences and competences (I recommend both). For example, if your personal DEI aim is to recognize your own biases, then you will need to assess your preferences, at a minimum. If your personal DEI aim is to improve your inclusive behaviors or intercultural competence, then you will need to assess your competences. By comparison, if your personal DEI aim is to mitigate your own biases, then you will need to both assess your preferences (to recognize your biases) and your competences (after having recognized your biases, to have the ability to mitigate them). Once you've determined whether you need to assess preferences or preferences and competences, you must complete three tasks.

Task 1: Choose Initial Personal DEI Core Preferences and Competences

The first task is to choose initial personal DEI core preferences and DEI core competences, that is, the specific preferences and competences you will focus on as a part of your DEI journey. Table 1.4 provides a list of 21 personal DEI core preferences and competences—"The ABCDEs of DEI"—and their definitions. You should choose preferences and competences that are most aligned with your DEI aims. And much like your DEI aims, as long as your choices are directionally correct, you will be just fine for now. You will have the opportunity to not only refine and finalize your choices in **Step 4: DEI Initiatives**, but you will also have the opportunity to inform those choices based on promising and proven practices summarized in **Step 3: DEI Insights**.

TABLE 1.4 List of Personal DEI Core Preferences and Competences ("The ABCDEs of DEI")

Category	Related to Preference? To Competence?	Definition
1. Awareness of Self*	Preference and Competence	Consciousness of one's own social identities, cultural influences, behaviors, values, and preferences and their relevance to internal and external interactions.
2. Awareness of Others*	Preference and Competence	Consciousness of other's social identities, cultural influences, behaviors, values, and preferences and their relevance to internal and external interactions.
3. Appreciation of Self*	Preference and Competence	Acknowledging the value and significance of one's own identities and contributions.
4. Appreciation of Others*	Preference and Competence	Acknowledging the value and significance of other's identities and contributions.
5. Affirming Others	Competence	Displaying approval, encouragement, or recognition of someone, their actions, or contributions.
6. Advocacy	Competence	Understanding and communicating the needs of others in support of a specific interest or cause.
7. Allyship	Competence	Action, behaviors, or practices in equal partnership with a marginalized group to actively and purposefully challenge, dismantle, and eliminate the personal (beliefs), interpersonal (behaviors), institutional (organizational culture), and systemic (societal structures) barriers to advance their interests.

(Continued)

TABLE 1.4 (Continued)

Category	Related to Preference? To Competence?	Definition
8. Antiracism	Competence	Action, behaviors, or practices in equal partnership with racial group to actively and purposefully challenge, dismantle, and eliminate racist beliefs (personal racism), behaviors (interpersonal racism), policies and practices (institutional racism), and societal systems (structural racism).
9. Bias Awareness	Preference and Competence	Acknowledging prejudices or unsupported judgments of individuals or groups.
10. Bias Mitigation	Competence	Decreasing or preventing the occurrence and/or impact of prejudices or unsupported judgments of individuals or groups.
11. Coaching, Mentoring, and Sponsoring	Competence	Coaching—facilitating skill development by providing clear behavioral-specific feedback, and by making or eliciting specific suggestions for improvement in a manner that builds the confidence and maintains the self-esteem of others. Mentoring—facilitating a reciprocal learning partnership by establishing mutually defined goals to develop skills, abilities, knowledge, or thinking over an extended period. Sponsoring—utilizing power and influence to advocate for an individual's promotion or advancement that aligns with specific personal and/or professional goals.
12. Collaboration	Competence	The ability to work with two or more people for a common purpose.
13. Common Language	Competence	The ability to define and describe common terms such as diversity, equity, inclusion, belonging, bias, prejudice, discrimination, racism, antiracism, allyship, privilege, and more.
14. Cross-Cultural Communication	Competence	The ability to recognize both differences and similarities in how cultural groups communicate and exchange information and meaning with people from different cultural backgrounds to effectively engage in a given context.
15. Courage	Competence	The ability to respond or act despite the presence of fear.
16. Cultural Adaptation	Competence	The ability to modify behavior or overcome changes with consideration of language, culture, environment, and context.

TABLE 1.4 (Continued)

Category	Related to Preference? To Competence?	Definition
17. Cultural Competence	Competence	The ability to understand, appreciate, and interact with people from cultures or belief systems different from one's own.
18. Cultural Humility	Preference and Competence	Respecting and not having a sense of superiority toward other people's cultural backgrounds.[16]
19. Cross-Cultural Conflict Resolution	Competence	The ability to recognize both differences and similarities in how cultural groups resolve conflict and objectively approach a challenge or issue between individuals from different cultural backgrounds.
20. Dialogue	Competence	The ability to exchange opinions and/or ideas with two or more people leading to greater mutual understanding.
21. Intelligence	Preference and Competence	The ability to understand, use, and manage one's own emotions in positive ways to relieve stress, communicate effectively, empathize with others, overcome challenges, and defuse conflict.

*Includes awareness of personality, culture, temperament, leadership style, communication style, conflict style, cognitive or thinking style, and other preferences.

While you are not limited to the preferences and competences listed in Table 1.4, the list does a good job of capturing some of the most common preferences and competences to consider. If you decide to only assess your preferences, then I recommend you choose a total of three to five preferences as your core focus. If you decide to assess your preferences and competences, then I recommend a total of five to seven preferences and competences as your core focus.

Task 2: Select the Personal DEI Assessment Tools That Map to Your Personal DEI Aims, Core Preferences, and Competences

The second task is to select one or more personal DEI assessment tools that map to your personal DEI aims, core preferences, and core competences. Table 1.5 walks you through the entire process for choosing initial personal DEI core preferences and competences and selecting the right personal DEI assessment tool. Later in **Step 4: DEI Initiatives**, when determining your personal DEI strategies and measures, we will apply a very similar process to selecting your final personal DEI core preferences and competences. While it's important to select personal DEI assessment tools that are appropriate for your personal DEI aims, what's most important is that you put in the time and effort to fully understand and explore the value a tool can deliver.

TABLE 1.5   Mapping Personal DEI Aims to Personal DEI Preferences and Competences to Personal DEI Assessments

If your personal DEI aims relate to . . .	Then you must assess your . . .	First, select from among the following personal DEI core preferences and core competences ("The ABCDEs of DEI") . . .	Second, choose one or more DEI assessments that map to the personal DEI preferences and competences you selected . . .
Diversity: The Range of Human Differences *(A Fact)*			
1. Appreciate differences	Preferences	Awareness of Self, Awareness of Others, Appreciation of Others, Cultural Humility, Emotional Intelligence	HBDI®, ICS®, MBTI®, KTS, DiSC, Birkman, TKI®, HVP, SOCIAL STYLES™, EQ-i 2.0, SEI®
2. Recognize own biases	Preferences	Awareness of Self, Appreciation of Others, Bias Awareness, Cultural Humility, Emotional Intelligence	IAT, EQ-i 2.0, SEI®
Inclusion: Involvement and Empowerment *(An Action)*			
3. Mitigate own biases	Preferences	Awareness of Self, Appreciation of Others, Affirmation of Others, Bias Awareness, Bias Mitigation, Cultural Humility, Emotional Intelligence	IAT, EQ-i 2.0, SEI®
	Competences	Adaptation, Communication, Cultural Competence, Cultural Humility, Emotional Intelligence	I3™, ILSA, EQ-i 2.0, LSI, SEI®, *Any Diverse 360°*
4. Navigate and bridge differences	Preferences	Awareness of Self, Awareness of Others, Appreciation of Others, Affirmation of Others, Bias Awareness, Bias Mitigation, Cultural Humility, Emotional Intelligence	HBDI®, ICS®, MBTI®, KTS, DiSC, Birkman, TKI®, HVP, SOCIAL STYLES™, EQ-i 2.0, SEI®
	Competences	Adaptation, Communication, Courage, Cultural Competence, Cultural Humility, Dialogue, Emotional Intelligence	I3™, IDI®, PASK, ILSA, LSI, EQ-i 2.0, SEI®, *Any Diverse 360°*
5. Be inclusive	Preferences	Awareness of Others, Appreciation of Others, Affirmation of Others, Bias Awareness, Bias Mitigation, Cultural Humility, Emotional Intelligence	IAT, EQ-i 2.0, SEI®

TABLE 1.5   (Continued)

If your personal DEI aims relate to . . .	Then you must assess your . . .	First, select from among the following personal DEI core preferences and core competences ("The ABCDEs of DEI") . . .	Second, choose one or more DEI assessments that map to the personal DEI preferences and competences you selected . . .
	Competences	Adaptation, Advocacy, Collaboration, Communication, Courage, Cultural Competence, Cultural Humility, Dialogue, Emotional Intelligence	I3™, ILSA, EQ-i 2.0, LSI, SEI®, *Any Diverse 360°*
6. Resolve conflict	Preferences	Collaboration, Emotional Intelligence	ICS®, TKI®, EQ-i 2.0, SEI®
	Competences	Conflict Resolution, Dialogue, Emotional Intelligence	EQ-i 2.0, SEI®, *Any Diverse 360°*
Equity: Fairness and Equality in Outcomes *(A Choice)*			
7. Be a mentor 8. Be a sponsor	Preferences	Awareness of Others, Appreciation of Others, Affirmation of Others, Cultural Humility, Emotional Intelligence	HBDI®, ICS®, MBTI®, KTS, DiSC, Birkman, TKI®, HVP, SOCIAL STYLES™, EQ-i 2.0, SEI®
	Competences	Advocacy, Coaching, Mentoring and Sponsoring, Collaboration, Communication, Cultural Competence, Cultural Humility, Dialogue, Emotional Intelligence	I3™, IDI®, ASI, IRI, ISI, WPT (26), WPT (30), WMPT (46), PASK, CliftonStrengths, StandOut, ILSA, LSI, EQ-i 2.0, SEI®, *Any Diverse 360°*
9. Be an ally 10. Be an antiracist	Preferences	Awareness of Others, Appreciation of Others, Affirmation of Others, Allyship, Antiracism, Bias Awareness, Bias Mitigation, Cultural Humility, Emotional Intelligence	IAT, EQ-i 2.0, SEI®
	Competences	Advocacy, Collaboration, Communication, Courage, Cultural Competence, Cultural Humility, Dialogue, Emotional Intelligence	I3™, ASI, IRI, ISI, WPT (26), WPT (30), WMPT (46), ILSA, EQ-i 2.0, LSI, SEI®, *Any Diverse 360°*

(Continued)

TABLE 1.5 (Continued)

If your personal DEI aims relate to . . .	Then you must assess your . . .	First, select from among the following personal DEI core preferences and core competences ("The ABCDEs of DEI") . . .	Second, choose one or more DEI assessments that map to the personal DEI preferences and competences you selected . . .
11. Improve performance 12. Increase compensation	Preferences	Awareness of Self, Awareness of Others, Appreciation of Others, Bias Awareness, Cultural Humility, Emotional Intelligence	IAT, HBDI®, MBTI®, KTS, DiSC, Birkman, HVP, SOCIAL STYLES™, EQ-i 2.0, SEI®
	Competences	Adaptation, Affirmation of Others, Bias Mitigation, Coaching, Mentoring and Sponsoring, Collaboration, Communication, Cultural Competence, Cultural Humility, Emotional Intelligence	I3™, IDI®, ISI, IRI, ASI, WPT (26), WPT (30), WMPT (46), PASK, CliftonStrengths, StandOut, ILSA, LSI, EQ-i 2.0, SEI®, *Any Diverse 360°*

Task 3: Generate Reports and Conduct a Debriefing The third and final step is to generate a report and conduct a debriefing. As shown in Table 1.3, some personal DEI assessments require that you work through a certified practitioner or qualified administrator or other approved third party. They will conduct your debriefing. In almost all instances, the work of generating a profile will be done for you and delivered in the form of an electronic or downloadable assessment report. Some reports also include tips, tools, and other insights based on your profile. You and/or your certified practitioner should take the time to conduct a detailed review of your personal DEI assessment results. The findings will serve as the basis for determining your personal DEI objectives and goals in **Step 2: DEI Imperatives**.

Mitigating Data Bias—Part 1

When administering an assessment tool, it is important to be mindful of how human biases can affect the implementation of the tool and interpretation of its results, and to take deliberate steps to mitigate those biases. Data carries and inherits its own assumptions and biases as a reflection of the human assumptions and implicit biases discussed earlier in this step. This phenomenon is referred to as "data bias" and "algorithmic bias." A famous example is when a team at Amazon built a computer program to improve their recruitment of women.

"The team had been building computer programs since 2014 to review job applicants' resumes with the aim of mechanizing the search for top talent," according to Reuters.[17] "Automation has been key to Amazon's e-commerce dominance, be it inside warehouses or driving pricing decisions. The company's experimental hiring tool used artificial intelligence (AI) to give job candidates scores ranging from one to five stars—much like shoppers rate products on Amazon. . . . But by 2015, the company realized its new system was not rating candidates for software developer jobs and other technical posts in a gender-neutral way. That is because Amazon's computer models were trained to vet applicants by observing patterns in resumes submitted to the company over a 10-year period. Most came from men, a reflection of male dominance across the tech industry." Essentially, the algorithm underlying Amazon's computer program inherited a gender bias, from among other problems, that disadvantaged women job seekers. Despite all their technological sophistication, even Amazon was undermined by a data and algorithmic bias. There are several ways that data and algorithmic biases can manifest themselves that you should be aware of, so they do not undermine your efforts. Three of the most common data biases—*researcher bias, confirmation bias*, and *attribution bias*—are described below along with steps you can take to mitigate them. I will further explore a third bias—*selection bias*—in the second part of **Step 1: DEI Inventory for Organizations**, and a fourth bias—*algorithmic bias*—in **Step 5: DEI Impact**.

Researcher Bias

Researcher bias shows up long before you employ an assessment tool. It affects how an instrument is conceived, designed, labeled, and presented. When they are developing instruments, scales, terminology, and phraseology, researchers make assumptions, and those assumptions can show up as a researcher bias.

For example, one of the tools we often use at BCT to help clients resolve conflicts and solve problems across cultural boundaries is the Intercultural Conflict Style Inventory® (ICS®). The ICS®, which measures your preference for intercultural conflict against four styles, was also developed by Dr. Mitchell R. Hammer of ICS Inventory, LLC.

In Western cultures there is a bias, or preference, for resolving conflict directly. This reflects an individualistic cultural orientation and a focus on tasks. For example, a common approach to resolving conflict in Western cultures is for both individuals to try to work out their differences one on one and, if that fails, to bring in a neutral third party to resolve the issues and complete the task. In non-Western cultures there is a bias, or a preference, for resolving conflict indirectly. This reflects a collectivistic cultural orientation and a focus on relationships. For example, a common approach to resolving conflict in non-Western cultures is to keep the individuals apart and use a third party who knows them both intimately to discuss the issue with them separately and inform them of the resolution to the issue separately, to maintain the relationship. The ICS® is predicated on a theoretical model that embraces both preferences for resolving conflict and, in doing so, mitigates researcher bias. It was intentionally developed by Dr. Hammer "to eliminate potential cultural bias by insuring that the theoretical model is grounded in research evidence that is generalizable and inclusive of a wide-range of cultural communities (e.g., individualistic to collectivistic cultural groups)."[18]

When evaluating an assessment tool, you want to be certain to ask questions such as the following:

- Is the model or framework for the assessment inclusive?
- Does it reflect diverse perspectives, racially, ethnically, culturally, domestically, and internationally in its conception, design, labeling, and presentation?
- If so, how was this accomplished?

This will help mitigate the potential of researcher biases to skew the assessment questions, methodologies, analysis, and results.

Confirmation and Attribution Bias

Confirmation bias occurs when we actively search for information or evidence that confirms our preconceived assumptions and hypotheses while ignoring information or evidence to the contrary. Prior to conducting an assessment, people often harbor expectations of the results. For example, imagine that you have always prided yourself on being an organized person, but your close friends and family regularly disagree and consider you a very disorganized person. If you were to assess your thinking preferences using the HBDI® and your results came back with a high profile score for "practical" thinking (organized/sequential/planned/detailed) it would very likely be interpreted as confirmation of your expectations, thus reflecting your confirmation bias. However, you should not ignore the feedback from your friends and family as it also represents valuable data that could cause you to have a blind spot. Moreover, you should recall that a preference is not a competence. Therefore, while the HBDI® may have assessed you as having a high preference for being organized, the feedback from you friends and family may suggest you have a low competence for being organized!

As another example, imagine you are assessing your implicit biases using the IAT. You may take the test believing you don't have any implicit biases because you incorrectly assume that a bias is a bad thing or says something negative about you (in fact, I've witnessed this "bias about bias" on countless occasions during trainings and facilitations) or that you could not possibly harbor any preferences, thus reflecting an attribution bias. As result, you are likely to reject the results if they come back with anything other than a neutral or positive finding. Stated simply, a confirmation bias may cause you to passively accept assessment results you like and/or vehemently reject assessment results you don't like.

To mitigate confirmation bias, attribution bias, or other forms of bias, you can employ a technique akin to Structured Free Recall (SFR).[19] SFR has proven to be successful in reducing the influence of bias when evaluating people or decisions. It suggests that you consider all the positives and negatives associated with the person or the decision before completing your evaluation. I think of SFR as a way to mitigate bias by first calibrating your brain to all possibilities both positive and negative. In this context, I recommend that you consider all the positives and negatives associated with you and your preferences and competences, including seeking feedback from a diverse set of colleagues, coworkers, and close friends and family, prior to completing a personal DEI assessment. This can help mitigate the potential influence of bias when you receive and interpret your personal DEI assessment results.

STEP 1

DEI Inventory for Organizations—Seek Understanding

Representation matters.

Meet people where they are.

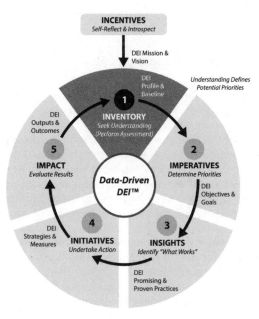

Data-Driven DEI—Step 1: DEI Inventory

A DEI inventory for organizations—an **organizational DEI assessment**—is like a personal DEI assessment in collecting data from your organization and producing data for your organization, typically in the form a profile or report summarizing insights, findings, and/or recommendations to improve organizational DEI. It also helps establish a baseline or a starting point, based on data, that helps you understand where you are organizationally, determine where you want to go, and the means to gauge progress along the way (i.e., to know if and how much progress you have made, you must first know where you started). Once again, as you will see in our final **Step 5: DEI Impact**, it is often by readministering the same organizational DEI assessment you identify here in **Step 1: DEI Inventory** that you evaluate results. You will also see that the data you report will only be as good the data you collect.

Organizational DEI Assessment Framework

Per BCT's DEI Assessment Framework: The 4 P's of People, Practices, Policies, and Performance shown in Figure 0.5, Figure 1.18 shows the **Organizational DEI Assessment Framework** we employ at BCT. It is essentially a focused subset of the Dimensions of Organizational Transformation, or more specifically, those dimensions that lie above the waterline of the iceberg in Figure 0.3 and the top three layers of the pyramid in Figure 0.5.

Our approach to organizational DEI assessment includes:

- **People:** Personal Preferences and Competences
- **People:** Personal Behaviors and Experiences (Organizational Culture and Climate)
- Management **Practices** and Organizational **Policies**
- Overall **Performance** Benchmark and/or Ranking

Organizational DEI assessments tend to have several moving parts because they seek to understand some or all of these four puzzle pieces that characterize your organization. **Step 1: DEI Inventory for Organizations** outlines how you can perform your own organizational DEI assessment of people, policies, practices, and performance. This step begins by focusing on how to assess the personal preferences and competences of people, followed by how to assess the behaviors and experiences of people within the context of your organizational culture and climate via surveys, interviews, and focus groups; how to assess management practices and organizational policies; and, finally, how to benchmark and/or rank performance. This step also includes a list of organizational DEI assessment tools to choose from along with specific advice for how to choose the best organizational DEI assessment tools that align with your objectives and suit your needs. As mentioned at the beginning of

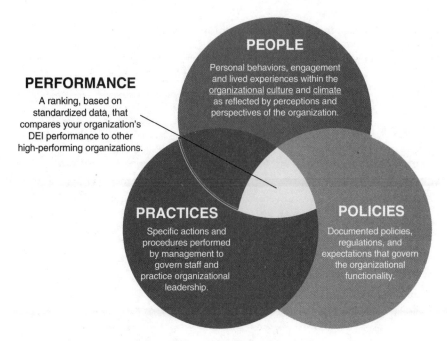

FIGURE 1.18   Organizational DEI Assessment Framework: The 4 P's

Step 1: DEI Inventory for People, your DEI strategic plan will only be as good as your DEI assessment. Similarly, your organizational DEI assessment (and subsequent data analysis and reporting) will only be as good as the quality of the quantitative and qualitative data you collect. Accordingly, this step includes important discussions about data collection, data sampling, data privacy, data confidentiality, data anonymity, data analysis, and data reporting, and it concludes by revisiting the topic of mitigating data bias.

Conducting an Organizational DEI Assessment

Based on the organizational DEI aims you crafted in **Step 0: DEI Incentives,** Table 1.6 can assist you by making clear whether you need an organizational DEI assessment tool that evaluates people, practices, policies, and/or performance.

As you can see, in all but a few instances, you should consider assessing people, practices, policies, and performance. Figure 1.19 illustrates the overall approach we employ at BCT to conduct an organizational DEI assessment of people,

TABLE 1.6	Mapping Organizational DEI Aims to Organizational DEI Assessments			
	Then your organizational DEI assessment should evaluate . . .			
If your organizational DEI aims relate to . . .	**People: Personal Preferences and Competences**	**People: Personal Behaviors and Experiences (Organizational Culture and Climate)**	**Management Practices and Organizational Policies**	**Overall Performance Benchmark and/or Ranking**
Diversity: The Range of Human Differences _(A Fact)_				
1. Increase diversity (representation)	X	X	X	X
2. Increase awareness of diversity and/or biases in people	X	X		
Inclusion: Involvement and Empowerment _(An Action)_				
3. Mitigate biases in people	X	X		
4. Increase engagement, inclusion, and/or belonging	X	X	X	X
5. Improve communication, teamwork, collaboration, and/or innovation	X	X	X	X
6. Manage conflict	X	X		
Equity: Fairness and Equality in Outcomes _(A Choice)_				
7. Foster development	X	X	X	X

TABLE 1.6 (Continued)

If your organizational DEI aims relate to ...	Then your organizational DEI assessment should evaluate ...			
	People: Personal Preferences and Competences	People: Personal Behaviors and Experiences (Organizational Culture and Climate)	Management Practices and Organizational Policies	Overall Performance Benchmark and/or Ranking
8. Promote advancement	X	X	X	X
9. Eliminate barriers and/or improve equity in policies and practices		X	X	X
10. Dismantle racism	X	X	X	X
11. Improve productivity	X	X	X	X
12. Increase profitability	X	X	X	X

practices, policies, and performance. It is comprised of seven phases across two major components:

1. **Personal DEI Assessment** (Step 1: DEI Inventory for People): A personal DEI assessment of preferences and competences for some or all people throughout your organization (Phase 0).

2. **Organizational DEI Assessment** (Step 1: DEI Inventory for Organizations): An organizational DEI assessment of the personal behaviors and lived experiences of people within the context of your organizational culture and climate, management practices, organizational policies, and overall performance benchmark and/or ranking (Phase I through Phase VII).

The following sections break down each of these phases in detail. As you will see, we espouse an approach to organizational DEI assessment that does not focus solely on weaknesses and/or problems. We embrace the tenets of "appreciative inquiry (AI)," which focuses on leveraging an organization's core strengths, rather than seeking to overcome or minimize its weaknesses. We also refer to these approaches as "strengths-based" and "asset-based" (versus "deficiency-based" or "limitations-based").

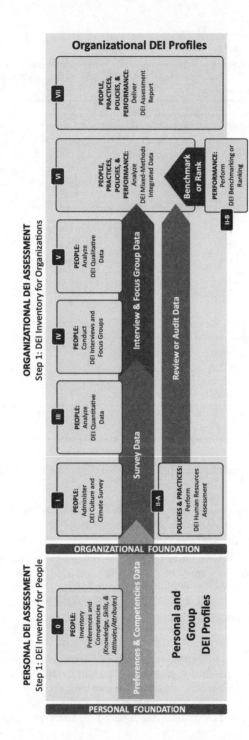

FIGURE 1.19 Personal and Organizational DEI Assessment Overall Approach

Phase 0: Inventory Preferences and Competences

The first phase of **Step 1: DEI Inventory for Organizations** is assessing the personal preferences and competences of some or all of the people throughout your organization. This can be accomplished using the same approach to personal DEI assessment outlined in **Step 1: DEI Inventory for People** with the added step of generating not only **personal DEI profiles**—reports summarizing the assessment results and any recommendations for individuals—but also **group DEI profiles** that aggregate the assessment results and recommendations for some or all of the following groups, which are not mutually exclusive:

- **Pairs:** Two people, including mentors and mentees, managers and direct reports, and peers
- **Leaders and Managers:** A subset or superset of executives, directors, managers, and supervisors
- **Teams:** A specific team or group, including committees, task forces, office locations, agencies, departments, and divisions
- **Organizations:** Any organizational entity

In each configuration, on an ongoing basis, the people who have completed the personal DEI assessment should familiarize themselves with their personal DEI profile, the personal DEI profiles of their colleagues (with permission), and the group DEI profile, as a part of their personal and organizational DEI journey. This can be supported by debriefing each individual on their personal DEI profile, debriefing each group on their group DEI profile, and/or providing DEI coaching, learning, and development for members of the group.

Administering a personal DEI assessment tool to different groups throughout your organization opens several new possibilities and delivers added value:

- Share a common tool, framework, and language based on the assessment tool's model
- Raise awareness and foster understanding of colleagues' preferences
- Identify potential blind spots based on composite preferences
- Identify areas of strength and areas for improvement based on composite competences
- Design and tailor DEI coaching, learning, and development based on individual, group, and organizational profiles
- Empower people to adapt to the preferences of others and integrate with the competences of others
- Empower groups to shift, stretch, flex, or expand into areas of low collective preference and increase competence in areas for collective improvement
- Empower leaders to better manage and optimize the activities of their teams
- Improve decision making, teamwork, communication, collaboration, conflict resolution, innovation, and performance

Several of the personal DEI assessment tools identified in the previous step provide reports that aggregate personal DEI profiles into group profiles along with additional insights specifically pertaining to the group (the final column of Table 1.3 indicates which tools provide group reports). Examples include the IAT full-service option (preferences), HBDI® Pair Profile and Team Profile (preferences), Intrinsic Inclusion Inventory™ (I3™) for Organizations (competences), and IDI® Group Profile Report (competences). Looking ahead to **Step 2: DEI Imperatives**, for example, if your organizational DEI objective is to improve your team's inclusivity then your organizational DEI goal could be to complete the I3™ for Organizations 12 months apart and see if your organization's score has moved from one level to the next.

Depending on the size of your organization, it may be cost prohibitive and/or logistically prohibitive to administer a personal DEI assessment to everyone. You should therefore align the size and scope of your Phase 0 inventory to what is affordable, appropriate, and aligned with your DEI aims. For example, it is quite common for organizations who are just embarking on their DEI journey to focus these efforts on executives only, so they can lead by example, and then expand from there to other groups.

Phase I: Administer DEI Culture and Climate Survey (Quantitative Data Collection)

Quantitative data clarifies what people think, feel, and do. As it relates to the prior Phase 0: Inventory Preferences and Competences, this includes data pertaining to the preferences, such as biases, and competences, such as inclusive behaviors, of people and/or groups throughout your organization. As it relates to this Phase I: Administer DEI Culture and Climate Survey, this includes data pertaining to the personal behaviors, engagement, perceptions, and perspectives of people throughout your organization and how they experience the organization's culture and climate. Among the most effective ways to assess the lived experiences of people throughout your organization is to administer an organizational DEI culture and climate survey. Organizational DEI culture and climate surveys can assess:

- Perceptions and perspectives on DEI
- Cultural norms and standards related to DEI
- Behaviors, practices, and expectations related to DEI
- Employee engagement, support for DEI, and feelings of inclusion and belonging
- Leadership engagement and commitment to DEI
- The relationship between DEI, performance, and results

We will now walk through the steps to design and deploy a DEI culture and climate survey including choosing subgroups, determining the survey sample size, selecting a survey instrument or designing a survey instrument, selecting the survey tool, launching the survey, monitoring survey responses, and sharing the survey findings as broadly as possible.

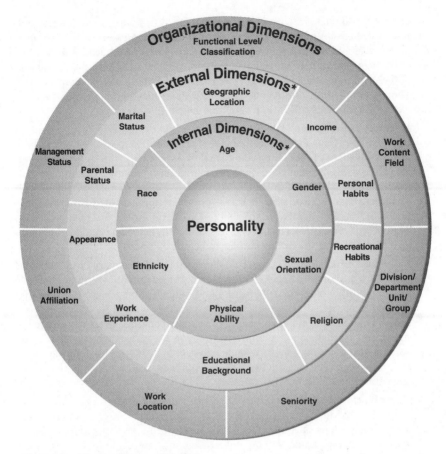

FIGURE 1.20 The Four Layers of Diversity
Source: **gardenswartzrowe.com.**

Choose Subgroups For an organizational DEI assessment of culture and climate, the value of your quantitative data will only be as good as the subgroups (i.e., identifiers and categories for respondents) you choose when collecting data. For any DEI surveys, questionnaires, forms, and so on, make certain up front that these data collection efforts are obtaining the right identifiers and categories from respondents to ensure that your data analysis efforts can produce the desired results. In other words, if there are certain subgroups you seek to understand (e.g., people of color, women, people with disabilities, employees in a specific office location, etc.), you will need to make certain your culture and climate survey is collecting the proper data from respondents (e.g., their race/ethnicity, gender, disability status, office location, etc.) to generate those insights. Here, Gardenswartz and Rowe's "four layers of diversity"—also known as the "diversity wheel" and the "identity wheel"—can be a helpful tool (see Figure 1.20):

- **Personality:** At BCT, we typically do not collect personality data from respondents to a DEI culture and climate survey. Instead, we focus on the internal, external, and organizational dimensions. However, it is worth noting that what was outlined in Phase 0: Inventory Preferences and Competences—assessing personal preferences and competences—represents exactly what is needed for some or all of the people in your organization to learn more about their personality, and that of their colleagues, leading to all of the benefits described in the previous section. The remaining three dimensions speak directly to data you should consider collecting for your DEI culture and climate survey.

- **Internal Dimensions:** The internal dimensions or "primary layer" includes characteristics for which people have little to no control and are largely born into, albeit with some variations based on lived experience and the ability to effectuate changes: age, gender, sexual orientation, physical ability, ethnicity, and race (these represent many of the federally protected classes—groups of people with a common characteristic who are legally protected from employment discrimination based on that characteristic—except for veteran status and religion/creed). At BCT, we typically ask respondents to self-identify according to all of these subgroups in this layer in our DEI culture and climate surveys.

- **External Dimensions:** The external dimensions or "secondary layer" includes characteristics for which people have a greater measure of control and include some atypical choices for DEI culture and climate survey data collection that should be considered: geographic location, income, personal habits, recreational habits, religion, educational background, work experience, appearance, parental status, and marital status. At BCT, we typically ask respondents to self-identify according to the subgroups of religion, educational background, languages spoken, and geographic location in this layer, and have also included marital status and parental status in certain instances.

- **Organizational Dimensions:** The organizational dimensions or "organizational layer" includes characteristics that are specific to your organization: functional level, work content field, division/department/unit/group, seniority, work location, union affiliation, and management status. From a DEI culture and climate survey data collection perspective, what to include and not include can vary dramatically based on your organization's size and structure. Based on our experience at BCT, a good rule of thumb is that the larger your organization's size, the more complex your organization's structure, and the broader your organization's geographic footprint, the more likely you will find value by asking respondents to self-identify according to some or all of the subgroups in this layer.

By expanding your range of subgroups during DEI quantitative data collection, you will set the stage for *data disaggregation*—stratifying the data by the subgroups you selected, and *data analysis and reporting*—identifying and disclosing statistically significant differences between subgroups (e.g., women vs. men vs. non-binary; people who are visually impaired vs. people who are deaf and hard of hearing; employees in the domestic office vs. employees in the overseas office; etc.) and between intersections of subgroups (e.g., domestic women who are visually impaired vs. international men who are deaf and hard of hearing). We will revisit this topic later in this step.

Determine the Survey Sample Size   The *population size* refers to the number of people that will be asked to complete the DEI culture and climate survey. Ideally, the population size for a DEI culture and climate survey should be everyone throughout the organization. However, there are circumstances when that is not preferred or permissible such as survey fatigue or other competing demands. While survey fatigue is real, I am critical of organizations that allow it to preclude distributing a DEI culture and climate survey to the entire organization, much less distributing it at all. At BCT, we have found that survey fatigue is often used as an excuse for not conducting a DEI assessment survey at all, to hide from the truth, and as a sign that there are other matters of higher priority. Your DEI strategic plan is only as good as your DEI assessment, so do not allow these excuses to rule the day! The truth shall set your organization free!

Having said this, in instances where it is simply not feasible to survey your entire organization, you can distribute the survey to a *sample* of the population, or a smaller group of the organization that can characterize your entire organization. By developing a *stratified sampling plan* that looks at the total number of people according to the subgroups you have chosen, you can determine the *sample size* or requisite number of people who should randomly receive the survey to ensure representative participation from each subgroup.

You must first determine if there are combinations of subgroups you want to be able to make valid claims against and then you must determine the sample size for each of those combinations of subgroups one by one. For example, if you want to make valid claims for a combination of subgroups by race and gender, then you will need to determine the sample size for all combined race-gender subgroups one by one (e.g., Asian American and Pacific Islander (AAPI) men, AAPI women, AAPI nonbinary, Latino men, Latina women, Latino and Latina non-binary, etc., etc., etc.). These calculations can be performed using a free "Sample Size Calculator" such as: **https://www .calculator.net/sample-size-calculator.html**. At BCT, we recommend the following inputs to the calculator:

- **"Confidence Level":** Determines how confident you can be that the responses from the subgroup lie within the survey's specified range of values. The higher the confidence level, the higher the sample size, and the lower the degree of uncertainty around the findings. We recommend a 95% confidence level.

- **"Sampling Error" or "Margin of Error" or "Confidence Interval":** Determines how confident you can be that your survey reflects the overall population. The larger the sampling error, the smaller the sample size. We recommend 3% to no more than 5% sampling error. If the sampling error is too high, you cannot trust that the findings represent the larger population.

- **"Population Proportion":** Defines the likelihood that responses are higher or lower than the true value. We recommend a 50% population proportion to suggest that any response is equally likely of being above or below the true value.

- **Population Size:** The total number of people in each combined subgroup entered one by one.

For example, if the number of AAPI women in the organization is 150, then you would need to randomly send the survey to 109 people within this subgroup at a 95%

confidence level, 5% sampling error, and 50% population proportion. Once you have performed a similar sample size calculation for each subgroup, you have a stratified sampling plan that informs how many people can be randomly selected from each subgroup to receive the survey.

Because representation matters, and is of paramount importance for an organizational DEI culture and climate survey, a stratified sampling plan ensures that you have enough respondents from each subgroup to make valid and statistically significant inferences about that subgroup during analysis and reporting. Since the results of your DEI assessments will be used to make important decisions related to people, practices, policies, and performance, not ensuring a representative sample and a high response rate for underrepresented groups and marginalized voices is analogous to voter suppression. That's how serious it is. For this reason and other reasons discussed later, such as organizational cultures with low trust or unaddressed DEI issues that have been left to fester, we also strongly recommend using a neutral, third party to design and administer your DEI culture and climate assessment. While using a neutral, third party does not guarantee a high response rate, it can help maximize the response rate because some respondents will have greater confidence that their responses will be anonymous, the data will remain private and confidential, and no data will be disclosed that can compromise their identity, thus addressing what may be any underlying concerns.

Select a Survey Instrument or Design a Survey Instrument   The next step, which is an important one, is to select a DEI culture and climate survey instrument. Here, you could choose an existing DEI culture and climate survey from a vendor or design your own.

Choosing the Right DEI Culture and Climate Survey Instrument   If you decide to use an existing DEI culture and climate survey from a vendor, it is of paramount importance to use a survey instrument that assesses organizational culture and climate *specifically through the lens of DEI*. Not all culture and climate surveys are created equal. For example, a growing number of employee engagement surveys can be augmented with a few DEI questions. At BCT, we have generally found them to be insufficient for a thorough and comprehensive organizational DEI assessment. Make certain that your survey not only has questions that are specific to DEI but that it was also designed with DEI front and center.

A List of Organizational DEI Assessment Tools

A list of organizational DEI assessment tools, including DEI culture and climate survey instruments, is provided in Table 1.7 with the following headings:

- **Name of Assessment Tool**—The name of the assessment tool.
- **Description**—A brief overview of the assessment tool.
- **What Does It Measure?**—A summary of what the assessment tool claims to measure. Where known and appropriate, validity and reliability are indicated.

TABLE 1.7   List of Organizational DEI Assessment and Other Related Tools

Assessment Tool	Description (What Does It Measure?)
People: Personal Preferences & Competences	
Personal Preference Assessments	See list of personal DEI assessments of preferences in Table 1.3.
Personal Competence Assessments	See list of personal DEI assessments of competences in Table 1.3.
People: Personal Behaviors & Experiences	
DEI Workforce and Workplace Assessment™ (DWWA™)	Assesses organizational culture and climate through a DEI lens in the following 10 categories: (1) Employee Satisfaction, (2) Support for Diversity—Generally, (3) Workforce Culture and Climate, (4) My Supervisor, (5) Diversity and Performance, (6) Belonging and Inclusion, (7) Diversity as a Strategic Management Competency, (8) Employment Law and Workplace Incivility Issues, (9) Open-ended Questions, and (10) Outcomes-related Questions. Valid and reliable. **https://www.bctpartners.com/dei-workforce-and-workplace-assessment**
Intrinsic Inclusion Inventory™ (I3™) of People and Organizations	Measures the competence or ability of people and organizations to be intrinsically inclusive according to the following four behaviors ("inclusion accelerators"): Shared Trust, Respectful Empathy, Significant Emotional Relationship/Event, and Connected Understanding. These behaviors can cultivate the Power of the Pause, upend patterned thinking, and reboot our biased brain. Valid and reliable. **https://www.intrinsicinclusion.com**
Q^{12}	Survey tool based on a hierarchy of employee development needs (growth, teamwork, individual contribution, basic needs) designed to measure engagement. Valid and reliable. **http://www.gallup.com**
Employee Engagement Survey Software	Organization hierarchy tool used to map employee feedback to an organization's unique structure. Custom software platform allows organizations to measure, design, and improve employee experiences. **http://www.qualtrics.com**
Employee Experience	Assessment platform designed to measure key engagement measures such as belonging, happiness, recognition, leadership, enablement, alignment, and development. **http://www.medallia.com**
Betterworks Engage	Platform designed to gather continuous feedback throughout the employee life cycle. **http://www.betterworks.com**

(Continued)

TABLE 1.7   (Continued)

Assessment Tool	Description (What Does It Measure?)
Kilmann-Saxton Culture-Gap® Survey (CGS)	Organizational culture gaps: Differences between actual norms versus desired norms. http://www.kilmanndiagnostics.com
Organizational Courage Assessment	Organizational courage: Whether members do the "right thing" or "look the other way" when experiencing challenging situations. http://www.kilmanndiagnostics.com
Vital Signs	Leadership Vital Signs: Rapid, compelling insights for vital leadership. Team Vital Signs: Real-time data on team vitality and a path to peak performance. Organizational Vital Signs: Actionable, rapid insight on the drivers of sustainable performance across the enterprise. Educational Vital Signs: Measure school climate to quickly and easily assess the context for learning. http://www.6seconds.org
Culture of Change Scan	Provides users with a better understanding of and detailed information on the differences between current and desired organizational cultures. It provides users a new way of dealing with the tensions raised by different organizational cultures. https://www3.thtconsulting.com/tools/culture-change-scan-dilemmas/
Inclusive Behaviors Inventory℠ (IBI)	An easy-to-use assessment that allows you to develop your own inclusion profile and get simple steps for improvement. http://www.globesmart.com
Go Culture	Measure and help organizations engage with employees and inclusivity in the workplace. http://www.goculture.com
Inclusive Intelligence Test (IIT)	Adapted from the New IQ, a tool for measuring inclusivity that was developed for numerous federal agencies: 20 salient questions that had the highest correlation to inclusive environments have been grouped into 5 Habits of inclusion (Fair, Open, Cooperative, Supportive, Empowering). https://inclusiveintelligencetest.org
Inclusion Assessment	A framework for measuring inclusion and pinpointing where organizations can focus their DEI resources. Leveraging Categories of Inclusion, the assessment can link the day-to-day experiences of employees to clear opportunities to drive change. http://www.aleriatech.com

TABLE 1.7   (Continued)

Assessment Tool	Description (What Does It Measure?)
Diversity Inclusion Belonging Survey (DIBS)	An assessment tool designed especially for arts organizations, firms, agencies, nonprofits, small businesses, and corporations that captures data on member engagement and their sense of belonging, the inclusive characteristics of the organizational culture, and the degree to which diverse groups experience inclusion. DIBS captures the interplay of identity, engagement, and inclusion within the organization and defines belonging in its dynamic state. Valid and reliable. **http://www.dibs.dlplummer.com**
Perceived Group Inclusion Scale	Conceptual framework used to measure perceptions of inclusion in the workplace that acknowledges authenticity and belonging as major determinants. **https://doi.org/10.1002/ejsp.2011**
Organizational CQ Instrument	An instrument that measures cultural intelligence at the organizational level using five factors: leadership behavior, adaptability, training and development, organizational intentionality, and organizational inclusion
Culture Amp	Culture Amp empowers your teams and fuels positive change with employee engagement, performance, and development tools—all in one intuitive platform. The platform offers DEI survey templates, analytics, inspirations, and bias mitigation techniques throughout our platform at no additional cost. **https://www.cultureamp.com/platform/solutions/diversity-inclusion**
Organizational Culture Inventory (OCI)	Assessment tool used to measure the attributes of organizational culture through shared behavioral norms, revealing what members collectively believe is expected of them. The OCI also highlights how behavioral norms influence team member engagement and effectiveness. **http://www.humansynergistics.com**
Color-Blind Racial Attitudes Scale (CoBRAS)	Survey tool designed to assess denial of the existence of racism and racial dynamics. **https://doi.org/10.1037/0022-0167.47.1.59**
The White Privilege Attitudes Scale (WPAS)	WPAS assesses the multidimensional nature of white privilege attitudes, reflecting affective cognitive and behavioral dimensions. **https://doi.org/10.1037/a0016274**
Gartner Inclusion Index	Gartner's Inclusion Index is seven questions that provide organizations with a measure of their ability to foster an inclusive work environment by testing their initiatives along seven key dimensions, including fair treatment, decision making, trust, and diversity. **http://www.gartner.com** **https://hbr.org/2021/05/how-to-measure-inclusion-in-the-workplace**

(Continued)

TABLE 1.7   (Continued)

Assessment Tool	Description (What Does It Measure?)
Psychological Climate and Effort Measures (PC&EM)	Designed to measure how employees perceive their organizational environment in connection to level of effort in the workplace. https://doi.org/10.1037/0021-9010.81.4.358
Quantum Workplace (QWP)	Questionnaire used to understand how employees view inclusion, fairness, equity, respect, and diversity to measure engagement. http://www.quantumworkplace.com
Workplace Culture Survey (WCS)	Two-part survey instrument designed to measure workplace culture, along with details associated with inclusive elements and/or actions. WCS can also be used as a planning tool. https://doi.org/10.1177%2F0034355214544750
The Workplace Exclusion Scale (WES)	Assessment tool used to assess the extent to which employees feel excluded in the workplace. Valid and reliable. https://doi.org/10.1080/13594320903025028
Organizational Culture Intelligence Survey (OCQ)	Assessment tool used to measure an organization's cultural knowledge and interactions. https://doi.org/10.1177/1470595815615625
Organizational Change Questionnaire–Climate of Change, Processes and Readiness (OCQ–C, P, R)	Questionnaire designed to assess an organization's readiness for change, climate for change, supervisor support, participation, cohesion, and politicking. http://dx.doi.org/10.1080/00223980903218216
Gender Roles Stereotypes Scale (GRSS)	Assessment tool designed to measure attitudes toward both men and women. Used to assess potential gender role stereotypes held by management. https://doi.org/10.1108/17542411211279715
Diversity Climate Survey (DCS)	Tool designed to survey the affective and achievement outcomes of employment to assist organizations with monitoring and assessing diversity management competences. https://www.academia.edu/3587648/Using_Diversity_Climate_Surveys_A_Toolkit_for_Diversity_Management
Workplace Diversity Survey (WDS)	The WDS measures an organization's diversity using five key dimensions—emotional reactions, judgment, behavior reactions, personal consequences, and organizational outcomes. https://doi.org/10.1002/1532-1096(200101/02)12:1<33::AID-HRDQ4>3.0.CO;2-P

TABLE 1.7   (Continued)

Assessment Tool	Description (What Does It Measure?)
Voices Cultural Assessment (VCA)	The VCA collects rich and relevant data and goes beyond what's available in an online cultural assessment or engagement survey. Findings include specific and nuanced feedback that can lead to direct action and behavior change. **https://wmfdp.com/customized-solutions/**
Management Practices & Organizational Policies	
DEI HR Policies & Practices Assessment	Review or audit of HR policies and practices through a DEI lens. **http://www.bctpartners.com**
Global Diversity, Equity & Inclusion Benchmarks (GDEIB)	The GDEIB is the well-researched, definitive picture of quality DEI work and is paired with useful tools to make it a living/working document for users. It provides a means of measurement, a strategic planning tool, and a set of actions that may be taken at an organizational and individual level, to do good DEI work. **https://centreforglobalinclusion.org/what-we-do/the-gdeib/**
PwC Diversity & Inclusion Benchmarking Survey	A short survey to diagnose the maturity of your organization's diversity and inclusion program and identify your program's strengths and areas for enhancement. At the conclusion of the survey, you'll also be able to see how your organization compares to others in your region and industry. **https://www.pwc.com/gx/en/services/people-organisation/global-diversity-and-inclusion-survey.html**
Textio.com	Textio brings the world's most advanced language insights into your hiring and employer brand content, every time you write. Textio's in-product language change reports analyze language trends across your public-facing job posts, helping you keep a pulse on whether your inclusive values are shining through and where you may have room to improve. **https://textio.com**
People, Practices & Policies Platforms	
Kanarys	Kanarys' tools and technology deliver the clear, comprehensive DEI data that companies need to diagnose, prioritize, and optimize their efforts to achieve healthy, equitable workplaces. Some of their key offerings include the following: Equity Innovation Solution (measures employees' perceptions from a DEI perspective), Supplier DEI Assessment (identifies third-party suppliers who rank highly in DEI and employ intentional inclusion practices), and Organizational Systems Assessment (a targeted review of your company policies and programs, and it covers the entire employee practices lifecycle). **https://www.kanarys.com**

(Continued)

TABLE 1.7 (Continued)

Assessment Tool	Description (What Does It Measure?)
Mathison	Mathison is a technology platform to give employers an end-to-end system to build, manage, and measure their DEI strategy, source underrepresented candidates, reduce bias, and build awareness across their organizations. It includes an Equal Hiring Index® (EHI) that assesses your entire hiring process to uncover gaps and identify bias, an Inclusive Text Analyzer and tools to reduce bias, a Diversity Pipeline Sourcing System to analyze skills and experiences, and a DEI Knowledge and Training Center with actionable resources to build awareness and change behavior across every step of the talent process. **https://www.mathison.io**
Blueprint Strategy Platform	Build, benchmark, and manage your diversity, equity, and inclusion efforts and track the metrics that matter with a platform created by the world's leading experts. Blueprint offers online assessment tools, key metrics benchmarking, expert recommendations, and an easy-to-understand analytics dashboard. **https://www.paradigmiq.com/blueprint/**
Pulsely	Pulsely helps companies measure and monitor the progress of their DEI efforts and the impact on business performance. Their suite of solutions includes diversity analysis, workplace inclusion diagnostic, inclusion competences assessment, leadership pipeline analysis, and a D&I organizational assessment. **https://pulsely.io**
Inclusion Insights	Inclusion Insights is a powerful online learning platform that keeps your leaders practicing and growing real-world inclusion skills with individually paced modules, tools, and resources throughout the year, all in the company of their peers. **https://wmfdp.com/online-learning/**
Emprising™	An employee survey platform to measure and monitor D&I, increase recruitment pipeline, cut employee turnover, and create a culture of innovation. **https://www.greatplacetowork.com/solutions/diversity-equity-inclusion-belonging**
Other Assessments	
Supplier Diversity Spend Analysis and Solutions	How much of procurement dollars are being spent with Tier 1 (direct suppliers/partners) and Tier 2 (subcontractors to direct suppliers/partners) diverse suppliers by category? **https://www.coupa.com/products/supplier-management/supplier-diversity-management** **https://www.supplier.io** **http://spendhg.com**

TABLE 1.7   (Continued)

Assessment Tool	Description (What Does It Measure?)
BirkmaND Report	What are needed workplace accommodations geared toward increasing inclusion of neurodivergent (ND) individuals with either Autism Spectrum Disorder or Attention-Deficit/Hyperactivity Disorder (ADHD) at work? **https://birkman.com/neurodiversity/**
The Coaching Development Assessment (CDA)	Designed to assess the competences of coaches and the effectiveness in managing coaching relationships. **http://www.globaldiversityservices.com**
Regretted Loss Assessment	Why did different groups of employees leave for whom the organization regrets the loss? **https://www.bctpartners.com/data-driven-dei**
Time-to-Promotion Equity Assessment	How long does it take different groups of employees to advance? **https://www.bctpartners.com/data-driven-dei**
Pay Equity Assessment	Is compensation for different groups fair and equitable? **https://www.bctpartners.com/data-driven-dei**

Note that almost all personal DEI assessment tools mentioned previously have the ability to generate both individual and team/organizational reports that can serve as tools for assessing the preferences and competences of people on a specific team or throughout an organization.

Designing Your Own DEI Culture and Climate Survey Instrument   While it can be tempting to design your own DEI culture and climate survey, you should strongly consider using a standardized instrument for the entire survey or a standardized set of questions for a given category. This is particularly important if you desire to benchmark your results now or in the future. Using standardized instruments or questions will allow you to draw comparisons to other organizations, of course, if you have (and/or the organization you are working with to conduct your organizational DEI assessment has) access to comparison data for benchmarking.

However, if you choose to design your own DEI culture and climate survey instrument, you should begin by identifying the major categories of interest, such as leadership commitment, inclusion and belonging, equitable outcomes, and so forth, and then identify a few questions in each category.

You should combine mostly closed-ended questions (i.e., quantitative data) with a few open-ended questions (i.e., qualitative data). Closed-ended questions should be phrased as statements where respondents are asked to choose from a list of preselected options such as a Likert rating scale (i.e., strongly disagree, disagree, neutral, agree, and strongly agree) relative to the statements. They are excellent in providing quantifiable data and for categorizing respondents. The responses represent very structured data that can be analyzed using quantitative data analysis techniques such as statistics (discussed later in this step) and data science techniques such as machine learning (ML), natural language processing (NLP), and natural language understanding (NLU) (discussed in the conclusion). The following are examples of closed-ended questions:

- **Commitment:** Leadership is committed to diversity, equity, and inclusion.
- **Differences:** Our organization values differences.
- **Diversity:** Leadership reflects the diversity of the organization.
- **Equity:** Promotions and compensation are given fairly at our organization.
- **Inclusion:** I feel empowered to contribute to our organization.
- **Belonging:** I feel like I belong at our organization.
- **Supervisor:** My supervisor handles diversity, equity, and inclusion issues effectively.
- **Retention:** I am considering leaving the organization.
- **Respect:** People treat each other with respect.
- **Psychological Safety:** I am comfortable speaking up in our organization.

Table 1.7 provides a list of DEI and other related survey instruments with standardized question sets that you can use. For example, if one of the categories you wanted to measure was the psychological climate of your organization, then you could use some or all of the 31 questions from the "Psychological Climate and Effort Measures (PC&EM)."

Open-ended questions should be phrased as questions that require a longer response in the respondent's own words. They are excellent for providing context and soliciting opinions. The responses represent unstructured data that can be analyzed using qualitative data analysis techniques such as coding (discussed later in this step) and data science techniques such as natural language processing (NLP) (discussed in the conclusion). The following are examples of open-ended questions:

- **Culture:** How would you describe our organization's culture?
- **Strengths:** What is working well related to diversity, equity, and inclusion?
- **Limitations:** What is not working well or could work better related to diversity, equity, and inclusion?
- **Environment:** How can our organization create an environment where everyone feels valued for their contribution? As individuals? Feels that they belong?
- **Recommendations:** What would improve DEI at our organization?

In her blog post, "7 Tips for Conducting Your Next DEI Survey," Lyssa Test of Lattice, a people-success platform, offers the following advice from Ashley Schwedt, Leadership Trainer & DEI Lead at LifeLabs, a New York-based consultancy firm specializing in leadership training for managers and executives: "Every question on your survey should have a clear, specific purpose. Only ask questions you can do something about. When designing your survey, for each question, ask [yourself], 'What will I do with this information?'," advised Schwedt. "If the answer is 'Nothing,' it isn't a good question to ask. The responses should drive [organizational] strategy by highlighting current gaps and helping the leadership team determine where to focus resources."[1] A good rule of thumb is that it should take no more than 20 to 30 minutes for respondents to complete the survey.

Example of an Organizational DEI Culture and Climate Survey: BCT's DEI Workforce and Workplace Assessment   BCT has created a statistically validated and reliable **DEI Workforce and Workplace Assessment™ (DWWA™)** instrument. This instrument assesses organizational culture and climate through the lens of DEI in the 10 categories shown in Figure 1.21. Designed by BCT's senior director of health equity, David Hunt, JD, a former employment lawyer and civil rights attorney and nationally recognized DEI subject matter expert, BCT has successfully used this tool with many leading corporations, nonprofit organizations; educational, academic, and faith-based institutions; hospital and health care systems; foundations and philanthropic organizations; and federal, state, and local government agencies.

FIGURE 1.21   BCT's DEI Workforce and Workplace Assessment™ (DWWA™)

The DWWA™ measures organizational DEI culture and climate along the following lines:

- Perceived areas of strengths and areas for improvement relative to your organization's culture
- Factors that characterize culture (i.e., improved performance, leadership qualities, organization, learning team members, learning environment, individuals empowered, individual values, departmental values, and teamwork)
- Needs and concerns of different stakeholder groups
- Social perceptions that might uncover any major biases that impact the culture and climate
- Cultural perceptions of your organization's manner and approach to diversity, equity, and inclusion associated with the above
- Legal and risk management issues related to uncivil or disrespectful treatment, DEI-related incidents of disrespect, workplace bullying, and discrimination

The DWWA™ is an online survey that saves time and collects valuable data to inform DEI program design and implementation. It is often combined with in-depth interviews (IDIs) and focus groups to gather anecdotal information and deeper insights from people.

Select the Survey Tool   There is a plethora of low-cost or no-cost survey tools such as Microsoft Forms, Zoho Survey, Mentimeter, Typeform, Pollfish, Google Forms, QuestionPro, Alchemer (formerly SurveyGizmo), and SurveyMonkey, as well as enterprise platforms such as Ambivista, AskNicely, Emprising™, and Qualtrics. When selecting a survey tool, in addition to cost, you should also consider the question formats that are supported (e.g., check boxes and ratings for closed-ended questions, text fields for open-ended questions, and more), the survey logic that is supported (e.g., "skip logic" to skip certain questions for certain people, and "display logic" to display certain questions only for certain people), multi-lingual support, customer support, the level of sophistication for analysis, and the level of detail for reports.

Launch the Survey   Prior to launching the survey, it is always a good practice to pilot it with 5 to 10 test users and solicit their feedback. This will not only ensure the questions are clear and can be answered effectively and in a reasonable amount of time, but also that the survey tool and logic are configured and functioning properly. Once again, a good rule of thumb is that it should take no more than 20 to 30 minutes for respondents to complete the survey.

You should also develop an outreach and communication plan to maximize the response rate. The plan should include a message from executive leadership, human resources, and/or the chief DEI officer about the importance of the survey, equip supervisors with talking points to carry the message further, maximize the use of available channels (e.g., e-mail, newsletters, intranets, town halls, etc.), establish a response deadline (typically two weeks from launch), send weekly reminders and advisory reminders as the deadline approaches, and deliver messaging that addresses the key questions of who, what, where, when, and why:

- Who will have access to the data?
- What is the purpose of the survey?
- Where will the results be shared?
- When will the survey close? When will results be shared?
- Why should the survey be important to people? To the organization?

Messaging should also be tailored to specific segments to motivate their participation. Three segments require distinctive messaging for a DEI survey.

The first segment, DEI supporters and champions, are passionate about DEI and connect to these issues through their "heart." This is perhaps the easiest segment to motivate. A potential message to this segment is "your input matters because the results of this survey will shape the development of our DEI strategic plan and new initiatives."

The second segment, DEI naysayers and detractors, are critical of, or resistant to, DEI and may only connect to these issues through their "head." Naturally, this is a difficult segment to motivate. Potential messages to this segment are, "we welcome all voices as we endeavor to create a more welcoming workplace for everyone," and "the organization is committed to this effort, so we invite everyone to participate," and "research has shown that DEI leads to improved organizational performance, so your response will help us improve our bottom line."

The third segment is DEI disadvantaged groups. DEI surveys are often the victim of the very issues they seek to address. In other words, if the lack of attentiveness to DEI matters has led to certain groups feeling isolated, excluded, targeted, or disadvantaged, it may inhibit them from responding to the survey truthfully, if at all, based on skepticism, distrust, and fear of reprisal. As mentioned previously, we recommend using a neutral, third party to administer the survey and the messaging to this segment (and all segments) is, "the survey is being administered by a neutral, third party with X years of experience in DEI. All responses will be anonymous, the data will remain private and confidential, and no data will be disclosed that can compromise a person's identity."

The execution of the outreach and communication plan will signal to prospective respondents that the survey is now live and will motivate their participation.

Monitor Survey Responses
You should actively monitor the survey response rate so you can adjust and adapt your outreach and communications plan accordingly. If there are specific subgroups with low response rates, you should consider extending the deadline another one to two weeks and tailoring your outreach and communication to those subgroups and, once again, enlist the voices of leadership, supervisors, human resources, and DEI. Our experience with DEI surveys suggests that 40% is considered a good overall response rate for relatively large organizations and 80% is a good overall response rate for relatively small organizations. However, there is no "one size fits all" when it comes to response rates. What is far more important than the overall response rate is the specific response rate for underrepresented subgroups and marginalized voices.

To avoid a double-edged sword, you should pay particular attention to the response rates of subgroups that are underrepresented or marginalized. The fact that these subgroups are underrepresented or marginalized already poses a challenge to ensuring that their voices are adequately captured in the survey sample. A low response rate has the potential to further disempower their voices unless deliberate steps are taken to boost their participation (and/or factor the response rate into the analysis, which is discussed later). Referring back to our prior conversation on data sampling, the inclusion of underrepresented subgroups and marginalized voices should be considered of paramount importance.

To increase the response rate with underrepresented subgroups, enlist the help of ambassadors that identify and/or have credibility with those subgroups, and partner with organizations that represent those subgroups, such as employee resource groups (ERGs), in designing and executing the outreach and communication plan.

Share the Survey Findings as Broadly as Possible   Later in this step, we will discuss sharing survey findings in the section "Phase VII: Deliver DEI Assessment Report" in the context of sharing the entire organizational DEI assessment results including quantitative and qualitative findings.

Phase II-A: Perform DEI Human Resources (HR) Policies and Practices Assessment

A DEI HR policies and practices assessment, when compared to a traditional HR policies and practices assessment, is conducted specifically through the lens of DEI. While organizations are comprised of a multitude of organizational policies and management practices, the following is a representative but not exhaustive list of HR policies and practices that could be evaluated from a DEI perspective:

- Recruitment and Hiring
- Learning and Development
- Advancement and Promotions
- Performance Management and Evaluation
- Succession Planning
- Compensation and Rewards Management
- Discipline, Terminations, and Exit Policy
- Retention, Turnover, and Support
- Discrimination, Harassment, and Bullying
- Affirmative Action and/or Office of Federal Contract Compliance Programs (OFCCP) Regulations
- Benefits and Assistance

- Family Medical Leave Act (FMLA) and Americans with Disabilities Act (ADA)
- Employee Attire and Grooming Standards
- Protected and Unprotected Speech, Religious and Political Expression

Based on the collection of all documents pertaining to a policy or practice, the assessment can be broadly performed as a review or audit. The distinction between the two is summarized in Table 1.8. The audit process can also be combined with in-depth interviews (IDIs) and/or focus groups (described later) to provide additional context and insight.

Conducting a DEI HR assessment yields the following benefits that are specific to DEI:

- Embrace diversity and unleash creativity within your workforce, spurring innovation
- Create an inclusive and equitable workplace, improving staff retention and helping to attract diverse talent
- Ensure compliance with applicable equal employment opportunity (EEO) and affirmative action laws
- Craft better HR and DEI strategies and organizational decisions, enhancing organizational performance

The deliverable is a final report that summarizes findings (review), recommendations (audit), and next steps regarding equity challenges and opportunities within each policy and practice examined.

TABLE 1.8 **DEI Human Resources (HR) Policies and Practices Assessment**

	Review	Audit
Key Objective	A discovery process for learning how you are doing on HR functions as they relate to DEI (i.e., diagnosis)	Identify problem areas and generate recommendations for HR functions as they relate to DEI (i.e., treatment)
Key Questions That Are Answered	Do we have any problems? What do the problems look like? What have been the consequences?	What should we do? Who should be accountable?
How It Works	Gather and analyze data and information (existing or new data) (i.e., get the evidence)	Apply expertise to explain problem areas and present conclusions and recommendations (i.e., provide a roadmap)
Final Report Contents	Fact-based findings and insights	Expert conclusions and recommendations

Example of a DEI HR Policies and Practices Assessment: BCT's DEI HR Policies and Practices Audit   BCT's DEI HR Policies and Practices Assessment evaluates an organization's policies and practices documentation relative to best practices for DEI appropriateness, inclusive language, and mitigating bias relative to gender, race, disability status, and more. Developed by BCT's DEI HR subject matter experts, Damita Byrd, Barry Thomas, Jerry Benston, Andera Moten, and Rebecca Ahmed, the policy language and practice evaluation involves a four-step process:

1. **Assessment and Evaluation**—Assessment and evaluation research of a comparable policy and language.

2. **Review**—A comparative analysis of policy language to similar policy descriptions researched, assessed, and evaluated.

3. **Determination**—A determination regarding adherence to best practice standards or not.

4. **Recommendation**—From a DEI perspective, suggested inclusive policy language and practice considerations aimed at improving the employee life cycle are presented.

Accompanying IDIs and focus groups focus on four stakeholder groups based on their relationship to the process: (1) impacted by the process, (2) responsible for the process, (3) observer of the process, and (4) oversight and/or influence on the process. In performing these steps, BCT seeks to unearth answers to the following key questions:

- **Promising Practices**—Does the organization already employ effective or promising practices to advance DEI in this area?

- **Potential Barriers**—Does the organization's workforce composition or workplace culture and climate survey data suggest that any potential barriers to DEI exist in this aspect of the organization's HR practices?

- **Root Causes**—What are the root causes of any potential barriers to DEI within organizational policies, practices, or programs?

- **Potential Solutions**—What solutions would help address barriers in this area, if any?

- **Resources**—What additional resources or capacity would the organization need to further address barriers and advance DEI in this area, if any?

We work with organizational stakeholders to ensure a clear understanding of the results, implications, and limitations of the final report, and help draw clear linkages from the findings and results to the organizational implications.

Phase II-B: Perform DEI Benchmarking or Ranking

Another useful DEI assessment tool is DEI benchmarking, which is an evaluation of your organization against best practices and/or other organizations. The benefits of DEI benchmarking are as follows:

- Establish a reference point relative to other organizations
- Compare your organization to others within your industry, sector, and/or geographic region including your peers and competitors
- Identify specific organizational areas of strengths and areas for improvement relative to others
- Drill down to specific divisions, departments, and other areas of your organization
- Focus on specific strategies and actions for organizational improvement

One approach to benchmarking is to assess your organization's capacity, maturity, ability, or "muscle strength" in specific categories that relate to DEI such as organizational structure, leadership involvement, approach, staffing and resources, measurement, and the like. These benchmarks are often based on a DEI maturity model, that is, a series of levels reflecting your DEI capacity and maturity to improve DEI (e.g., Level 1: Basic, Level 2: Intermediate, and Level 3: Advanced). The benchmarking process involves data collection, typically via a survey of organizational stakeholders, and/or submission of DEI data or organizational policy and practice documents. This data is reviewed and analyzed to establish a series of scores reflecting your level of maturity in each category. Once you've completed a DEI benchmarking, you essentially have a scorecard by which you can measure capacity and a reference point to assess maturity. We will revisit scorecards (and dashboards) in **Step 4: DEI Initiatives**.

Another approach to benchmarking is to engage with one of several entities that have established DEI and DEI-related rankings such as *DiversityInc's* Top Companies for Diversity®, *Black Enterprise's* Best Companies for Diversity, *DiversityMBA's* Inclusive Leadership Index, Bloomberg's Gender-Equality Index, Careers & the disABLED Top Employers, Disability:IN's Disability Equality Index, Hispanic Association on Corporate Responsibility Corporate Inclusion Index, DEI Disability Equity Index™ of the Best Place to Work for Disability Inclusion, Human Rights Campaign Corporate Equality Index™ of the Best Places to Work for LGBTQ Equality, *Working Mother* Best Companies for Working Mothers and Best Companies for Dads, Military Friendly, *MilitaryTimes* Best for Vets Employers, to name a few. These rankings are compiled based on the submission of a standardized set of data that is then analyzed and compared to the submissions of other organizations. For example, some rankings can tell you exactly how you compare to peers in your industry and/or geography such as an exact number (e.g., 5th out of 1,000 organizations) and/or a percentile (e.g., 95th percentile). Rankings are different from benchmarking in that they tell how well you are doing but may not necessarily go deeper to provide insights to recommended strategies for your organization.

Example of DEI Benchmarking: The Global Diversity, Equity & Inclusion Benchmarks (GDEIB)   One of our favorite benchmarking tools at BCT is the Global Diversity, Equity & Inclusion Benchmarks (GDEIB): Standards for Organizations Around the World, which is published by the Centre for Global Inclusion.[2] Authored by Nene Molefi, Julie O'Mara, and Alan Richter, GDEIB is a free, downloadable, international instrument, developed and refined by 112 expert panelists, that contains 266 benchmarks in four primary processes (groups) and 15 concrete actions (categories), which cover the important elements that need to be addressed to create a world-class DEI initiative (see Figure 1.22 and Table 1.9).

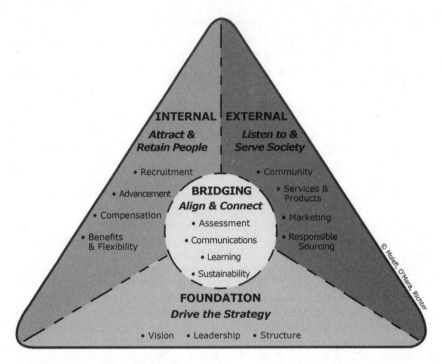

FIGURE 1.22 The Global Diversity, Equity & Inclusion Benchmarks (GDEIB) Model for Organizational DEI Benchmarking

Among the characteristics of the GDEIB are:

- The well-researched, definitive picture of quality DEI work.
- Use it to determine the level of your organization and set achievement goals.
- Use it to measure progress. Compare your organization to proven practices and outcomes.
- Agreed-upon definitions of diversity, equity, and inclusion.
- Content crosses cultures and continents.
- Both global and local in scope; it is useable anywhere.
- Useable for all sectors, industries, types, and sizes of organizations.
- Useable for various approaches to DEI: Competence, Compliance, Dignity, Organization Development, and Social Justice.
- Focus on two ultimate goals of DEI: Creating a Better World and Improving Organization Performance.
- Can be customized.
- In English and Portuguese. Spanish and French coming soon.

Each of the 15 categories is rated according to five levels, summarized in Table 1.10, with the benchmarks at Level 5 considered best practice.

TABLE 1.9 The Four Groups and 15 Categories of the GDEIB Model for Organizational DEI Benchmarking

THE FOUNDATION GROUP: Drive the Strategy	THE BRIDGING GROUP: Align & Connect
Foundational elements that are necessary to build a strong DEI initiative and for the effective operation of all other categories	Provide critical linkages that bridge foundational work with the internal and external focus of DEI in the organization
Category 1: Vision, Strategy, and Business Impact	Category 8: Assessment, Measurement, and Research
Category 2: Leadership and Accountability	Category 9: DEI Communications
Category 3: DEI Structure and Implementation	Category 10: DEI Learning and Development
	Category 11: Connecting DEI and Sustainability
THE INTERNAL GROUP: Attract & Retain People	**THE EXTERNAL GROUP: Listen To & Serve Society**
Focus primarily on strengthening policies, systems, and processes to advance DEI	Relate to how the organization offers its services and products to and interacts with its customers, clients, communities, and other stakeholders
Category 4: Recruitment	Category 12: Community, Government Relations, and Philanthropy
Category 5: Advancement and Retention	Category 13: Services and Products Development
Category 6: Job Design, Classification, and Compensation	Category 14: Marketing and Customer Service
Category 7: Work, Life Integration, Flexibility, and Benefits	Category 15: Responsible Sourcing

TABLE 1.10 The Five Levels of the GDEIB

Level	Global Benchmark	Description
Level 1	Inactive	No DEI work has begun; diversity, equity, and inclusion are not part of organizational goals.
Level 2	Reactive	A compliance-only mindset; actions are taken primarily to comply with relevant laws and social pressures. Doing the bare minimum.
Level 3	Proactive	A clear awareness of the value of DEI; starting to implement DEI systemically. This is what is required and expected of all organizations.
Level 4	Progressive	Implementing DEI systemically and showing improved results and outcomes beyond what is required or expected.
Level 5	Best Practice	Demonstrating current global best practices in DEI; exemplary.

At BCT, we have operationalized the GDEIB into an online assessment survey that can be easily completed by anyone who manages people and is, therefore, familiar with and responsible for policies and practices—such as managers, supervisors, and executives—to quickly evaluate your organization's capability or maturity to improve DEI. We determine an organizational score (i.e., from Level 1 through Level 5) within each of the 15 categories, four groups, and overall. This gives organizations the ability to not only know how their organization ranks against global best practices but also to discover the strength of their capacity and maturity to improve DEI. We interpret the results as both a way to compare organizations to others, including within their sector/field/industry, as well as to right-size their DEI program to their DEI capacity, so they are not undertaking more than they can reasonably accomplish. The GDEIB will reappear several times throughout the book, including **Step 3: DEI Insights**, as a "What Works" model for DEI benchmarking.

Phase III: Analyze DEI Quantitative Data

The next phase of the organizational DEI assessment process is analyzing the DEI quantitative data. The following three tips and techniques will aid you in your quantitative data analysis:

1. **Compare current data with past data to identify trends**—*Longitudinal data* tracks the same data at multiple points in time. When longitudinal data is available, a fairly straightforward way to analyze DEI quantitative data is to compare current data with past data over multiple points in time (e.g., months, quarters, years, etc.). Is the data increasing, decreasing, or remaining flat? Is the data changing at a rapid pace, a slow pace, or not at all? The answers to these simple questions can help illuminate key trends and identify important developments.

2. **Use cross-tabulations to better understand different subgroups**—*Cross-tabulations* ("crosstabs" or "contingency tables") are data tables that can be used to analyze the correlation between two or more variables. A cross-tabulation table groups variables together to better understand the relationship between the variables by producing various breakdowns according to your chosen subgroups from the internal, external, and organizational dimensions of Four Layers of Diversity (previously shown in Figure 1.23). These breakdowns can be extraordinarily helpful to understanding perceptions, perspectives, and lived experiences of different subgroups. For example, Table 1.11 shows a cross-tabulation between race (internal dimension) and lived experiences with different forms of incivility rank ordered by disrespectful behavior. The table not only clearly shows the relationship between race and multiple variables but also that people of color are more likely to experience disrespect, bullying, and discrimination. As another example, Table 1.12 shows a cross-tabulation between management status (organizational dimension) and responses to a statement about the organization benefitting from increased diversity using a five-point Likert scale (i.e., strongly disagree, disagree, neutral, agree, and strongly agree) rank ordered by level of management status. The table suggests there is a high level

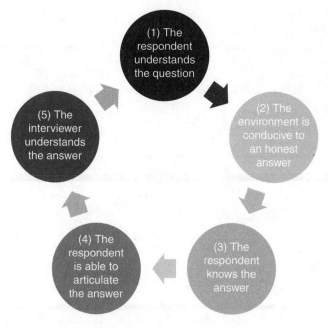

FIGURE 1.23   Successful Moderation of a DEI Focus Group

of commitment to diversity among executives that drops off precipitously among directors, managers, supervisors, and team leaders.

3. **Identify statistically significant differences to illuminate possible challenges and opportunities of different subgroups**—As mentioned earlier in the context of data sampling, when conducting a DEI culture and climate survey it is of paramount importance that you have enough respondents from each subgroup to make valid and statistically significant inferences about that subgroup because representation matters. Moreover, it is of paramount importance when analyzing the quantitative data from your DEI culture and climate survey that you identify where there are statistically significant differences between the perceptions, perspectives, and lived experiences of different subgroups. A statistically significant difference can suggest that a subgroup is experiencing your organization's culture and climate in a markedly different way—positively or negatively—when compared to others. This can be indicative of deeper, underlying issues, strengths, and areas for improvement. The quantitative research (i.e., DEI culture and climate survey) can help describe "what" challenges and opportunities exist and be suggestive of the need for further qualitative research (i.e., in-depth interviews and focus groups) to understand "why" they exist. For example, if the employees at a specific work location (organizational dimension) are found to have a statistically significant higher score on the Intrinsic Inclusion Inventory™ for Organizations, then there may be something very special happening there to foster an environment of inclusion and belonging that your organization would benefit from a deeper understanding and to potentially adopt more broadly.

TABLE 1.11	Example of Cross-Tabulation between Race and Forms of Incivility				

Please indicate which ethnicity(ies) best describe you:	N %	Disre-spectful Behavior	Diversity-Related Disrespect	Work-place Bully-ing	Dis-crimi-nation
African American or Black	867	64%*** ↑	43%** ↑	27%	22%
	13.4%				
American Indian or Alaska Native	84	47%	19%	26%	10%
	1.3%				
Asian	382	42%	20%	20%	11%
	5.9%				
Hispanic, Latino, or Spanish Origin	1197	49%	20%	27%	11%
	18.5%				
Middle-Eastern or North African	58	41%	12%	18%	4%
	0.9%				
Native Hawaiian or Other Pacific Islander	32	46%	18%	24%	9%
	0.5%				
Some other race	97	41%	11%* ↓	18%	3%* ↓
	1.5%				
Two or more races	136	48%	19%	26%	10%
	2.1%				
White, Not Hispanic or Latino	3617	40%	11%* ↓	17%	3%* ↓
	55.9%				
TOTAL	**6471**	**44%**	**19%**	**23%**	**12%**
	100.0%				

***Statistically significant at the $p < 0.001$ level
**Statistically significant at the $p < 0.01$ level
*Statistically significant at the $p < 0.05$ level

By comparison, if the employees at that work location are found to have a statistically significant lower score on the Intrinsic Inclusion Inventory™ for Organizations, then issues may be unfolding that warrant deeper understanding to address them.

- To determine statistical significance, you will need to determine the *p-value* (or probability value) for each data point, which indicates the likelihood that your data would have occurred by random chance or the likelihood that the

TABLE 1.12	Example of Cross-Tabulation between Management Status and Commitment to DEI

| Management Status | N % | My organization would benefit from increased workforce diversity. | | |
		Strongly Agree or Agree	Neutral	Disagree or Strongly Disagree
Executive/Vice President/Associate Vice President	98 ——— 1.5%	100%	0%	0%
Location, Unit, or Division Director	212 ——— 3.3%	62%	32%	6%
Manager/Supervisor	568 ——— 8.8%	45%	39%	16%
Team Leader	1524 ——— 23.6%	40%	42%	18%
Staff	4069 ——— 62.9%	65%	30%	5%
TOTAL	**6471 ——— 100.0%**	**62%**	**29%**	**9%**

"null hypothesis" of there being no correlation or relationship between the two variables being studied is true (i.e., one variable does not affect the other), and establish a threshold or significance cutoff also known as an *alpha value*. An alpha value of 0.05—a *p*-value of less than 0.05 ($p \leq 0.05$)—is generally recognized as statistically significant. Here are some good rules of thumb to establish alpha values and interpret *p*-values:

- An alpha value of 0.05—that is, *p*-value less than 0.05 ($p \leq 0.05$)—represents moderate statistical significance (1 in 20 chance of being random)
- An alpha value of 0.05—*p*-value less than 0.01 ($p \leq 0.01$)—represents high statistical significance (1 in 100 chance of being random)
- An alpha value of 0.05—*p*-value less than 0.001 ($p \leq 0.001$)—represents very high statistical significance (1 in 1,000 chance of being random)

As you can see, the lower your *p*-value threshold, the higher the likelihood that your results are not random. Looking back at Table 1.11, you can see the results of statistical significance tests at $p \leq 0.05$, $p \leq 0.01$, and $p \leq 0.001$. The arrows point up for results that are significantly higher and down for significantly lower. These results suggest that the experiences of African American or Black employees with disrespectful behavior and diversity-related disrespect reflect very high statistical significance that warrant further investigation and likely action.

There are several software applications that can automate comparing current data with future data, generating cross-tabulations, and performing tests of statistical significance such as SAS, SPSS, Stata, SUDAAN, and WesVar. Moreover, if you leverage a standardized DEI culture and climate survey from a vendor, it is very likely that they have also automated these analyses into their standard reporting. Later in this step, in the section "Phase VII: Deliver DEI Assessment Report," we will explore organizational DEI assessment reporting in the context of sharing both the quantitative and qualitative findings together. A detailed discussion of how to visualize quantitative data can be found in **Step 5: DEI Impact**.

Phase IV: Conduct DEI Interviews and Focus Groups (Qualitative Data Collection)

While quantitative data is effective in understanding what people think/feel about a DEI topic, qualitative data is helpful in understanding why people think/feel a certain way about that topic, such as their experiences or personal observations and feelings of inclusion and belonging (or exclusion and marginalization). Qualitative data is an essential part of a DEI assessment because it provides a different and valuable lens to the lived experiences of others when compared to quantitative data.

Qualitative data captures the opinions, experiences, perceptions, and perspectives of people. It can be collected in a variety of ways including interviews, observation, focus groups (or listening sessions), and written documents. Here, I will focus on the two most prevalent ways to collect DEI qualitative data: *in-depth interviews (IDIs)* and *focus groups*, while drawing directly from *Focus Groups: A Practical Guide for Applied Research*, fifth edition, by Richard A. Krueger and Mary Ann Casey.[3]

IDIs are one-on-one sessions between a moderator and a person and focus groups are one-to-many sessions between a moderator and several people. The moderator creates a safe psychological space that encourages participants to share perceptions and points of view.

IDIs and focus groups have four characteristics:

1. They involve people who possess certain characteristics
2. They take place in a physical or virtual setting
3. They engender focused discussion
4. They product qualitative data

The purpose of an IDI or focus group for an organizational DEI assessment is to better understand how people feel or think about issues relating to DEI. The intent of IDIs and focus groups is not to infer but to understand; not to generalize but to determine the range of perspectives; and not to make statements about the population but to provide insights about how people in the groups perceive an issue. IDIs and focus groups work when participants feel comfortable, respected, and free to give their opinions without being judged.

Ideally, the IDIs and focus groups are conducted several times with similar types of participants, so the moderator can identify trends and patterns in perceptions. Then, careful and systematic analysis of the discussion provides clues and insights as to how a topic is perceived by individuals and members of the group.

We will now walk you through the steps of conducting IDIs and focus groups for an organizational DEI assessment including determining the purpose, developing questions, establishing timing, selecting the number of participants, selecting and sampling the type of participants, moderating and debriefing, and coding and analyzing data. Because an IDI is essentially a focus group with one participant, hereafter I will only refer to focus groups but please be aware that each step equally applies to IDIs. The step will then conclude with how to report integrated findings from an organizational DEI assessment that combines quantitative and qualitative data.

Determining the Purpose   The objective of a DEI focus group is to understand DEI issues based on the lived experiences of participants. The first step, determining the DEI focus group purpose, means identifying which aspects of DEI you seek to understand more deeply. Your organizational DEI aims may be valuable in this regard as they can direct your attention to the topics that matter most. For example, if your organizational DEI aim is to improve teamwork and collaboration leading to greater innovation, then you will want to glean insights into how effectively people are or are not working together and generating ideas. By comparison, if your organizational DEI aim is to identify or confirm and dismantle institutional and structural barriers to racism and improve equitable outcomes for people of color, then your DEI focus groups will necessarily delve into the lived experiences of people of color, their allies, and, if possible, their detractors. Other questions to answer in determining the purpose of the DEI focus groups:

- What kinds of information do you want?
- Who wants the information?
- How will you use the information?
- What is the next step your organization wants to take with the information?

This pattern of questioning lets the moderator get a better picture of the information needs of intended users and thereby keeps the organizational DEI assessment on target. Determining the purpose of the DEI focus groups is the most important step of the process because:

- It guides the planning.
- It suggests how much time and resources should be put into the focus groups.
- It gives clues as to what type of people should be recruited to participate.
- It guides the development of questions.
- It helps the moderator know what to focus on.
- It helps set the analytic framework.
- It helps the qualitative data analyst separate what is important from what is not.

The purpose shapes and guides all the remaining steps for focus groups.

Developing Questions The second step is developing a series of DEI focus group questions or a *DEI focus group questioning route* (that will be incorporated into a DEI focus group protocol that is described later). Not all questions are created equal. Open-ended questions allow the respondents to determine the direction of the response. The answer is not implied and the type or manner of response is not suggested. Individuals are encouraged to respond based on their unique perspective and lived experiences. The major advantage of open-ended questions is that they reveal what is on the participant's mind as opposed to what the moderator suspects is on their mind. For example, consider these open-ended questions:

- Think back to when you were first hired. What was that experience like?
- Who cares about DEI and how do you know they care?
- Does the organization's diversity reflect the community it serves?
- Do you feel included as a part of the organization?
- What do you like best about the organization's culture?
- What do you like least about the organization's culture?
- Where do you get information about new opportunities for development? Advancement and promotions?
- Do you think development decisions are made equitably? Advancement and promotions?

Another way to ask open-ended questions but limit the response options is listing things (e.g., *"What could lead to more equitable hiring? Write down your answers and be prepared to share."* or *"Jot down three characteristics of a more inclusive culture."*). Some questions are deceptive and appear to be more open-ended but are really closed-ended questions in disguise. Compare the question, "How satisfied were you with the hiring and onboarding process?" to "How did you feel about the hiring and onboarding process?" The former, more closed-ended question, implies there is a level of satisfaction. The latter, more open-ended question, invites more description and explanation.

Closed-ended questions aren't totally off limits. They can provide very helpful information and can also be productive to narrow the types of responses and bring greater focus to the answers and especially when followed by an open-ended question. Examples of closed-ended questions, followed by open-ended questions, that engage participants include:

- **Rating Items:** "How would you rate leadership's demonstrated commitment to DEI? Excellent, Good, Fair, or Poor. What have you experienced or observed that led to that rating?" or "Please indicate whether you strongly agree, agree, are neutral, disagree, or strongly disagree with the following statement: Managers fairly evaluate talent for promotions/advancement. What have you experienced or observed that led to that rating?"
- **Choosing Among Alternatives:** "Which of the following strategies do you think will be most effective for improving DEI? (1) conduct organization-wide DEI training, (2) incorporate DEI into performance evaluations, or (3) establish employee resource groups (ERGs). What have you experienced or observed that led to that opinion?"

Keep questions simple, make them sound conversational, and be cautious about giving examples because they can limit thinking.

We use different types of questions at different times during the DEI focus group for different reasons. Each question has a distinct purpose: some to help people get prepared to answer more important questions later. Essentially there are several categories of questions, each with a distinctive function in the flow of a DEI focus group, that are administered in the following order:

Opening Question—All participants are asked to answer the opening question at the beginning of the focus group. The purpose of the question is to get everyone to talk early in the discussion. The opening question is designed to be easy and to be answered quickly (in about 30 seconds). Usually, it is best to ask for facts as opposed to opinions. For example, *"Tell us your name, your title, your department/division, and how long you have been employed with the organization?"*

Introductory Questions—Introductory questions introduce the topic of discussion and get people to start thinking about their connection with the topic. Sometimes the introductory question asks participants to remember when they first experienced or encountered the organization or topic under investigation and to describe the experience. For example, *"Describe your experience when you first joined the organization."*

Transition Questions—Transition questions move the conversation into the key questions that drive the focus group. They serve as logical links between the introductory questions and the key questions. During these questions, the participants are becoming aware of how others view the topic. These questions set the stage for productive key questions. For example, *"What were your first impressions of the organization's culture?"*

Key Questions—Key questions drive the focus group. Typically, there are four to six questions in this category. These are the questions that require the greatest attention. While only a few minutes might be allocated for each of the earlier questions, the key questions may need as much as 20 minutes each. Furthermore, the moderator will likely need to use different moderation techniques, such as pauses, probes, parrots, pivots, and practices (described later under "Moderating and Debriefing"), more frequently with key questions. Examples of key questions include:

"Tell me about how you have experienced the organization's culture. What does it feel like to work here?"

"Have you heard people talk about DEI? When people talk about DEI, what do they say?"

"Do you think people face barriers in getting hired? What are some of the barriers that people face to hiring? What about barriers to development? Promotions and advancement?"

"Do people have the opportunity to be mentored in your organization? How does one obtain a mentor? What keeps some people from being mentored?"

"Are there incentives or benefits to supporting DEI? What are they?"

"What would cause you or others to be a DEI champion or supporter? What would discourage you or others from becoming a DEI champion or supporter?"

Ending Questions—These questions bring closure to the discussion, enable participants to reflect back on previous comments, and are critical to the analysis. Three types of ending questions can be valuable:

"All Things Considered Question"—Moderator seeks to determine the final position of participants on critical areas of concern by asking, *"Of all the needs related to DEI that we discussed, which one is most important to you?"*

"Summary Question"—Moderator provides a two- to three-minute summary and asks, *"Does that capture what was discussed or shared here?"*

"Final Question"—Moderator provides a short overview of the purpose of the focus group and asks, *"Is there anything else you would like to add, in addition to what has already been shared?"*

A good ending question can be the moderator's best friend because it invites participants to help do their job by summarizing main points, prioritizing key issues, and making sure important topics were not overlooked.

The moderator may move through some questions more rapidly and devote more time to others. The level of importance influences the amount of time spent on the question as well as the intensity of the analysis. Not all questions are analyzed in the same way. Some questions, like the opening question, may not be analyzed at all.

Establishing Timing
Focus groups are typically 90 minutes to two hours long. Successful focus groups have been conducted in less time, particularly with very focused topics. The two-hour time limit, however, is a physical and psychological limit for most people. Don't go beyond two hours unless there is a special event or circumstance that makes it comfortable for participants, such as providing a meal. Once you have a draft questioning route, you should estimate how much time you will spend on each question, typically 5, 10, 15, or 20 minutes, add up the time you have assigned to the questions, and decide if you need to add or remove questions. Prioritize the "must ask" or key questions to ensure that data is collected.

Once the draft questioning route is completed, ask others to provide feedback and revise the questions into a revised draft. I recommend testing the question in a mock focus group, which can be as simple as finding a few people who fit the target focus group profile and asking them the questions as if you were conducting an IDI. The moderators should pay attention to the ease of asking the question and the ease of mock participants understanding the question. After the questions have been tested with a few people, you are ready to hold the first focus group.

Table 1.13 shows a DEI focus group questioning route to understand why there is a lack of diversity (representation) of people of color at all levels of the organization. The participants are seven people of color that have been with the company three years or more. Table 1.14 shows a corresponding DEI focus group questioning route for supervisors to understand their perspective on the same issue. The participants are 7 supervisors that have been with the company 10 years or more.

TABLE 1.13   **DEI Focus Group Questioning Route for People of Color Example**

Category	Question	Minutes
Opening	1. Tell us your name, your title, your department/division, and how long you have been employed with the organization.	5
Introduction	2. What is your definition of diversity?	5
Transition	3. What do you hear people saying about diversity:	
	a. Over coffee breaks?	5
	b. At staff meetings?	
	Commitment	
	4. Who cares about diversity, and how do you know they care?	5
	5. Is diversity a priority for management? How can you tell?	5
Key	Retention	
	6. In the past three years [or ask 12 months, 18 months, etc.], have you considered leaving the company? If so, what caused you to consider leaving?	10
	7. What has caused you to stay with the company?	10
	Barriers	
	8. Have you experienced any barriers to your development? Advancement?	10
	9. Have you seen barriers for other people of color to their development? Advancement?	10
	Supervisor Effectiveness	
	10. How effective are supervisors in managing people of color?	10
	11. How effective are supervisors in handling difficult diversity issues?	10
	Improvements	
	12. What could be done to make the workplace more inclusive for you?	10
	13. What could the organization do to better support you?	10
Ending	14. If you had one minute to give advice to the CEO about how to improve the development and advancement of people of color, what would you say?	5
	15. Is there anything else we should have talked about or you want to make sure we capture related to the discussion topic?	10
	Total	**120**

TABLE 1.14 DEI Focus Group Questioning Route for Supervisors Example

Category	Question	Minutes
Opening	1. Tell us your name, your title, your department/division, and how long you have been employed with the organization.	5
Introduction	2. What is your definition of diversity?	5
Transition	3. What do you hear people saying about diversity: a. Over coffee breaks? b. At staff meetings?	5
	Commitment	
	4. Who cares about diversity, and how do you know they care?	5
	5. Is diversity a priority for management? How can you tell?	5
Key	Retention	
	6. What makes people of color stay?	10
	7. What makes people of color leave?	10
	Barriers	
	8. As supervisors, what incentives or benefits are there for you to create and maintain a diverse workforce?	10
	9. As supervisors, what makes it difficult to create and maintain a diverse workforce?	10
	Supervisors' Resources	
	10. How comfortable are you with your knowledge and skills to manage people of color?	10
	11. Do you have resources for handling difficult diversity issues or conversations? If so, where do you go?	10
	Improvements	
	12. What could be done to make the workplace more inclusive for people of color?	10
	13. What could the organization do to help improve supervisors' effectiveness in managing people of color?	10
Ending	14. If you had one minute to give advice to the CEO about how to improve the development and advancement of people of color, what would you say?	5
	15. Is there anything else we should have talked about or you want to make sure we capture related to the discussion topic?	10
	Total	**120**

Selecting the Number of Participants   Focus groups are typically five to eight people—but the size can range from as few as four to as many as 12. The focus group must be small enough for everyone to have an opportunity to share insights and yet large enough to provide diversity of perspectives. Some other factors that influence the number of people per focus group are summarized in Table 1.15.

The accepted rule of thumb is to plan for three or four focus groups with each participant subgroup (i.e., each demographic group, role, level, location, etc., warrants three or four focus groups). After you have conducted these first three or four focus groups, determine if you have reached saturation. *Saturation* is the term used to describe the point where you have heard the range of ideas and aren't getting new information. If, after three or four groups, you were still getting new information, you would conduct more groups. The reason you plan for three to four groups is that focus groups are analyzed across groups. The qualitative data analyst looks for patterns and themes across groups. For example, if you wanted to know how men's and women's experiences are similar or different in receiving mentorship, sponsorship, and allyship, you would conduct three focus groups with men and three focus groups with women. That way, you can analyze across the men's groups, analyze across the women's groups, and then compare and contrast the findings.

Also, when planning groups, you should avoid mixing people who may feel they have disparate levels of expertise or power related to the issue. If there is an expertise or power differential, some participants may be reluctant to talk. When structuring focus groups, you should probably avoid putting supervisors and their direct reports in the same focus group. You should probably not put teachers and students or teachers and parents in the same focus group. You should probably not put new hires and senior leaders in the same focus group. Our experience at BCT has taught us that, in most cases, these kinds of configurations are not a good idea because the power dynamics decrease or eliminate the likelihood of honest, candid, and unfiltered discussion from those of lesser power (i.e., a direct report is unlikely to disclose negative comments about their supervisor if they are in the same focus group). Authority bias, which is the tendency to be influenced by authority figures, can also be a factor in suppressing authenticity. I say you should *probably* avoid these kinds of configurations, but I wouldn't say that you should never pursue these kinds of configurations. Ultimately, the purpose of the focus groups should dictate what should happen.

TABLE 1.15   **Factors to Influence the Number of DEI Focus Group Participants**

Factor	Recruitment
Complexity of Topic	More complex, invite fewer people
Participants' Level of Experience	More experience, invite fewer people
Participants' Level of Passion	More passion, invite fewer people
Number of Questions	More questions, invite fewer people

Selecting and Sampling the Type of Participants When deciding who to invite to DEI focus groups, think back to the purpose. Usually, the purpose is to describe how certain people—who have something in common—think or feel about something related to DEI. The purpose should guide the invitation decision. Questions to consider:

- What kind of people do you want to make statements about?
- What kind of people can give you the information you are looking for?
- What kind of people are most negatively affected by an issue?
- Who are the people who have power or influence over the issue?
- What kind of people are most advantaged or disadvantaged by an issue?

Caution is needed when the focus group participants represent diverse categories of people. It is a fallacy to assume that any one individual can represent his or her race, gender, or culture. Each person speaks for themselves. When asked, however, these individuals may attempt to offer insights about the opinions of an entire category of people. If you want to capture the opinions of a certain category of people, then you will need to conduct a sufficient number of focus groups with that particular category of people. A single focus group comprised of a diverse group of people is not sufficient to pick up trends of subcategories of people.

Here are some good rules of thumb that we embrace at BCT for when selecting DEI interview and focus participants:

- Use the DEI culture and climate survey results to inform the selection of IDI and focus group participants for whom the organizational DEI assessment would benefit from a deeper understanding of their lived experience.
- Conduct IDIs with senior leaders and executives.
- Conduct focus groups with specific subgroups (e.g., people representing the same geographic location, demographic identifies, positions, levels, functions, etc.) to understand dynamics that may be specific to the subgroup.
- Conduct focus groups with cross-cutting subgroups (e.g., people representing different geographic locations, demographic identifiers, positions, levels, functions, etc.) to understand organization-wide dynamics.
- Consider matching the identifiers of the interviewer to the identifiers of the interviewee or the identifiers of focus group moderator to the identifiers of the focus group.

With respect to sampling participants for a DEI focus group, the primary factor for selecting participants is to be purposeful—to determine what issues you want to more deeply understand, and which people and groups are most appropriate to provide insights to those issues. Keep in mind that the intent of IDIs and focus groups is not to infer but to understand, not to generalize but to determine the range of perspectives, and not to make statements about the population but to provide insights about how people in the groups perceive an issue. While a degree of randomization may be used, it should only be to eliminate the selection bias inherent in some forms of personal recruitment, such that all participants within the purposeful sample possess an equivalent chance to be involved in the organizational DEI assessment. Caution is needed because randomization of participants without the preliminary purposeful sample can lead to inaccurate findings. For example, let's say the purpose of a DEI focus group is to understand the experiences of AAPI employees as they are overrepresented in technical positions but underrepresented in managerial positions. The target participants or purposeful sample is AAPI employees who transitioned from technical positions to managerial positions within the past two years. It is recommended that you first identify the pool of prospective participants who meet this criterion and then use a random procedure to select individuals from that pool to participate in the focus groups.

Moderating and Debriefing   At BCT, we always use a moderation team when conducting focus groups: a moderator and an assistant moderator. Each person performs certain tasks:

- The moderator is primarily concerned with directing the discussion and keeping it flowing.
- The assistant moderator is responsible for the audio recording (with permission), handles the environmental conditions and logistics (e.g., refreshments, lighting, and seating for physical or in-person focus groups and web conferencing setup, configuration, and management for virtual or online focus groups), responds to unexpected interruptions, and takes comprehensive notes.

Near the end of the discussion, the moderator may request the assistant moderator to ask additional questions or follow up on topics of interest. The assistant moderator may also be asked to give a short (two to three minutes) summary of the key points of the discussion. In addition, the assistant moderator plays an important part in the debriefing session that follows the focus group.

While it may seem simple, the moderator is responsible for ensuring that five activities take place, as shown in Figure 1.23.

If any of these links are broken, the quality of the focus group suffers. A good moderator:

- Respects the participants and shows it
- Communicates clearly
- Is open and not defensive
- Is the one who can get the most useful information

Successful moderation involves four phases: beginning the focus group, facilitating the focus group, concluding the focus group, and debriefing the focus group.

Beginning the Focus Group   The first few moments of a focus group discussion are critical. In this brief time, the moderator must give enough information so people feel comfortable with the topic, create an atmosphere of psychological safety, provide the ground rules, and set the tone of the discussion. Beginning the focus group has five parts shown in Table 1.16.

Much of the success of focus groups can be attributed to this three- to five-minute introduction. Being too formal or rigid can stifle interaction among participants.

.16   Beginning the Focus Group

Part	Example
The Welcome	Offer welcoming remarks and introduce the moderation team: *"Good afternoon and welcome. Thank you for taking the time to join our discussion of diversity, equity, and inclusion. My name is Anita Nossek. I am a member of the DEI council and I have the pleasure of serving as your moderator today. I am joined today by Dale Walker who will be assisting me and taking notes to make certain that we capture the key themes from our conversation."*
The Overview of the Topic	Provide an overview of the topic and explain why participants were selected. *"The purpose of this focus group is to understand the reasons why a growing number of millennials voluntarily leave the company within 6 to 12 months of being hired. You all represent former millennial employees that have voluntarily left the company within 6 to 12 months of being hired and departed within the last 6 to 18 months."*
The Ground Rules	Explicitly ask for permission to record the audio and/or video. Offer commentary to set the tone, establish expectations, and create psychological safety to set participants at ease and help the discussion go smoothly (emphasis mine): *"We're taking notes because we don't want to miss any of your comments. No names will be included in any reports. Your comments are confidential. We would also like to record this focus group for research purposes only. Neither the recorded focus group nor the transcripts will be shared beyond the research team who will analyze the data and prepare the summary report. Please indicate that you consent to the focus group being recorded by stating 'I consent' or 'I do not consent' aloud . . . thank you.* *"There are no wrong answers. We expect that you will have differing points of view. Please share your point of view even if it differs from what others have said. Do not feel like you have to respond to me all the time. If you want to follow up on something that someone has said, you want to agree, or disagree, or give an example, feel free to do that. Feel free to have a conversation with one another about these questions. I am here to ask questions, listen, and make sure everyone has a chance to share. We're interested in hearing from each of you. So if you're talking more than others, I may ask you to give others a chance. And if you aren't saying much, I may call on you. We just want to make sure all of you have a chance to share your ideas."*
The Context	Provide any background information to help frame and/or ground participants in the topic. This could include definitions, data, statistics, trends, previous findings, etc. that offer perspective on the topic. This could also be used to further set the tone and the mood for the conversation, such as to communicate its importance, seriousness, gravity, severity, etc.: *"We have had a difficult time retaining millennials as 30% that have been hired within the past year have voluntarily left the company within 6 to 12 months of being hired. This represents three times the company average and we are committed to learning and understanding how we can do better to retain this important population."*

TABLE 1.16   (Continued)

Part	Example
The Questions	Administer the DEI focus group questioning route including:
	1. Opening Question
	2. Introductory Questions
	3. Transition Questions
	4. Key Questions
	5. Ending Questions

By contrast, too much informality and humor can cause problems because participants might not take the discussion seriously.

Facilitating the Focus Group   DEI focus group moderators should be familiar with five essential techniques ("The Five P's"):

1. **The Pause**—A five-second pause can be used after a participant comment. This short pause often prompts additional points of view of agreement with the previously mentioned position, especially when coupled with eye contact from the moderator. There is a tendency for novice moderators to talk too much or to move too quickly from one topic to another, usually because they feel uncomfortable with silence.

2. **The Probe**—A request for additional information. Some people may offer phrases or vague comments that could have multiple meanings, or say, "I agree." These answers aren't very useful and don't give the moderator much to work with. A probe is used to draw out additional information. Common probes include questions and statements like these:

   a. Would you explain further?

   b. Can you give us an example?

   c. Would you say more?

   d. Tell us more.

   e. Say more.

   f. Is there anything else?

   g. Please describe what you mean.

   h. I'm not sure I understand.

      Use the probe a few times early in the focus group to communicate the importance of elaboration. Excessive probing can be time-consuming, annoying, and unnecessary.

3. **The Parrot**—Parroting is when you repeat what you have heard from a participant to confirm understanding and help them clarify their thoughts. This is particularly helpful when a participant makes a point that is unclear or when a participant's thoughts are not fully formed. According to *Verywell Mind* in their blog post, "How Parroting is Used in Therapy: An Effective Conversational Technique," "When parroting, it is important not to go too far. It is much better to repeat only the last few words than to attempt to repeat several sentences. Repetitive parroting can become annoying. It can also make the [participant] feel nervous or edgy."[4]

4. **The Pivot**—A pivot is a transition from one topic to the next and can be accomplished as follows:

   - **Preview the pivot by stating your intentions**—Make clear your intentions to pivot from one topic to the next (e.g., "Unfortunately, I only have a few minutes remaining on this topic, so I'll have time for two more comments.").

   - **Begin the pivot using an "internal summary"**—Summarize the most important point(s) from the current topic (e.g., "Thank you for sharing key insights about how we can foster greater diversity such as . . .").

   - **Complete the pivot using an "internal preview"**—Highlight the next topic (e.g., "In this next segment, we are now going to explore challenges and opportunities to create a more inclusive culture.").

5. **The Practices**—The following are other useful practices when facilitating a focus group:

   - Nod your head (slow not fast)
   - Provide short verbal responses (e.g., "Okay," "Yes," or "Uh-huh" but not "That's good" or "Excellent," which may imply judgments about the quality of the comment.)
   - Smile and embrace humor (when appropriate)

It is not uncommon in a DEI focus group for participants to share difficult, painful, or traumatic experiences and/or for participants to get frustrated or angry if a question touches on a sensitive or hot-button topic. DEI focus groups are often specifically geared toward unearthing these experiences and emotions. The moderation team should be prepared for how to respond in these circumstances. The following are ways the moderation team can support participants that have expressed difficult experiences:

- **Express Gratitude**—Simply say "Thank you" for their honesty, transparency, vulnerability, willingness to share, and so forth. If relevant, make clear that their openness has honored the ground rules that were established at the beginning of the session and will likely inspire others to do the same. Example: *"Thank you for your honesty in sharing your experiences. Thank you also for honoring ground rules we established at the beginning of the focus group around honesty and transparency."*

- **Embrace the Collective**—Speak on behalf of the entire group that their courage does not go unnoticed and that the group is collectively sorrowful that they had to endure the experience. Example: *"We all appreciate what you have shared. Our hearts go out to you, and we regret what you experienced."*
- **Emphasize the Value**—If appropriate, articulate how valuable their insights will be to understanding the issues and hopefully addressing the issues to help others. Example: *"Your deeper insights are exactly what we need to get to deeper solutions that can actually make a difference for you and others."*

The following are do's and don'ts for supporting angry/frustrated participants:

Do's	Don'ts
Acknowledge the anger/frustration and express compassion	Get defensive (on your own behalf or on behalf of the organization)
Honor the anger/frustration by thanking the person for bringing up the issue	Diminish or minimize the anger/frustration
	Express anger/frustration back
Seek to understand the source of the anger/frustration and not just the symptom(s)	Shy away from the anger/frustration or move on too quickly; others may share similar experiences that lead to deeper and powerful insights
Pivot the anger/frustration by indicating that the hope is to avoid future anger/frustration for others	

Concluding the Focus Group   Conclude the focus group by posing one or more of the aforementioned ending questions (e.g., "All Things Considered Question," "Summary Question," and "Final Question"). When posing the summary question and presenting the brief summary, the moderation team should watch the participants for signs of agreement, hesitation, or confusion. When the two- to three-minute summary is completed, the moderator should invite comments, amendments, or corrections. A variation to the final question is useful if participants are reluctant to talk because of sensitivity to the recording of the focus group. An alternative is to turn off the recording of the focus group, indicate that the discussion is now completed, thank them for their assistance, and then ask, "Do you think we've missed anything in the discussion?" This gesture may uncover some avenues of thought that were not anticipated.

Debriefing the Focus Group   The moderation team should conduct a 15- to 30-minute debriefing after participants leave the physical or virtual room. This gives the team a chance to compare notes, share highlights, and consider what others on the team have observed or heard. Questions to consider when debriefing:

- What were the themes?
- What are the most important points that we've learned from this group?

- What was surprising or unexpected?
- What quotes were particularly helpful?
- How was this group similar to or different from earlier groups?
- Does anything need to be changed to the focus group questions, format, or structure before the next focus group?

Audio or video record the debriefing. If an oral or written report is needed following the focus group, the moderation team can use the debrief to summarize key points.

Transcribing the Focus Group   If permission was granted to record, the audio or video recording of the focus group (and possibly the debriefing) should be transcribed to aid the analysis. While this can be done manually, there are a growing number of options that can help automate the process. For example, virtual focus groups using web conferencing platforms such as Zoom, Microsoft Teams, Google Meet, and others offer automated transcription services that are built in or can be installed as an extension at no additional cost using artificial intelligence (AI). There are also fee-based services such as **Rev.com**, Otter.ai, and Trint. The features vary and are constantly evolving across these services and include easy integration with certain web conferencing platforms to provide live transcription and importing audio/video files for transcription. The transcription can either be fully automated, also using AI, for a relatively lower cost with approximately 90% accuracy, or performed by humans, who are scaffolded by AI, for a relatively higher cost with approximately 99% accuracy. At BCT, we've had the best experience with the latter and especially with a high volume of transcripts and/or a sufficient budget, whereas the former can suffice for a low volume of transcripts and/or a limited budget.

Coding Qualitative Data   Coding qualitative data is a precursor to analyzing it. *Coding* consists of placing similar labels on similar things. The task is to sort comments into similar categories. The job is best performed by several people working together ("the qualitative data analysis team") and ideally those who were physically present when the focus groups were conducted. It's been estimated that 80% of the content is found in the transcript and the remaining 20% are all other things that occur in the physical or virtual room. Being in the focus groups gives the qualitative data analysis team a sense of the energy, passion, and emotion that doesn't come through the transcript.

Throughout the coding and analysis process, remember the purpose of the DEI focus groups. The purpose will guide the direction, depth, and intensity of the analysis. Beginning DEI focus group moderators can get overwhelmed with the vast quantity of qualitative data and distracted by all the details. Some have a hard time getting started because the task seems daunting. Some get started but can't decide what to pay attention to. Everything seems interesting. Everything might have potential. If you get bogged down or stuck, go back and reread the purpose. This should help you decide how to move forward. If that doesn't work, talk to colleagues.

The coding process entails the following steps:
Review:

1. Take the first set of notes and/or transcript.
2. Read the entire set of notes and/or transcript.

Initial Coding:

3. Select the first question you want to analyze.
4. Examine the first response.
5. If it is an answer to the question, then give it a title or a "code" that describes the comment.

Final Coding:

6. Examine the subsequent responses and if it is a similar answer, give it the same title or code or give it a title or code that is abstracted and broader while still encompassing of all similar answers.
7. If it differs give it another title or code that best describes the response.

This process continues with all the responses until the data are exhausted and then move on to the next question. Figure 1.24 illustrates this qualitative data coding process by depicting a focus group scenario where the responses from two participants have been coded for the following two questions: "Have you seen barriers for women and people of color to their development and advancement?" and "What can be done to address the barriers?"

Phase V: Analyze DEI Qualitative Data

When all qualitative data have been coded and categorized, the qualitative data analysis team must get a sense of the frequency of themes and findings, but the analytic process is more than arriving at the number of times a comment was said. At this stage, the qualitative data analysis team should give thought to a cluster of concepts:

- **Frequency**—How often was a concept mentioned?
- **Extensiveness**—How many different people mentioned the concept?
- **Intensity**—How much passion or force was behind the comments?
- **Specificity**—How much detail was provided by respondents?
- **Internal Consistency**—Did individual participants remain consistent in their views?
- **Participant Perception of Importance**—Did participants cite this as an important concept?

Question #1: Have you seen barriers to the development and advancement of women and people of color?
Question #2: What can be done to address the barriers?

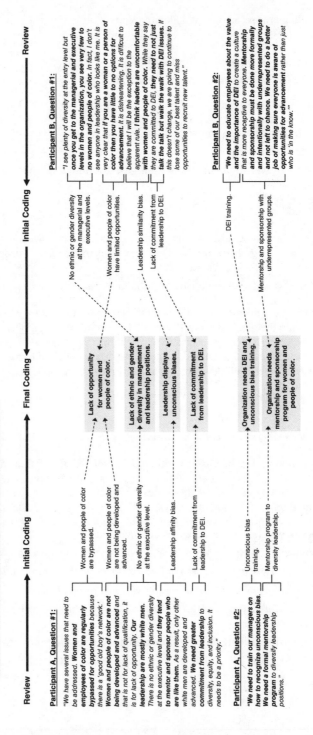

FIGURE 1.24 Qualitative Data Coding Process Example

To more easily arrive at integrated and consolidated answers to these questions, give thought to various analytic frameworks. These frameworks allow you to examine the problem from different vantage points and have the potential for bringing focus to your qualitative data analysis. Base your choice of framework on the purpose of the DEI focus groups and what you are seeking to discover. There is no right or wrong framework.

The examples of analytic frameworks in Table 1.17 are not intended to be exhaustive but rather to point out how your qualitative data collection strategies and process of qualitative data analysis will differ depending on the purposes of your DEI focus groups. For example, if you are intent on uncovering factors that might influence change, then you will need more note-taking strategies that allow you to identify the participant who makes each comment. And then you will need to trace that individual's comments throughout the discussion to identify indications of consistency or change. Moreover, keep in mind that your quantitative data can help you

TABLE 1.17   **DEI Focus Group Analytic Frameworks**

Analytic Framework	Objective	Key Task
1. Constant Comparative	Identify patterns in the data and discover relationships among ideas or concepts.	Compare one segment of data with another to identify similarities and differences.
2. Identifying Individual Change	Identify change or movement in opinions, preferences, or attitudes.	Track an individual's comments throughout the course of the focus group. Ask participants if their views have changed.
3. Critical Incidents	Discover important and critical events that have shaped later decisions. Less emphasis on patterns and more on the logic and rationale offered by each individual.	Identify important ingredients related to success or failure of a program, organization, or concept. Ask participants to identify critical incidents.
4. Key Concepts	Identify the factors that are of central importance, not critical, but of moderate importance toward understanding how participants view a topic.	Identify a limited number of important ideas, experiences, or preferences that illuminate the topic. Ask participants to help identify the key concepts.
5. Testing Alternatives	Identify the most preferred choice among several alternatives.	Show participants examples, descriptions, etc., and ask them to choose. Encourage participants to identify their choices and then provide reasons.

better understand your qualitative data. For example, if 70% of Latina women have expressed a desire to leave the organization, much information like this could help guide the focus group discussion, it can also help focus your analysis on comments that help explain why.

There are several software applications that can aid and automate qualitative data analysis including NVivo, Atlas.ti, and MAXQDA. As it specifically relates to DEI, co:census (**cocensus.io**) is an all-in-one text analysis and data visualization studio powered by patent-pending natural language processing (NLP), aimed to reduce biases and prioritize ethical analysis. It offers templates, tailored for different use cases, and multiple integrations (e.g., SurveyMonkey, Twitter, etc.) to connect feedback from surveys, public comments, audio transcriptions, and social media and produce streamlined analytics and real-time insights. In the conclusion of this book, I discuss a genre of tools that leverage Big Data and NLP to offer the next generation of qualitative data analysis that will offer unparalleled analysis and insights.

Here is some final advice for analyzing DEI focus group data:

- Much analysis is based on pattern identification.
- Sometimes pattern identification might not be appropriate. In certain situations, such as critical incidents, an event might occur only once and yet be of great consequence.
- Beware of personal bias and preexisting opinions about the topic.
- *Remember that you are the voice of the participants!*

A detailed discussion of how to visualize qualitative data can be found in **Step 5: DEI Impact**. We will explore how to report qualitative data later in the section "Phase VII: Deliver DEI Assessment Report" in the context of sharing the entire organizational DEI assessment results including quantitative and qualitative findings.

Phase VI: Analyze DEI Mixed-Methods Integrated Data

If you have undertaken some or all preceding phases, then you are now sitting on a lot of mixed-methods (quantitative and qualitative) data that forms the basis for your organizational DEI assessment according to the "4 P's" framework including:

- **People:** Personal Preferences and Competences
  - **Preferences and Competences Data**—You have quantitative data from the personal and team DEI inventories that characterize the preferences and/or competences of the people and teams that comprise your organization. This offers a lens to individual and organizational blind spots (via preferences) and areas of strength and improvement (via preferences and competences).
- **People:** Personal Behaviors and Experiences (Organizational Culture and Climate)

- ○ **Survey Data**—You have quantitative data from your DEI culture and climate survey that characterize what people are experiencing with your organizational culture and climate.

- ○ **Interview and Focus Group Data**—You have qualitative data from your IDIs and focus groups that characterize why people throughout your organization think and feel a certain way about how they experience your organizational culture and climate.

- Management **Practices** and Organizational **Policies**

- ○ **Review or Audit Data**—You have qualitative data from your DEI HR policies and practices review or audit including fact-based findings and insight (review) or expert conclusions and recommendations (audit) relative to your HR functions as they relate to DEI.

- Performance

- ○ **Benchmarking Data**—You may have data that assesses your organization's capacity, maturity, ability, or "muscle strength" in specific categories that relate to DEI such as organizational structure, leadership involvement, approach, staffing and resources, measurement, and the like.

- ○ **Ranking Data**—You may have ranking data, based on a standardized submission, that compares your organization's DEI performance to other organizations or peers in your industry—regionally, nationally, and/or internationally.

Naturally, this can be a lot of data to process and interpret! As shown in Table 1.18, we use a simple mixed-methods integrated data analysis framework at BCT—*Findings, Evidence, Implications, and Recommendations*—to translate what can be a multitude of data into actionable recommendations.

Leveraging this framework necessitates a close review of the reports and findings across all the organizational DEI assessments to identify the consistent themes and insights. We have found the four groups and the 15 categories of the GDEIB to be extremely helpful in organizing the analysis into useful categories. In other words, the GDEIB is not just a useful tool for benchmarking purposes, it also provides useful categories for analyzing and reporting assessment findings (and, as you will see in **Step 2: DEI Imperatives** and **Step 4: DEI Initiatives**, these categories are also useful for developing a DEI strategic plan). We have also found it helpful to engage a DEI Council—a diverse and inclusive body representing different functions, levels, roles, identities, and responsibilities throughout the organization—to aid in reviewing and interpreting the results.

For illustrative purposes, Table 1.19 provides an example of a mixed-methods integrated data analysis based on the four groups of the GDEIB. However, do note that a comprehensive mixed-methods integrated data analysis might necessitate a further breakdown into some or all of the 15 categories of the GDEIB.

Please note that the findings, evidence, implications, and recommendations generated from the organizational DEI assessment you have performed here in **Step 1: DEI Inventory** are critical to the proceeding steps of the *Data-Driven DEI* cycle. During **Step 2: DEI Imperatives**, the findings will help you establish clear DEI objectives;

TABLE 1.18   **Mixed-Methods Integrated Data Analysis Framework**

Term	Definition	Questions to Answer	Example
Findings	Key discoveries and takeaways from the organizational DEI assessment. Complete the sentence: *One of the key discoveries and takeaways was . . .*	*What are the key discoveries and takeaways?*	Lack of diverse representation in executive leadership positions.
Evidence (Source)	Information, data, and facts that support the key findings. Quantitative, qualitative, and expert-driven insights derived from the organizational DEI assessment (reference the source, where applicable). Complete the sentence: *The findings are supported by evidence such as . . . (from the following source . . .)*	*What specific information, data, and facts support the findings?*	Only 2% of executive leadership positions are held by BIPOC employees *(Survey)*. *"Managers are the problem. They only hire and promote people like them." (Focus Groups)*
Implications	Insights and conclusions based on the findings and evidence. Complete the sentence: *Based on the key findings and the evidence, it is clear that . . .*	*What have we learned?*	The organization needs to foster an environment of greater fairness and equity; managers must play a central role.
Recommendations	Detailed and specific things to do based on the implications. Complete the sentence: *As a result of the implications, the organization should . . .*	*What should we do?* *How should we proceed?*	Implement DEI and unconscious bias training for all managers.

the evidence, data, and results will establish a profile and baseline from which you can set specific DEI goals and determine impact; and the recommendations will inform which strategies you pursue to achieve your DEI objectives and goals. However, that is only after you complete **Step 3: DEI Insights**, which will identify promising and proven strategies that have worked for others. It is not until **Step 4: DEI Initiatives** that you will make a final determination of your DEI strategies and the measures to gauge progress.

TABLE 1.19   Mixed-Methods Integrated Data Analysis Framework Example

Findings	Evidence (Source)	Implications	Recommendations
THE FOUNDATION GROUP: Drive the Strategy			
• Lack of effective communication and accountability for leadership, particularly in supervisory and managerial roles. • Lack of leadership communication follow-through on DEI initiatives	• 63% of employees completing the DWWA™ indicated that leadership is not committed to DEI. *(DWWA™ Culture and Climate Survey)* • "Leadership is not effective in creating an environment of inclusion and belonging." *(Focus Groups)* • The organization scored at Level 2: Reactive on the GDEIB in the Foundation Group *(GDEIB Benchmarking)*	• The organization must enhance the inclusive leadership competences of leadership to create an environment of inclusion and belonging.	• Establish a competence-based inclusive leadership framework for all leaders (i.e., Intrinsic Inclusion™) • Implement learning and development to reinforce the inclusive leadership framework (i.e., Intrinsic Inclusion™). • Establish Employee Resource Groups (ERGs).
THE INTERNAL GROUP: Attract & Retain People			
• Lack of diverse representation in executive leadership positions.	• Only 2% of executive positions are held by BIPOC employees. *(Human Resources Information System)* • "Managers are the problem. They only hire and promote people like them." *(Focus Groups)* • The performance management process, which forms the basis for promotion and advancement decisions, is too subjective. Criteria are unclear and the ways of evaluating against those criteria are unstructured and lack consistency. *(DEI HR Policies and Practices Evaluation Audit)* • The organization scored at Level 1: Inactive on the GDEIB in the Internal Group. *(GDEIB Benchmarking)*	• The organization must reform its performance management process to be more structured and objective.	• Implement recommendations from the DEI HR Policies and Practices Audit for performance management.

(Continued)

TABLE 1.19 (Continued)

Findings	Evidence (Source)	Implications	Recommendations
THE BRIDGING GROUP: *Align & Connect*			
• The organization has a welcoming culture but could improve with underrepresented groups. • Employees and managers need to increase their DEI competences.	• The DWWA™ reported a statistically significant lower commitment to DEI by managers and supervisors when compared to all people. *(DWWA™ Culture and Climate Survey)* • The average employee scored at the second level and the average manager and supervisor scored at the lowest level on the Intrinsic Inclusion Inventory™ for People. *(I3™ for Organizations)* • The Intrinsic Inclusion Inventory™ (I3™) for Organizations found that 43% of employees demonstrated intrinsically inclusive behaviors. *(I3™ for Organizations)* • "The organization has a welcoming and friendly culture but far less so for underrepresented groups." *(Focus Groups)* • The organization's current training curriculum does not include any DEI-specific topics; there are no Employee Resource Groups (ERGs). *(DEI HR Policies and Practices Evaluation Audit)* • The organization scored at Level 3: Proactive on the GDEIB in the Internal Group. *(GDEIB Benchmarking)*	• The organization needs to foster an environment of greater fairness and equity; all employees can play a role and managers must play a central role.	• Implement Intrinsic Inclusion™ training for all people. • Implement an inclusive leadership program for all managers and supervisors.

TABLE 1.19   **(Continued)**

Findings	Evidence (Source)	Implications	Recommendations
THE EXTERNAL GROUP: Listen To & Serve Society			
• The organization does not invest significant procurement dollars in diverse suppliers.	• 2% of procurement dollars are spent with minority- and women-owned businesses (MWBEs). *(Supplier Diversity Spend Analysis)*	• The organization must establish a formal supplier diversity program.	• Hire a supplier diversity director. • Implement a formal supplier diversity program. • Establish partnerships with the National Minority Supplier Development Council (NMSDC) and the Women's Business Enterprise National Council (WBENC).

Phase VII: Deliver DEI Assessment Report

The final phase is to deliver an integrated DEI assessment report that combines the quantitative and qualitative results and shares the findings as broadly as possible and as transparently as possible. This process may begin with a briefing of executive leadership, HR, and general counsel to mitigate any organizational or legal risks and then more broadly throughout the entire organization. Lyssa Test further advises, "Next, you'll need to share your analysis and action plan with your employees. Oftentimes, Human Resources teams or a [senior executive leader] will present . . . results during an [all-hands] meeting, so they can walk employees through the findings and add context. These presentations should include an overview of participation rates, survey scores, organizational strengths, opportunities for growth, key findings, and historical or benchmark comparisons. You should end the meeting by reviewing your detailed action plan, showing employees exactly what your [organization] will be doing to address any issues raised by the survey."[5] Very few organizations emerge from an organizational DEI assessment unscathed but *do not bury the truth*. The more transparent your organization is with the results, the more you will engender trust, uplift the very tenets of DEI, and set the tone for the DEI journey that lies ahead.

An outline of a sample organizational DEI assessment report is shown in Figure 1.25.

Organizational DEI Assessment Report

  I. Introduction

  II. DEI Assessment Framework: The 4 P's

    a. People, Practices, Policies & Performance

  III. DEI Assessment Approach and Results

    a. People: DEI Quantitative Data Results (Culture and Climate Survey)

    b. People: DEI Qualitative Data Results (In-depth Interviews and Focus Groups)

    c. Policies and Practices: DEI HR Policies and Practices Results (Review or Audit)

    d. Policies and Practices: DEI Benchmarking Results (GDEIB)

    e. Performance: DEI Ranking (DiversityInc)

  IV. DEI Integrated Data Analysis

  V. Findings and Recommendations

    a. The Foundation Group: *Drive the Strategy*

    b. The Internal Group: *Attract & Retain People*

    c. The Bridging Group: *Align & Connect*

    d. The External Group: *Listen To & Serve Society*

  VI. Conclusions

FIGURE 1.25   DEI Assessment Report Outline

For personal DEI assessments that leverage the kinds of tools highlighted in **Step 1: DEI Inventory for People**, in almost all cases, reporting work will be done for you and delivered in the form of an electronic or downloadable assessment report. For **Step 1: DEI Inventory for Organizations**, the form and fashion of organizational DEI assessment reports can vary. Organizations that specialize in conducting organizational DEI assessments will very likely have processes that semi-automate or fully automate the data analysis and data reporting processes.

Once again, I cannot emphasize enough the critical relationship between data collection, data analysis, and data reporting. As mentioned earlier, by establishing your range of subgroups during data collection, you set the stage for *data disaggregation*— stratifying the data by the subgroups you selected, and *data analysis and reporting*— identifying and disclosing statistically significant differences between subgroups (e.g., women vs. men vs. nonbinary; married vs. single; people who are vision impaired vs. people who are hearing impaired, etc.) and between intersections of subgroups (e.g., married men who are vision impaired vs. single women who are hearing impaired). In other words, your data analysis and reporting can only be as detailed as the subgroups you have selected.

If disaggregated data may reveal a respondent's identity, it must be further aggregated to protect their privacy, confidentiality, and anonymity. For example, if your organization only has one female Hispanic employee, then results should not be disaggregated by ethnicity and gender because doing so will reveal the employee's responses simply by the process of elimination. Additionally, if the pool of Hispanic employees or female employees are sufficiently large to maintain privacy, confidentiality, and anonymity as separate pools, then the results can be stratified and disaggregated by ethnicity *or* gender but not by ethnicity *and* gender together. At BCT, our rule of thumb is that the number of respondents in a disaggregated group must be greater than 5 to 10 people to justify disaggregation.

Mitigating Data Bias—Part 2

In the previous **Step 1: DEI Inventory for People**, I discussed how data carries and inherits its own assumptions and biases as a reflection of human assumptions and biases known as "data bias" and "algorithmic bias." I introduced three forms of data bias—*researcher bias, confirmation bias*, and *attribution bias*—that pertain to people and how to address them. Here, I introduce a fourth form of data bias—*selection bias*—that pertains to people and processes, and I outline steps you can take to address it. I will address the topic of *algorithmic bias* in the conclusion.

Selection Bias

Selection bias occurs when the respondent pool is not representative of the target population. For example, if your DEI culture and climate survey had a low or no response from persons with disabilities, then the results would reflect a selection bias. The traditional way to mitigate selection bias in research studies is to randomly assign respondents to the intervention and control groups (i.e., a randomized controlled trial or RCT, which will be further explored under "Distinguishing Between Correlation and Causation" in **Step 5: DEI Impact**). Random assignment is generally untenable for an organizational DEI assessment. We have, however, found effective engagement outreach and monitoring to be among the best strategies to mitigate selection bias when conducting an organizational DEI assessment. A modern and more practical approach is BCT's Equitable Analytics™, which will be introduced as a "What Works" model in **Step 3: DEI Insights** and discussed further in the conclusion.

As mentioned earlier, effective engagement is about having a communication plan that makes the DEI assessment's value clear to all stakeholders and with different messages for difference audiences, such as supporters and naysayers, along with regular reminders to participate. For example, potentially effective messages to supporters are that the assessment will help pinpoint challenges and opportunities and that these efforts will lead to a more informed and more effective strategic plan for DEI transformation. Potentially effective messages to naysayers are that input from all voices is invited and valuable; a focus on DEI does not lower standards, but rather, better enables the organization to attract and retain the best and brightest; and these efforts are intended to make a better workplace for everyone, improve performance, and enhance results.

Effective outreach means enlisting the voices of executive leaders, thought leaders and DEI ambassadors, council members, champions, and trusted intermediaries such as employee resource groups (ERGs) to conduct outreach to groups that may be susceptible to low response or participation rates, once again, armed with messaging that is tailored to the perceptions and challenges that are unique to those groups.

Lastly, effective monitoring involves very closely examining the response and participation rates to the organizational DEI assessment once it is underway and comparing to them the target population's representation data. For example, if women are 50% of the total target employee base but only 25% of the respondents to your organizational DEI assessment survey, then you have a selection bias problem! Mitigating selection bias necessitates that you quickly adjust your engagement and outreach efforts accordingly to maximize the likelihood of a representative respondent pool.

Having reflected on your DEI incentives, and completed your DEI inventory, you are ready to determine your DEI imperatives.

STEP 2

DEI Imperatives—
Determine Priorities

If you don't know where you're going, any road will take you there.

Your DEI strategy is only as good as your DEI assessment.

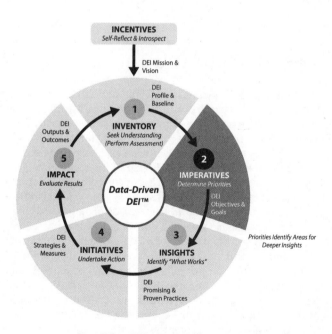

Data-Driven DEI—Step 2: DEI Imperatives

The first opening quote is commonly, but inaccurately, cited from Lewis Carroll's classic children's tale, *Alice in Wonderland*, and an exchange between Alice and the Cheshire Cat. In "Lessons from the Cheshire Cat," Donna Tinberg, an educational consultant, clarifies the actual exchange:[1]

> *In Carroll's altered reality, the conversation between the disoriented Alice and the mysterious Cheshire Cat actually went like this: "Would you tell me, please, which way I ought to go from here?" "That depends a good deal on where you want to get to," said the Cat. "I don't much care where—" said Alice. "Then it doesn't matter which way you go," said the Cat. "—so long as I get SOMEWHERE," Alice added as an explanation. "Oh, you're sure to do that," said the Cat, "if you only walk long enough."*

Even though the opening quote was never uttered by the Cheshire Cat, it represents timeless and sage wisdom for any journey and certainly your DEI journey. In fact, the reason your DEI journey started with **Step 0: DEI Incentives** was to establish a general direction or aims for the journey. The reason your journey continued with **Step 1: DEI Inventory** was to establish your starting point for the journey. With these two steps completed, you are now ready for **Step 2: DEI Imperatives** and determining where you want to go for the journey (**DEI objectives**) and how you will know you have arrived there (**DEI goals**). And if you are willing to walk long enough, you'll be certain to get somewhere very special.

DEI Objectives and Goals

An imperative is something of essential or vital importance. It is here in **Step 2: DEI Imperatives** that you will determine your DEI priorities: The things that matter to you and/or your organization and the clarion call that flows directly from your DEI aims in **Step 0: DEI Incentives** and the results of your **Step 1: DEI Inventory.**

Completing a DEI assessment (Step 1) is what enables you to translate your DEI aims (Step 0) into DEI objectives and goals (Step 2). As mentioned in the previous steps, the deeper understandings from your assessment define potential, if not advised, priorities. However, oftentimes you have blind spots and "you don't know what you don't know." An assessment can lead to new and/or unanticipated understandings that refine or completely reshape your DEI aims into DEI objectives and goals. Also mentioned previously is that the purpose of a DEI assessment is to identify areas of strength, areas for improvement, risks, synergies, challenges, opportunities, and, above all, to generate findings and/or recommendations. Your DEI objectives should necessarily reflect areas of focus stemming from the DEI assessment: areas of strength you want to amplify, areas for improvement you want to bolster, challenges you want to address, opportunities you want to pursue, and recommendations you choose to heed. Completing a DEI assessment is also what enables you to fully set goals because you have established a profile and a baseline from which to set those goals. This further explains the logic behind why **Step 1: DEI Inventory** precedes **Step 2: DEI Imperatives.**

The framework we will use to establish your DEI Strategic Plan is the OGSM Strategic Planning Framework, as shown in Figure 2.1. OGSM is an acronym that stands for objectives, goals, strategies, and measures. It is a method that guides people and organizations through the strategic planning process:

- Each objective should have one or more goals to evaluate results and determine impact.
- Each goal should be evaluated against one or more metrics or key performance indicators (KPIs).
- Each objective should have one or more strategies to fulfill the objective and achieve the corresponding goals.
- Each strategy should be evaluated against one or more measures.

At BCT, we use this method to connect broader aspirations to concrete and actionable steps that can be integrated into daily behaviors. We frequently apply the OGSM framework to DEI strategic planning. Another framework to be aware of that may be useful is Objectives and Key Results (OKR).[2]

Go to **www.datadrivendei.com** to download templates for developing a personal DEI strategic plan, called the Crawl-Walk-Run Personal Action Plan, and an organizational DEI strategic plan. You can enter your objectives, goals, strategies, and measures directly into these templates.

Here in **Step 2: DEI Imperatives**, you will build out the first half of a personal and/or organizational DEI strategic plan by establishing DEI objectives and setting DEI goals. Later in **Step 4: DEI Initiatives**, you will build out the second half of your DEI strategic plan(s) by determining DEI strategies and defining DEI measures.

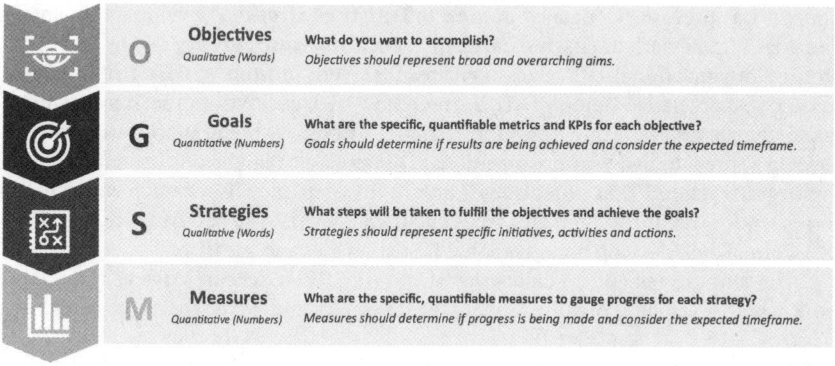

O	**Objectives** *Qualitative (Words)*	What do you want to accomplish?	*Objectives should represent broad and overarching aims.*
G	**Goals** *Quantitative (Numbers)*	What are the specific, quantifiable metrics and KPIs for each objective?	*Goals should determine if results are being achieved and consider the expected timeframe.*
S	**Strategies** *Qualitative (Words)*	What steps will be taken to fulfill the objectives and achieve the goals?	*Strategies should represent specific initiatives, activities and actions.*
M	**Measures** *Quantitative (Numbers)*	What are the specific, quantifiable measures to gauge progress for each strategy?	*Measures should determine if progress is being made and consider the expected timeframe.*

FIGURE 2.1 The OGSM Strategic Planning Framework

Establishing DEI Objectives

To begin **Step 2: DEI Imperatives**, you want to craft an *objective statement*, or a series of DEI objective statements, representing your broad and overarching aspirations. In fact, B.R.O.A.D. is also a great acronym describing guidelines for developing objectives:[3]

- **B**old—Think big. Shoot for the stars and not the mountaintop. Establish objectives that defy conventional thinking and push beyond expectations. Establish some "stretch" objectives that create a positive and healthy tension and catalyze others.

- **R**esponsive—Make certain that your objectives reflect the needs of all stakeholders and that no one is being overlooked or marginalized.

- **O**verarching—Your objectives should be all-encompassing (for people) and organization-wide (for organizations). They should also address the challenges and opportunities deemed as priorities from your DEI assessment.

- **A**spirational—Develop goals that inspire the head (i.e., clearly articulated) and the heart (i.e., powerfully engaging). Balance realism with optimism and short-term wins, that may be low-hanging fruit and build momentum, with long-term gains, that may require several years.

- **D**ynamic—Galvanize personal engagement (for people) and engagement across the organization (for organizations). Be flexible and willing to adjust as new circumstances arise.

For people, I generally recommend one to three **personal DEI objectives**, potentially in the categories of diversity, equity, and inclusion. In fact, in this step I will group personal DEI objectives and goals into the categories of diversity, equity, and inclusion.

For organizations, it is typically at this juncture of the DEI journey that we once again engage a DEI Council/Committee/Task Force/Steering Committee, that is, a diverse, representative, and inclusive body to guide the organizational DEI strategic planning process in partnership with the organization's executive leadership. The DEI Council was previously engaged in **Step 0: DEI Incentives** to develop an organizational DEI framework or charter and **Step 1: DEI Inventory** to help review and interpret the organizational DEI assessment results. Here in **Step 2: DEI Imperatives**, based on Appreciative Inquiry (AI), a strengths-based, positive approach to organizational change and strategic innovation, the DEI Council should work intensively to develop a three- to five-year organizational DEI strategic plan beginning with three to five **organizational DEI objectives**. Later in this step, the DEI Council will develop corresponding organizational DEI goals and then later, in **Step 4: DEI Initiatives**, the DEI Council will develop organizational DEI strategies and measures.

The four groups and 15 categories of the GDEIB model can serve as the framework when developing organizational DEI objectives and goals (the three categories of diversity, equity, and inclusion, or one of its variations such as JEDI and IDEA, can also serve as an appropriate framework). This model was previously introduced in **Step 1: DEI Inventory** as a tool for DEI benchmarking (refer back to Figure 1.22 and Table 1.9), and it will reappear in **Step 3: DEI Insights** in this same context as a promising and proven practice for DEI benchmarking. Here in **Step 2: DEI Imperatives**, the same GDEIB model is re-introduced in a completely different context: as a framework for establishing organizational DEI objectives and goals. In other words, the four groups and 15 categories represent eligible areas in which to establish organizational DEI objectives and goals. For example, the DEI Council could create one organizational DEI objective for each of the foundation, internal, bridging, and external groups of the GDEIB, resulting in at least four organizational DEI objectives. The GDEIB will reappear in this same context in **Step 4: DEI Initiatives** as a framework for determining organizational DEI strategies and measures. Hereafter, I will group organizational DEI objectives, goals, strategies, and measures by the four groups—foundation, internal, bridging, and external—and the 15 categories of the GDEIB.

While it is recommended that you cover all four groups, you do not have to address all 15 categories when establishing DEI objectives and goals. The four groups and 15 categories of the GDEIB model represent the eligible categories for developing your organizational DEI objectives and goals. The determination of which groups and categories are relevant to your organization should be based on your DEI aims and the results of your DEI assessment. You should develop organizational DEI objectives and goals only in those categories that directly relate to your DEI aims and address the results of your DEI assessment.

Formatting Your DEI Objective Statements

Here is a simple format for a *DEI objective statement*:

[Action verb] [an outcome].

Examples of action verbs include: "strengthen," "create," "enhance," "improve," "achieve," "expand," "promote," and "tie."

To determine your outcomes, let's break down the difference between outputs and outcomes.

Outputs vs. Outcomes

Table 2.1 summarizes the difference between *outcomes* and *outputs*. Personal and organizational DEI objectives should be centered on outcomes and not outputs (in **Step 4: DEI Initiatives**, you will see how DEI strategies should be centered on outputs).

A good way to think about outputs vs. outcomes is that outcomes represent the ultimate results you are seeking for you and/or your organization, while outputs represent the interim milestones along the way. Outcomes are about the destination while outputs are about the journey.

TABLE 2.1 Outputs vs. Outcomes

Outputs	Outcomes
Outputs are immediate results.	Outcomes are short-term or mid-term results.
Outputs are **often referred as first-level or intermediate results**.	Outcomes are **often referred as second-level or final results**.
Outputs are linked to strategies.	Outcomes are linked to objectives.
Outputs indicate completion of a strategy.	Outcomes indicate achievement of an objective.
Outputs are **easy to measure/report** or validate. They are usually **tangible**.	Outcomes are **difficult to measure or validate**. They are usually **intangible**.
Outputs are the **means to end**. They are actions/activities/items that contribute to achieve an outcome.	Outcomes are the **end results**. They are what a project/business/organization wants/desires to achieve.
Outputs do not show the level of **performance/achievement**.	Outcomes show the level of **performance/achievement** due to the activity/services provided.
Outputs **result** in outcomes (i.e., they lead to outcomes).	Outcomes **are the result** of output (i.e., they are achieved after the outputs).

Source: S. Adhikari, adapted from Public Health Notes, **https://www.publichealthnotes.com/outputs-vs-outcomes-15-differences/**.

Examples of DEI Objective Statements Some examples of personal DEI objective statements centered on outcomes (extending the same personal DEI aims previously introduced in **Step 0: DEI Incentives**) are shown in Table 2.2.

Some examples of organizational DEI objective statements centered on outcomes are shown in Table 2.3.

Here are examples of awesome organizational DEI objectives partly courtesy of Ongig:[4]

The Foundation Group: *Drive the Strategy*

McDonald's: Executives will be measured on their ability to champion our core values, improve representation within leadership roles for women and historically underrepresented groups, and create a strong culture of inclusion within the Company.

Microsoft: Cash money to diversity and inclusion.

National Basketball Association: Our goal is to move from a diversity reflex to an inclusion instinct. The NBA strives to cultivate a workplace in which everyone feels welcomed and empowered to bring their whole selves to work.

TABLE 2.2   Examples of Personal DEI Objectives Statements

DEI aims related to. . .	Can translate to DEI objectives such as . . .
Diversity: The Range of Human Differences *(A Fact)*	
1. Appreciate differences.	Increase my awareness of different cultures across the globe.
2. Recognize my biases.	Increase self-awareness of my unconscious biases and how they impact others.
Inclusion: Involvement and Empowerment *(An Action)*	
3. Mitigate my biases.	Increase my intercultural competence to deal with cultural differences in a bias-free manner.
4. Navigate and bridge differences.	Increase my intercultural competence to work effectively with people who are different from me.
5. Demonstrate inclusive behaviors.	Be an inclusive leader who personalizes individuals, treats people and groups fairly, and leverages the thinking of diverse groups.
6. Resolve conflicts.	Increase my awareness of intercultural conflict styles to resolve conflicts effectively and harmoniously.
Equity: Fairness and Equity in Outcomes *(A Choice)*	
7. Be a mentor.	Be an effective and supportive mentor to women within my division.
8. Be a sponsor.	Be an effective sponsor and advocate for people of color within my division.
9. Be an ally.	Be an ally and exercise my voice in equal partnership with women within my department.
10. Be an antiracist.	Be an active, not passive, antiracist in equal partnership with people of color throughout my division.
11. Improve my performance.	Be a top performer in the organization and improve my performance evaluation ratings in the areas of interpersonal skills, teamwork, and innovation.
12. Increase my compensation.	Be a top earner in the organization and increase my total compensation including salary and bonus.

National Institutes of Health (NIH), National Heart, Lung and Blood Institute (NHLBI): Create and sustain a workplace environment that encourages collaboration, flexibility, and fairness. Foster an atmosphere focused on seeking staff input and unique perspectives from all levels within the NHLBI.

Nike: Tie diversity goals to executive compensation.

U.S. Department of State: Enhance accountability to ensure that all Department work creates and sustains a diverse, equitable, and inclusive workforce and an accessible workplace culture.

TABLE 2.3   **Examples of Organizational DEI Objective Statements**

DEI aims related to . . .	Can translate to DEI objectives such as . . .
Diversity: The Range of Human Differences *(A Fact)*	
1. Increase diversity (representation).	Renew a diverse, representative, and high-performing workforce that represents all segments of society.
2. Increase awareness of diversity and/or biases.	Educate all colleagues on diversity awareness, unconscious bias, and appreciating different cultures.
Inclusion: Involvement and Empowerment *(An Action)*	
3. Mitigate the impact of biases.	Educate all colleagues on strategies to mitigate the impact of bias and affirm one another.
4. Improve communication, teamwork, collaboration, and/or innovation.	Create a culture of transparent communication, effective teamwork, and psychological safety leading to innovation.
5. Increase engagement, inclusion, and/or belonging.	Cultivate an inclusive workplace culture that fully leverages unique perspectives and empowers all voices.
6. Manage conflict.	Foster awareness of different conflict styles to manage conflict more effectively.
Equity: Fairness and Equity in Outcomes *(A Choice)*	
7. Foster development.	Foster the comprehensive development of women as leaders within the organization.
8. Promote advancement.	Promote the advancement of people of color to become executives within the organization.
9. Eliminate barriers and/or improve equity in policies and practices.	Promote equitable policies, practices, and outcomes across the entire career lifecycle including recruitment, hiring, development, advancement, retention, and support.
10. Dismantle racism.	Become an antiracist organization that addresses the personal, interpersonal, institutional, and structural dimensions of racism both within our organization and the communities we serve.
11. Improve productivity.	Harness differences to improve employee productivity within our distribution facilities.
12. Increase profitability.	Embrace an equity-driven lens for the design and delivery of our products and services, expand market share, and increase net income.

Verizon: Verizon ties executives' pay to diversity and inclusion goals.

The Internal Group: *Attract & Retain People*

Accenture: Create a gender-balanced workforce.

Amazon: Increase the number of women and Black employees in senior roles and create a more inclusive workforce for retention of employees of underrepresented groups.

Citi: Increasing Black and female representation in leadership.

Standard Chartered Bank: Increase ethnic representation in UK and U.S. senior leadership teams.

Starbucks: Increase the workforce by hiring people who identify as Black, Indigenous, or people of color.

VMWare: No hire unless an underrepresented group is interviewed.

Workday: Hiring and developing diverse talent, cultivating a culture of belonging, building inclusive products and technologies, and strengthening communities.

Yum! Brands: Increase representation of Black, Latinx, people of color, and women among its executive and management ranks, franchisees and suppliers; and ensure Black, Latinx, and diverse representation in leadership and account teams at Yum's U.S. agencies.

The Bridging Group: *Align & Connect*

Hewlett-Packard Enterprise: Establish a Global Inclusion and Diversity Council & more diversity training for managers.

University of California, Davis: Promote diversity and inclusion in research, teaching, public service, and training across campus and in neighboring communities.[5]

Rutgers University: Develop an institutional infrastructure to drive change.[6]

The External Group: *Listen To & Serve Society*

American Red Cross, The Tiffany Circle: Become one of the leading "charities of choice" for women philanthropists.

AT&T: Working with Black-owned businesses.

Bristol Myers Squibb: Expand capacity in diverse businesses, create jobs, lift communities, and drive supply chain innovation.

The Bill and Melinda Gates Foundation: Achieve the impact we want to have in the world by actively listening to our partners and the communities they work within and serve, investing in and elevating their voices and ideas.

Facebook: Monetary support for Black-owned businesses.

Royal Bank of Canada: Donating to support BIPOC (Black, Indigenous, and Persons of Color) and committing more summer jobs to BIPOC youth.

Setting DEI Goals

The final part of **Step 2: DEI Imperatives** is to set goals. The way you evaluate results and determine impact against an objective is by setting well-constructed goals. Each objective must have one or more goals.

Goals should be S.M.A.R.T., which is another great acronym:

- **S**pecific—The more specific you can be the better. Whenever possible, use real numbers to quantify the goal.
- **M**easurable—Make certain the goal can be measured and tracked, which includes identifying the source of the data or the mechanisms you will establish to generate the data.
- **A**ttainable—Ensure that the goal can be achieved but, once again, balance realism with optimism by not setting the bar so low that it is easily accomplished.
- **R**elevant—Think back to **Step 0: DEI Incentives** and the intrinsic and/or extrinsic motivations that spawned your DEI journey and affirm that your DEI objectives and goals are directly relevant to those values, needs, and wants.
- **T**ime-bound—Every goal should have a target date or deadline. This will engender focus and discipline. Here, also be certain to space out deadlines based on priority and capacity to avoid overlapping deadlines that outstrip your ability to meet them.

DEI goals should go further from S.M.A.R.T. to S.M.A.R.T.I.E.

- **I** is for inclusive.
- **E** is for equitable.

A blog post from the Management Center entitled "From SMART to SMARTIE: How to Embed Inclusion and Equity in Your Goals"[7] is a powerful reminder that not all goals are created equal through the lens of DEI. It is therefore important to establish the proper language and guardrails to maximize the likelihood that goals will achieve their desired outcome and not have an unintentional disparate impact. The Management Center offers three principles for developing S.M.A.R.T.I.E. goals:

- **Mind the "how"**—Evaluate the extent to which the outcome specified in the goal is explicit about improving DEI.
  - Examples:
    - Your development team may have an outcome goal to "raise $X by Y to cover this year's budget and three months' operating reserve." There are many ways to do this, and one of them might include this activity goal: "recruit, retain, and develop a total of 30,000 dues-paying members," which can be improved by adding, ". . . at least X% of whom identify as [people of color / women / trans or gender non-conforming / poor / Spanish-speaking]."
    - Your policy team might have a goal to create and disseminate X policy briefs on immigration by the end of the year. In order to be more inclusive and equitable in the process, you might say explicitly: "We will consult with X coalition or Y community leaders to get feedback before finalizing."

- **Check for unintentional disparate impact**—Consider the missing stakeholders, disparate impact, and unintended consequences that might result from the goal.
  - ○ Examples:
    - ○ "Lower overhead costs by $X by [date]" can be improved by adding ". . . with quarterly check-ins with staff to check for negative disparate impact of cost savings."
    - ○ "Increase representation of staff with marginalized identities in our hiring processes by [date]" can be improved with the addition of ". . . with checks to ensure staff with marginalized identities aren't carrying an unequal share of the work."
- **Make your [measures and] metrics matter via inclusion and not tokenism**—Closely examine the goal to confirm that it is helping to build power, mitigate disparities, and/or address inequities.
  - ○ Example:
    - ○ "Build a volunteer team of 100 door-to-door canvassers by May, with at least 10% people of color" is a much different goal than "Build a volunteer team of 100 door-to-door canvassers by May, with at least 10 people of color recruited as volunteer leaders first, so that they can help shape the way we run the canvasses."

The Management Center provides an excellent worksheet for developing S.M.A.R.T.I.E. goals.[8]

Each DEI objective should have one or more S.M.A.R.T.I.E. DEI goals that adhere to the following guidelines:

- Distinguish between disparities and inequities
- Represent a combination of DEI metrics and DEI key performance indicators (KPIs)
- Capture a mix of leading and lagging indicators

Next, I will differentiate between disparities and inequities; explain the difference between measures, metrics, and KPIs; delineate leading indicators from lagging indicators; and, finally, explain how to format your goal statements along with several examples to close out this step.

Disparities vs. Inequities   Within the context of S.M.A.R.T.I.E. DEI goals, it is important to understand the difference between disparities and inequities:

- *Disparities* are differences in experiences or outcomes between different populations.
- *Inequities* are unfair and unjust differences in experiences or outcomes between different populations.

Disparities can be expected. For example, if women and men are found to react differently to a drug or therapy, that is a disparity that can often be expected based on their biological differences. Similarly, if the mortality rate is higher for the elderly than it is for children, that is also an expected disparity due to aging. By comparison, inequities are unexpected or unfortunate. For example:

- In a study of actual racial hiring bias in Chicago and Boston, where resumes were sent to actual wants ads, resumes with "white-sounding" names were 50% more likely to get a callback in response to their resume than resumes of equal quality with "Black-sounding" names.[9]
- According to the Centers for Disease Control and Prevention (CDC), American Indian/Alaska Native and Black women are two to three times as likely to die from a pregnancy-related cause than white women.[10]
- As late as 1970, the "Big Five" orchestras in the United States—New York, Boston, Chicago, Philadelphia, and Cleveland—had fewer than 5% women. In the 1970s and 1980s, orchestras began using blind auditions, which increased women musicians in the Big Five orchestras by 500% from 1970 to 2000.[11]

These outcomes are not expected—or are, sadly, expected but should not be tolerated—and represent inequities as they imply a state of being unfair and unjust. DEI goals, including racial, gender, and other equity goals, are sometimes centered on closing gaps, such as those outlined above. Be mindful in both your understanding of your DEI goals and the language used when constructing your DEI goals, to be clear about whether the gap you are closing is a disparity or an inequity. Whereas you may have little to no control over certain disparities, it may require root-cause analysis to fully understand and begin to address certain inequities.

Measures vs. Metrics vs. KPIs
Jonathan Taylor at Klipfolio does a wonderful job explaining the difference between a measure, a metric, and a KPI, in his blog post, "What is a KPI, Metric or Measure?"[12] Taylor writes, "As KPI, metric and measure are terms that in many ways serve as the building blocks for how . . . performance is both assessed and achieved, it's paramount to have a fundamental understanding of them." Leveraging Taylor's definition and his focus on performance, I will define these terms within the context of DEI performance.

A *DEI measure* is a number or value related to a DEI process, activity, program, effort, or initiative that can be summed and/or averaged according to a particular category. A measure is unit specific. For example:

- Diversity (Representation) Measures:
  - **People:** Preference scale on the Implicit Association Test (IAT) or the Herrmann Brain Dominance Instrument® (HBDI®).
  - **Organizations:** The number of employees at different levels of the organization according to different demographic subgroups.
- Inclusion Measures:
  - **People:** Competence score on the Intrinsic Inclusion Inventory™ (I3™) or the Intercultural Development Inventory® (IDI®).

- o **Organizations:** Employee self-reported ratings of feelings of inclusion and belonging via DEI culture and climate survey.
- Equity Measures:
  - o **People:** Peer rating in the "fairness" category of a diverse 360° assessment (i.e., relates to equitable behavior).
  - o **Organizations:** Compensation levels of employees according to different demographic subgroups (i.e., relates to pay equity).

Measures are the building blocks for metrics and KPIs as metrics and KPIs are calculated based on measures.

A *DEI metric* is a measure that is used to track a DEI-related process, activity, program, effort, or initiative. When you think of metrics think *numerous and broad*: there are a plethora of DEI metrics that can be tracked. For example, consider all the possible results from all the available IATs that measure your implicit biases relative to sexuality, skin tone, Arab-Muslims, gender-career, religion, race, disability, Native American, Asian American, gender-science, age, transgender, weight, and more. Or think about the number of people hired by your organization broken down according to each of the internal, external, and organizational dimensions of the "Four Layers of Diversity" previously shown in Figure 1.20 such as race, ethnicity, age, sex, national origin/ancestry, physical ability, mental ability, educational background, religion/creed, income, veteran status, and beyond. These examples alone represent a significant number of metrics.

While any measure can be used as a metric, metrics can also be derived or calculated from one or more measures and therefore expressed as a percentage, a composite score, an index, a difference, a gap, a rate, and the like. For example:

- For People:
  - o If your HBDI® profile code for practical thinking is a 69 under normal circumstances and a 31 under pressure, then the difference, 38, is a metric that is calculated from two measures and depicts a significant shift in your practical thinking preference under pressure.
  - o If your IDI® Perceived Orientation is significantly higher than your Developmental Orientation, the difference—your Orientation Gap—is a metric that is calculated from two measures, which indicates that you may be overestimating your level of intercultural competence.
- For Organizations:
  - o The percentages of women and people of color at the executive level is a metric that is calculated by dividing the number of women and people of color by the total number of executives.
  - o The GDEIB can be used to produce a composite score and level within each of the four groups and 15 categories by aggregating and averaging the responses from several people.
  - o If the average compensation for men who are supervisors within your organization is $50,000 and the average pay for women at the same level with the same qualifications is $40,000, then the difference, $10,000, is calculated from two measures and demonstrates a significant gap in equitable compensation.

- For People and Organizations
  - All the personal inclusion assessments, including I3™, provide a composite inclusivity score or index across multiple categories of inclusive behavior (for people), which can also be stratified and disaggregated by demographics, departments, divisions, etc. (for organizations).

Finally, a *DEI key performance indicator (KPI)* is a measurable value that demonstrates how effectively an organization is achieving key DEI objectives. KPIs are selected from among the many eligible metrics. When you think about KPIs think *few and deep*: much like DEI objectives, there should only be approximately one to two DEI KPIs for people and three to seven DEI KPIs for organizations representing those DEI metrics considered most essential to success. While DEI goals are likely to include metrics, they should be certain to include KPIs.

"Without establishing and tracking proper key performance indicators, [organizations] would be left in the dark about their performance. They might feel that they are having success, but what kind of success? And compared to what? They may know which metrics are trackable, but which ones should they track? With KPIs in place you can set appropriate goals, develop strategies to reach them and evaluate your progress, and eventually have a historical record of your [organizational] performance," writes Taylor.[13] A measure and a KPI are both an *indicator*—a gauge of change. As the name implies, a KPI is a *key* indicator because it focuses your DEI measures on the few that are most valuable.

Go to **www.datadrivendei.com** to access an extensive and comprehensive list, or menu, of personal and organizational DEI measures, metrics, and key performance indicators (KPIs).

Leading vs. Lagging Indicators
Again, a measure and a KPI are both an indicator (i.e., a gauge of change). In addition to understanding the difference between outputs and outcomes, it's also important to understand the difference between leading indicators and lagging indicators.

In his article "What is a Leading and a Lagging Indicator? and Why You Need to Understand the Difference," Bernard Marr, an influencer and thought leader in the fields of business and technology, writes, "The best way to manage performance is to merge the insights from backward-looking indicators (your 'lagging' indicators) with more forward-looking insights and predictions (your 'leading' indicators). Therein lies the main difference between the two:

- A *leading indicator* looks forward at future outcomes and events.
- A *lagging indicator* looks back at whether the intended result was achieved.

Imagine your organization is a car. Leading indicators look forwards, through the windshield, at the road ahead. Lagging indicators look backwards, through the rear window, at the road you've already travelled. Leading indicators are important for building a broad understanding of performance because they provide information on likely future outcomes. But they aren't perfect. For one thing, they aren't always accurate. Lagging indicators tell you about what has already happened. They're typically easy to identify, measure, and compare against elsewhere in your industry or sector, which makes lagging indicators very useful. Another downside is that lagging indicators encourage a focus on *outputs* (a number-based measure of what has happened), rather than *outcomes* (what we wanted to achieve)."[14]

Generally speaking, diversity-related metrics (i.e., representation numbers) are lagging indicators. They look backward at what has happened, are excellent for benchmarking, yet offer little insight on future outcomes because they change slowly. By comparison, inclusion-related metrics (i.e., inclusive behaviors) and equity-related metrics (i.e., equality in outcomes) are leading indicators. They are suggestive of performance improvements as they are directly linked to culture, climate, engagement, teamwork, innovation, and much more. In the article "Diversity is a Lagging Measure of Inclusion" in *Medium*, Lisa Russell writes, "In *Atomic Habits* James Clear says, 'Your outcomes are a lagging measure of your habits.' He continues with examples:

'Your net worth is a lagging measure of your financial habits.

Your knowledge is a lagging measure of your learning habits.

Your clutter is a lagging measure of your cleaning habits'."[15]

She continues:

- "Diversity metrics change slowly. The numbers can only change as employees leave or join the team. But while you're working to recruit a diverse workforce, so much can be done to improve the sense of inclusion within your organization and, as a result, improving employee satisfaction and retention.

- "Inclusion doesn't require a year or two to see progress. You can measure progress more frequently, gauge progress as you go and adjust your focus throughout the year as needed."

Diversity manifests itself as a result of inclusion and equity. Inclusion and equity can change at a much faster pace than diversity. Diversity is therefore a lagging measure of inclusion and equity.

Your goals should incorporate both leading and lagging indicators to paint a complete picture of your DEI performance. This is particularly relevant to organizations that will typically have multiple objectives, but it is also helpful for people who have multiple objectives.

Formatting Your Goal Statements
You will recall earlier that when we established our DEI objective statements, we adhered to the following simple format:

[Action verb] [an outcome].

A simple format for a *DEI goal statement* is as follows:

[Action verb] [a metric or KPI] *to* [target] *within/by* [timeframe].

Now that we have defined metrics and KPIs, we can break this down. For each DEI objective, you should undertake these steps to finalize its corresponding DEI goal statement(s):

1. Determine appropriate metrics or KPIs to evaluate results and determine impact against the DEI objective. Remember that a DEI objective can have one or more DEI goals.

2. Identify the *data source* to confirm that you have the necessary data to track your metrics and KPIs. Whether it is data from an assessment of preferences or competences, a test score, a seminar evaluation, an employee engagement survey, a payroll system, or a human resources information system (HRIS), you can only set goals for what you can measure, and you can only measure that for which you have the requisite data.

3. Choose an appropriate *action verb* for your goal such as "achieve," "increase/ decrease," "improve/mitigate/eliminate," "extend," "spend," "grow/eliminate," "reduce/close," or simply "change."

4. Determine a *target*—a mark you hope to achieve—for each metric or KPI.

5. Select a *timeframe*—a time period—within which you plan to reach the target.

6. Decide on the *frequency* upon which the data can/will be collected and analyzed. We recommend that most metrics and KPIs are best analyzed on an annual or quarterly basis, while other metrics and KPIs, particularly those related to culture and climate such as engagement, inclusivity, and belonging, are best analyzed quarterly or monthly and especially via "pulse surveys" (i.e., short surveys administered to only a subset of the entire organization).

To the extent that a DEI objective is being evaluated or measured using a DEI assessment tool, at least one of your DEI goals for that DEI objective should be related to the DEI assessment tool. Once again, this demonstrates the importance of **Step 1: DEI Inventory** because it makes the job of setting goals and selecting metrics and KPIs significantly easier.

If you visit **www.datadrivendei.com** you will find an extensive and comprehensive list, or menu, of DEI measures, metrics, and KPIs, organized by outputs and outcomes, that you and/or your organization can use when setting DEI goals. Once again, for your purposes here of setting DEI goals, you should generally focus on outcomes, a combination of metrics and KPIs, and a mix of leading and lagging indicators. In **Step 4: DEI Initiatives**, you will generally focus on outcomes and measures.

Examples of DEI Goal Statements   Let's look at some examples of personal and organizational DEI goals statements. For example, if your personal DEI objective is related to mitigating bias and you're measuring bias using the IAT, then one of your personal DEI goal statements could be to:

> Mitigate the impact of my Gender-Science IAT results being a "slight preference" of associating women with science and men with liberal arts by improving my diverse 360° assessment scores by 10% with women in science, technology, engineering, and math (STEM) over the next 12 months.

If your personal DEI objective relates to being an inclusive leader and you are measuring inclusive behavior using I3™, your personal DEI goal statement could be:

Increase my I3™ rating by one level within one year.

If your organizational DEI objective relates to improving equity in policies and practices, then one of your organizational DEI goal statements could be to:

Eliminate statistically significant pay equity gaps between women, men, and non-binary employees by the end of the fiscal year.

In circumstances where a DEI objective relates to the accomplishment of a task or reaching a milestone, the format for your goal statement could simply be:

Complete [task or milestone] *by* [timeframe].

For example, if your objective is "to be an ally" and you have conducted a 360° assessment, but you have yet to perform a diverse 360° assessment, your goal statement could be, "Complete diverse 360° assessment to identify other areas for DEI personal development by the end of the year." Or, if your organization has completed a DEI culture and climate survey but has yet to conduct a pay equity assessment, your goal statement could be, "Complete pay equity assessment to identify strategies for reducing or eliminating gaps by the end of the first quarter."

Table 2.4 summarizes full examples of personal DEI objectives and goals based on the preceding examples and Table 2.5 summarizes full examples of organizational DEI objectives and goals based on the preceding examples, along with the corresponding and potential DEI assessments, and organized by the four groups of the GDEIB model.

It is at this juncture that your DEI Council will now set one to three goals for each of your organizational DEI objectives. To aid in your process, if you visit **www .datadrivendei.com**, you will find an extensive and comprehensive list, or menu, of DEI metrics, organized by outputs and outcomes, according to the four groups and 15 categories of the GDEIB model, that you and/or your organization can use when setting DEI goals. Once again, for your purposes here of setting DEI goals, you should generally focus on outcomes, a combination of metrics and KPIs, and a mix of leading and lagging indicators. In **Step 4: DEI Initiatives**, you will generally focus on outcomes and measures, and you will also round out your organizational DEI strategic plan with organizational DEI strategies and measures to fulfill your organizational DEI objectives and achieve your organizational DEI goals.

Here are the corresponding DEI goals for a sampling of the awesome DEI objectives presented earlier, partly courtesy of Ongig:[16]

The Foundation Group: Drive the Strategy

- McDonald's:
  - **Objective:** Executives will be measured on their ability to champion our core values, improve representation within leadership roles for women and historically underrepresented groups, and create a strong culture of inclusion within the Company.[17]

TABLE 2.4 Full Examples of Personal DEI Objectives and Goals with Personal DEI Assessments

Personal DEI Objective Statements	Personal DEI Assessments	Personal DEI Goal Statements
Diversity: The Range of Human Differences (*A Fact*)		
Mitigate bias: "Treat people fairly by mitigating the impact of unconscious bias in my behaviors toward others."	• **Preferences:** The Implicit Association Test (IAT), which measures implicit bias (preferences).	• Mitigate the impact of my Gender-Science IAT results being a "slight preference" of associating women with science and men with liberal arts by improving my diverse 360° assessment scores by 10% with women over the next 12 months.
Inclusion: Involvement and Empowerment (*An Action*)		
Navigate differences: "Work effectively with people of different cultural backgrounds by raising my self-awareness and increasing intercultural competence."	• **Preferences:** The Implicit Association Test (IAT), which measures implicit bias (preferences). • **Competences:** The Passions, Awareness, Skills, and Knowledge Inventory (PASK), which measures self-efficacy for discussions about differences, and the Intercultural Development Inventory® (IDI®), which measures intercultural competence.	• Mitigate the impact of my Race IAT results being a "slight automatic preference" for white people over Black people by improving my diverse 360° assessment scores by 10% with people of color over the next 12 months. • Increase my PASK level from "Developing" to "Mastering" within two years. • Increase my IDI® level from "Acceptance" to "Adaptation" within two years.
Be inclusive: "Be an inclusive leader who personalizes individuals, treats people and groups fairly, and leverages the thinking of diverse groups."	• **Preferences:** The Implicit Association Test (IAT), which measures implicit bias (preferences). • **Competences:** Intrinsic Inclusion Inventory™ (I3™), which measures inclusive behaviors.	• Mitigate the impact of my Gender-Science IAT results being a "slight preference" of associating women with science and men with liberal arts by improving my diverse 360° assessment scores by 10% with women in science, technology, engineering, and math (STEM) over the next 12 months.

TABLE 2.4   (Continued)

Personal DEI Objective Statements	Personal DEI Assessments	Personal DEI Goal Statements
		• Mitigate the impact of my Race IAT results being a "slight automatic preference" for white people over Black people by improving my diverse 360° assessment scores by 10% with people of color over the next 12 months. • Increase my I3™ rating from Level 2 to Level 3 by the end of the year.
Improve equity in policies and practices: "Be an inclusive leader who personalizes individuals, treats people and groups fairly, and leverages the thinking of diverse groups by demonstrating inclusive behaviors."	• **Preferences:** The Herrmann Brain Dominance Instrument® (HBDI®), which measures thinking preferences. • **Competences:** Intrinsic Inclusion Inventory™ (I3™) for Individuals, which measures inclusive behavior.	• Stretch my HBDI® thinking preference into the "relational" quadrant and increase my "relational" profile score by 10 points over the next three years. • Increase my I3™ rating from Level 2 to Level 3 within one year.
Equity: Fairness and Equality in Outcomes (A Choice)		
Be an ally: "Be an ally in equal partnership with women and people of color within my division by being active and not passive in dismantling barriers."	• **Preferences and Competences:** 360° assessment, possibly with specific questions that are tailored to advocacy, support, and sponsorship of women and people of color. • **Competences:** Antiracist Style Indicator (ASI), which self-assesses efficacy to dismantle racism in systems and within yourself and the Internalized Sexism Inventory (ISI), which assesses attitudes and behaviors toward sexism.	• Increase my diverse 360° assessment scores for leadership, communication, teamwork, and development of others by 10% from women and people of color. • Improve my ASI from "Underfunctioning Antiracist" to "Functioning Antiracist" by the end of the calendar year. • Increase my ISI from 20/40 (50%) to 30/40 (75%)

TABLE 2.5 Full Examples of Organizational DEI Objectives and Goals with DEI Assessments

Organizational DEI Objectives	Organizational DEI Assessments	Organizational DEI Goals
The Foundation Group: *Drive the Strategy*		
Category 1: Vision, Strategy, and Business Impact: Cultivate an inclusive workplace culture by creating and sustaining an atmosphere of psychological safety and trust that fully leverages unique perspectives and empowers all voices.	• **BCT DEI Workforce and Workplace Assessment™ (DWWA™)**, which evaluates organizational culture and climate. • **Intrinsic Inclusion Inventory™ (I3™)** for Organizations, which measures inclusive behaviors. • **The Global Diversity, Equity & Inclusion Benchmarks (GDEIB)**, which provides a global benchmark of DEI capability and maturity.	• Eliminate statistically significant difference in DWWA™ scores between people with disabilities and all employees with respect to the organization's commitment to diversity. • Increase I3™ scores for inclusive behaviors by 10% by the end of the next fiscal year. • Increase our GDEIB overall benchmark from Level 2 ("Reactive") to Level 3 ("Proactive") within three years.
Category 2: Leadership and Accountability and Category 3: Structure and Implementation: Tie executive compensation to meeting diversity, equity, and inclusion goals for representation of persons with disabilities and Indigenous people.	• Collect, analyze, and report employee **representation data** that is stratified and disaggregated by the primary, secondary, and organizational layers of diversity.	• 10% of annual bonus compensation contingent on meeting representation goals of 10% for persons with disabilities within two years and 5% for Indigenous people within three years.
The Internal Group: Attract and Retain People		
Category 4: Recruitment: Renew a diverse, representative, and high-performing workforce that draws from all segments of society by achieving diverse representation at every level throughout the organization.	• Collect, analyze, and report employee **representation data** that is stratified and disaggregated by the primary, secondary, and organizational layers of diversity.	• Increase representation of persons with disabilities across the organization to 10% within two years. • Increase representation of Indigenous people in leadership positions to 5% within three years.
Category 4: Recruitment and Category 5: Advancement and Retention:	• **BCT DEI HR Policies and Practices**, which evaluates HR policies and practices through a DEI lens.	• Implement changes in all 13 DEI HR policy and practice areas to have 100% adherence with best practices.

TABLE 2.5   (Continued)

Organizational DEI Objectives	Organizational DEI Assessments	Organizational DEI Goals
Promote equitable policies, practices, and outcomes by mitigating or eliminating barriers across the entire career lifecycle including recruitment, hiring, development, advancement, retention, and support to achieve fairness in outcomes for all employees.	• **The Global Diversity, Equity & Inclusion Benchmarks (GDEIB),** which provides a global benchmark of DEI capability and maturity • **BCT Time-to-Promotion Equity Assessment,** which evaluates how long it takes different groups of employees to advance equitable • **BCT Pay Equity Assessment,** which evaluates whether compensation for different groups is fair and equitable.	• Increase our GDEIB overall benchmark from Level 3 ("Proactive") to Level 4 ("Progressive") within two years. • Increase the time-to-promotion for LGBTQIA+ employees by two years over the next three years. • Eliminate statistically significant pay equity gaps between women, men, and non-binary employees by the end of the fiscal year.
The Bridging Group: *Align & Connect*		
Category 10: Learning and Development: Educate all colleagues on strategies to mitigate the impact of bias and affirm one another.	• **BCT DEI Workforce and Workplace Assessment™ (DWWA™),** which evaluates organizational culture and climate. • **Intrinsic Inclusion Inventory™ (I3™)** for Organizations, which measures inclusive behaviors.	• Complete mandatory training of all employees within 12 months. • Administer a Kirkpatrick evaluation in a pre/post manner resulting in an average score of 4.5/5.0 or greater on a Likert scale (Level #1: Reaction) and an average grade of 80% or greater (Level #2: Learning).
Category 11: Connecting DEI and Sustainability: Mitigate the effects of environmental racism by addressing climate change given its disproportionate impact from adverse events on communities of color.	• **Quantitative Research** (i.e., surveys) and **Qualitative Research** (i.e., in-depth interviews and focus groups) to understand the impact of climate change adverse events on communities of color.	• 100% renewable energy across operations within 15 years. • Net-zero greenhouse gas emissions within 15 years. • Net-zero carbon emissions within 15 years.

(Continued)

TABLE 2.5 (Continued)

Organizational DEI Objectives	Organizational DEI Assessments	Organizational DEI Goals
The External Group: Listen To and Serve Society		
Category 12: Community, Government Relations, and Philanthropy: Invest in social justice, anti-poverty, and economic empowerment organizations working in five target predominately Black, Indigenous, and other People of Color (BIPOC) communities.	• **Quantitative Research** (i.e., surveys) and **Qualitative Research** (i.e., in-depth interviews and focus groups) to evaluate the impact of philanthropic investments and giving.	• Invest $500K in social justice, anti-poverty, and economic empowerment organizations. • Achieve 2-to-1 match with employee giving program. • Reduce the racial wealth gap by 10% in the five targeted and predominately BIPOC communities.
Category 15: Responsible Sourcing: Increase diverse supplier spend to foster supply chain innovation and promote economic development.	• **Supplier Spend Analysis**, which analyzes Tier 1 and Tier 2 procurement spend with diverse suppliers by category.	• Increase procurement spend with diverse suppliers, including minority-, women-, veteran-, and LGBTQIA+-owned suppliers, to 30% by the end of the next calendar year. • Grow the revenues of minority-, women-, veteran-, and LGBTQIA+-owned suppliers by 25%.

- **Goal:** 15% of top executive bonuses being tied to human capital measures including improving the number of women and minorities in the company, i.e., 45% of international senior directors and higher managers should be women and 35% in the United States are to be held by racial and ethnic minorities, up from 37% and 29% according to the reporters.[18]

- Nike:
  - **Objective:** Increase minority representation in leadership and tie diversity goals to executive compensation.
  - **Goals:**
    - A 49.5% increase in female employees across the company by 2025.
    - At least 29% increase in the U.S. VP leadership for racial and ethnic minorities by 2025.

- Verizon:
    - **Objective:** Verizon ties executives' pay to diversity and inclusion goals.
    - **Goals (2019):**
        - In order to receive the 5% of the short-term incentive award related to ESG metrics, the executives had to hit the following goals: have at least 60% of U.S.-based workforce comprised of minority and female employees; direct at least $5.2 billion of overall supplier spending to minority- and female-owned firms; reduce carbon intensity—the amount of carbon the business emits divided by the terabytes of data it transports over networks—by at least 10% compared to the prior year.

The Internal Group: Attract and Retain People

- Accenture:
    - **Objective:** Create a gender-balanced workforce.
    - **Goal:** A top-ranking global company on the Reuters Diversity & Inclusion Index, Accenture has set a diversity goal around creating a gender-balanced workforce by 2025.
- Amazon:
    - **Objective:** Increase the number of women and Black employees in senior roles and create a more inclusive workforce for retention of employees of underrepresented groups.
    - **Goals:**
        - For the second year in a row, double the number of U.S. Black employees at L8–L10 (Directors and VPs) year-over-year from 2020 numbers.
        - Increase hiring of U.S. Black employees at L4–L7 by at least 30% year-over-year from 2020 hiring.
        - Increase the number of women at L8–L10 (Senior Principals, Directors, VPs, and Distinguished Engineers) in tech and science roles by 30% year-over-year.
        - Increase the number of U.S. Black software development engineer interns by at least 40%.
- Citi:
    - **Objective:** Increasing Black and female representation in leadership.
    - **Goals:**
        - Increase the representation of women in leadership positions to 40% by the end of 2021, up from 37% in 2018.
        - Increase the representation of Black people in leadership roles to 8% in the same time frame, up from 6% in 2018.
- Microsoft
    - **Objective:** Cash money to diversity and inclusion, increased diversity in management positions, and increase the number of Black leaders.

- **Goals:**
  - Adding $150 million to its diversity and inclusion investment.
  - Doubling the number of Black and African American people managers, senior individual contributors, and senior leaders in the United States by 2025.
- Standard Chartered Bank:
  - **Objective:** Increase ethnic representation in UK and U.S. senior leadership teams.
  - **Goals:** The global bank has set diversity goals for its leadership team to meet by 2025:
    - U.S. Market
      - Increase percentage of Black or African American senior leadership from 4% to 8%.
      - Increase percentage of Hispanic or Latino senior leadership from 10.4% to 14%.
    - UK Market
      - Increase percentage of Black senior leadership from 1.3% to 5%.
      - Increase percentage of Black, Asian, and Minority Ethnic (BAME) senior leadership from 12.7% to 20%.
- Starbucks:
  - **Objective:** Increase the workforce by hiring people who identify as Black, Indigenous, or people of color.
  - **Goals:**
    - Starbucks has set a diversity goal to add more diversity to its workforce by 2025.
    - Along with having people of color represent 30% of corporate employees at all levels . . . the company is also aiming to have them occupy at least 40% of retail and manufacturing jobs at all levels by 2025.

The Bridging Group: Align and Connect

- Hewlett Packard Enterprise (HPE)
  - **Objective:** Establish a Global Inclusion and Diversity Council & more diversity training for managers.
  - **Goal:** HPE managers will also be required to attend diversity and inclusion training.
- University of California, Davis:[19]
  - **Objective:** Promote diversity and inclusion in research, teaching, public service, and training across campus and in neighboring communities.
  - **Goal:** Embed cultural competence in all academic and training programs, administrative units/programs, and workplaces to support diversity and inclusion.

The External Group: Listen To & Serve Society
- American Red Cross, The Tiffany Circle:[20]
  - **Objective:** Become one of the leading "charities of choice" for women phi-lanthropists.
  - **Goals:**
    - Grow to 1,200 members
    - Increase year-over-year revenue: FY21—$11,200,000; FY22—$11,800,00; and FY23—$12,400,000
    - Increase influenced donations by 5% annually: FY21—$10,800,000; FY22—$11,300,000; FY23—$11,900,000
- Facebook:
  - **Objective:** Monetary support for Black-owned businesses.
  - **Goal:** $200 million to support Black-owned businesses and organizations.
- Bristol Myers Squibb:
  - **Objectives:**
    - Increase clinical trial diversity
    - Expand supplier diversity program
  - **Goals:**
    - Extend the reach of clinical trials into underserved patient communities in urban and rural U.S. geographies by building infrastructure and training and mentoring 250 racially and ethnically diverse clinical investigators.
    - Spend $1 billion globally by 2025 with Black/African American and other diverse-owned businesses to help create jobs and generate positive economic impact in diverse communities often hard hit financially by systemic injustices.

As you can see, the goals represent a combination of DEI metrics and KPIs and a mix of DEI leading and lagging indicators.

In **Step 4: DEI Initiatives**, we will complete the OGSM strategic planning framework. You will determine DEI strategies to achieve each DEI goal and define DEI measures to gauge progress against each DEI strategy. As you will see even more clearly, whereas here when establishing DEI goals, we generally focused on outcomes, when defining measures, you will generally focus on outputs. However, before we go there, next, in **Step 3: DEI Insights**, we will look to promising and proven practices to help you determine the optimal DEI strategies to pursue.

STEP 3

DEI Insights—Identify "What Works"

What's fair is not equal and what's equal is not fair.

Equity is giving people what they need.

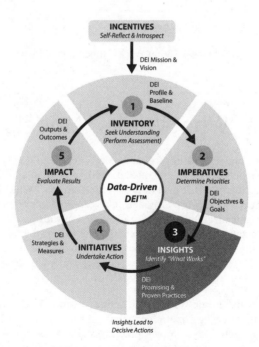

Data-Driven DEI—Step 3: DEI Insights

Th则here is something very powerful about learning from the experience of others. It's been said many times and many ways by many people:

- "Where there are experts there will be no lack of learners."—Swahili proverb
- "Don't reinvent the wheel, just realign it."—Anthony J. D'Angelo
- "The shortest distance between two points is a straight line."—Archimedes
- "Learn from the mistakes of others. You can't live long enough to make them all yourself."—Eleanor Roosevelt
- "One thing you can't recycle is wasted time."—Taiichi Ohno

Before you determine your DEI strategies and measures in **Step 4: DEI Initiatives**, you will greatly benefit from taking the time to see what has worked in other contexts that might work for you and/or your organization. The benefits are as numerous as the above quotations:

- Leverage research, science, and the experience of others who have "been there, done that, and got the T-shirt."
- Take advantage of the work others have done to create solid wheels.
- Optimize your path and accelerate your progress.
- Learn from the successes and mistakes of others.
- Save yourself time, energy, and effort.

This leads us to the idea of a "What Works" model, which is a core idea for **Step 3: DEI Insights**.

What Are "What Works" Models?

An *insight* is a deep understanding of a person or thing. A *DEI insight* is a deep understanding of a concept, technique, tool, model, methodology, or approach for improving DEI. More succinctly, a DEI insight is encapsulated in a "What Works" model.

Simply defined, "What Works" models have caused an improvement in DEI for another person or organization and have a likelihood of causing an improvement for you or your organization. Think of an archer trying to aim the bow and arrow at a target. If you are the archer holding the bow and arrow and your target is improving DEI, then a "What Works" model improves your aim and increases your likelihood of hitting the center of the target. Here are more formal definitions:

- A **"What Works" model for people** defines a concept, technique, technology, tool, model, methodology, or approach that has been reasonably (i.e., a promising practice) or reliably (i.e., a proven practice) found to be effective in expanding personal *preferences* and/or building personal *competences* leading to improved DEI based on research, science, and/or the experience of expert practitioners. For example, a "What Works" could include coaching for behavioral change, a toolkit that helps prepare you for courageous conversations, or a competence model for inclusive leadership.

- A **"What Works" model for organizations** defines a concept, technique, technology, tool, model, methodology, or approach that has been reasonably (i.e., a promising practice) or reliably (i.e., a proven practice) found to be effective in enhancing *people* experiences, management *practices*, and/or organizational *policies* leading to improved DEI based on research, science, and/or the experience of expert practitioners. For example, a "What Works" model could include people experiences such as Virtual Reality or ERGs; management practices such as mentorship and sponsorship; and organizational policies such as inclusive recruiting and hiring.

One definition of equity is giving people what they need. Equity is about understanding what works, for whom, and under what circumstances. "What Works" models can promote equity by giving people what they need to maximize their likelihood of improving DEI.

Here in **Step 3: DEI Insights** you will be introduced to several "What Works" models for people and for organizations, but they are not meant to be applied in a cookie cutter fashion. The "What Works" models outlined in this step are all flexible and must be adapted to your unique personal and/or organizational DEI journey. To be clear: While each model is based on research, science, and/or the experience of expert practitioners, they are all practical and have been embraced by people and organizations alike.

What follows are overviews and profiles of "What Works" models for people and organizations. Before we fully embark upon our exploration into what works for people and organizations, one point must be made at the onset: Above all else, what works for people is a personal commitment, incentives, resources, and accountability, and what works for organizations is leadership commitment, incentives, resources, and accountability. All the things we discussed in **Step 0: DEI Incentives** with respect to self-reflection and introspection, intrinsic and extrinsic incentives, and holding yourself and others accountable are paramount. Without these elements, all of what remains to be discussed is moot.

"What Works" Models for People

First, we will look at "What Works" models for people, which are summarized in Table 3.1. The list is by no means exhaustive, but rather, illustrative of the models that are available.

Go to **www.datadrivendei.com** to find much more detailed descriptions of the "What Works" Models for People including the lead developer, vendor, website, key takeaways, and how we know it works. You can share your "What Works" models for people and see those shared by others.

TABLE 3.1 "What Works" Models for People

"What Works" Model	Lead Developer/Vendor	Brief Description
Coaching	Various including: • Institute for Professional Excellence in Coaching (iPEC) **www.ipeccoaching.com** • CoachDiversity Institute **www.coachdiversity.com** • Institute of Coaching **www.instituteofcoaching.org** • The Coaching Habit **www.boxofcrayons.com** • Association for Coaching **www.associationfor-coaching.com**	Professional DEI coaching services include personalized, one-on-one support to help people stretch their DEI preferences, build their DEI competences, develop diverse relationships, overcome challenges, accelerate cross-cultural development, improve dialogue and communication, facilitate inclusive behavioral change, actively foster equity, and achieve DEI objectives.
Intrinsic Inclusion™	Dr. Janet Reid and Mr. Vincent Brown **www.intrinsicinclusion.com**	Four "inclusion accelerators"—Shared Trust, Significant Emotional Relationship/Event, Connected Understanding, and Respectful Empathy—define competences for intrinsically inclusive behaviors.
The Inclusion Habit™	Dr. Amanda Felkey **www.theinclusionhabit.com**	An incentive-based inclusion solution that helps individuals change behaviors and habits to be more inclusive via Microcommitments (small daily actions, to which users make commitment), social accountability, and community building.
Through My Eyes™ Virtual Reality (VR) Immersions	Steve Mahaley, Red Fern, and Dr. Randal Pinkett, BCT Partners **www.throughmyeyesvr.com**	A library of 360° video-based immersions that puts people in actual situations (i.e., real people, not avatars) where they have to confront some of their own obvious or implicit biases.
The Whole Brain® Thinking Model	Ned Herrmann, Herrmann International **www.thinkherrmann.com**	A time-tested framework to decode and harness the cognitive diversity of individuals, teams, and organizations.
The Ally Conversation Toolkit (ACT) and the RACE Method for Antiracism	Dr. David Campt and Allison Mahaley, The Dialogue Company **thedialoguecompany.com**	ACT helps antiracism allies learn how to have more effective conversations with people who think racism is not real. The RACE Method—Reflect, Ask, Connect, Expand—represents steps that an ally should take before and during authentic conversations about race.

TABLE 3.1 (Continued)

"What Works" Model	Lead Developer/Vendor	Brief Description
The Six Signature Traits of an Inclusive Leader	Bernadette Dillon and Juliet Bourk, Deloitte **www2.deloitte.com/ us/en/ insights/topics/talent/ six-signature-traits-of- inclusive-leadership.html**	Specific capabilities—*Cognizance of Bias, Curiosity, Cultural Intelligence, Collaboration, Commitment and Courage*—for becoming an inclusive leader.
Are You Ready to Talk? Toolkit for Discussions about Difference	Stanford Center for Social Psychological Answers to Real-World Questions (Stanford SPARQ) **sparqtools.org/areyouready- totalk/**	A toolkit made up of exercises for people to have or lead a conversation about different identities, experiences, or viewpoints.
IDI Guided Development®	Dr. Mitchell R. Hammer, IDI **www.idiinventory.com**	A proprietary, proven approach for designing training and other interventions that substantially increases intercultural competence for groups and organizations based on IDI® profile results.
The Bias Progress Model	Pamela Fuller and Mark Murphy with Ann Chow and Franklin Covey **www.franklincovey.com/ unconscious-bias-book/**	Four parts help move beyond awareness of unconscious bias to specific action: (1) identify bias, (2) cultivate connection, (3) choose courage, and (4) apply across the talent lifecycle.
Intercultural Conflict Style® (ICS®) Model	Dr. Mitchell R. Hammer, ICS **www.icsinventory.com**	The innovative, four-quadrant ICS model provides a roadmap to how people use specific culturally grounded strategies for communicating ideas, resolving disagreements, and dealing with emotional upset.
Emotional Intelligence (emotional quotient or EQ)	John Mayer, Peter Salovey, Daniel Goleman, and Dr. Reuven Bar-On **www.eiconsortium.org**	The ability to understand, use, and manage your own emotions in positive ways to relieve stress, communicate effectively, empathize with others, overcome challenges, and defuse conflict.[1]
Mentorship and Sponsorship	N/A	Mentors and sponsors are invaluable to both career support and psychosocial support, which can lead to several benefits for the mentees, mentors, and the organization including career outcomes, employee engagement, commitment, retention, and inclusion.

"What Works" Models for Organizations

The "What Works" models that were just introduced for people can be used by anyone for their personal and/or professional DEI journey, which includes both inside and outside of an organizational context. We now shift our attention to "What Works" models specifically for organizations, with a reminder of my earlier remarks that what ultimately works for organizations is leadership commitment, incentives, resources, and accountability. Along these lines, there are a growing number of DEI initiatives that have sought to formalize commitments from leaders and organizations. Here are just a few examples:

- **CEO Action for Diversity & Inclusion™ (www.ceoaction.com)**—CEO Action for Diversity & Inclusion™ is the largest CEO-driven business commitment to advance diversity and inclusion in the workplace. More than 2,200 CEOs and presidents have made pledges to support a more inclusive workplace for employees, communities, and society at large.

- **CEO Action for Racial Equity (www.ceoaction.com/racial-equity)**—The CEO Action for Racial Equity Fellowship is a first-of-its-kind, business-led initiative that mobilizes CEO Action for Diversity & Inclusion™ signatory organizations to advance policy change at the federal, state, and local levels. The mission is to identify, develop, and promote scalable and sustainable public policies and corporate engagement strategies that will advance racial equity, address social injustice, and improve societal well-being.

- **Institute for Diversity and Health Equity (IFDHE) of the American Hospital Association's (AHA) #123ForEquity (ifdhe.aha.org/123forequity)**—To accelerate progress on eliminating health and health care disparities in America's hospitals and health systems, the AHA launched its #123forEquity pledge campaign in 2015. It asks hospital and health system leaders to make a pledge to increase the collection and use of race, ethnicity, language preference, and other sociodemographic data, increase cultural competency training, increase diversity in leadership and governance, and improve and strengthen community partnerships. More than 1,705 hospitals and health systems have made the pledge thus far.

- **The Fifteen Percent Pledge (15percentpledge.org)**—The Fifteen Percent Pledge is a call to action for major retailers and corporations to create sustainable and supportive ecosystems for Black-owned businesses to succeed. The Fifteen Percent Pledge works with companies to comprehensively reevaluate their organizational structures, ways of working, funding, and resourcing in order to implement meaningful change and create greater equity for Black businesses.

These and other industry- and sector-wide initiatives can be helpful not only in galvanizing the support of leaders, but also in addressing institutional and systemic DEI and racial equity issues that are not particular to any one organization.

Table 3.2 summarizes "What Works" models for organizations. Once again, the list is by no means exhaustive, but rather, illustrative of the models that are available.

Go to **www.datadrivendei.com** to find much more detailed descriptions of the "What Works" Models for Organizations including the lead developer, vendor, website, takeaways, and how we know it works. You can share your "What Works" models for organizations and see those shared by others.

In the next **Step 4: DEI Initiatives**, not only will you determine which specific DEI strategies to pursue along with associated DEI measures, but you will also receive guidance on how to choose the right "What Works" model to suit your personal and/ or organizational needs.

TABLE 3.2 **"What Works" Models for Organizations**

"What Works" Model	Lead Developer/Vendor	Brief Description
Inclusive Recruiting and Hiring	N/A	Inclusive recruiting and hiring refers to a broad range of strategies to cast a wide net and engender fairness in recruiting and hiring processes including job postings, outreach, screening, and interviewing.
Employee Resource Groups (ERGs)	N/A	Groups of employees in an organization formed to act as a resource for both members and the organization.[2]
Human-Centered Behavior Change Experience: The Rali Platform and Learn-Do-Inspire Methodology	Larry Mohl, founder and chief transformation officer and Rich Cannon, CEO, Rali **www.getrali.com**	Rali's Change Experience Platform (CxP) provides an integrated suite of methods and features all designed to drive group-based behavior change that shapes culture and results in organizational impact at a large scale.
Scenario-based Microlearning	N/A	Addresses the "holy trinity" of skills that every person must be adept in for personal and organizational productivity: *hard skills* (subject-specific skills and abilities), *soft skills* (people and interpersonal skills), and *situational awareness* (understanding how decisions impact the present and the future).

(Continued)

TABLE 3.2 (Continued)

"What Works" Model	Lead Developer/Vendor	Brief Description
High Performance Learning Journeys® (HPLJ) and the Promote® Learning Transfer Platform	Dr. Robert O. Brinkerhoff, Promote International **www.hplj.org/** and **www .promoteint.com**	HPLJ is an instructional design approach that puts emphasis on targeted application of learning to bring about performance improvement and business impact. Promote® is a learning transfer platform that enables you to design and execute HPLJs.
Global Diversity, Equity & Inclusion Benchmarks (GDEIB)	Nene Molefi, Julie O'Mara, and Alan Richter, PhD and 112 expert panelists, The Centre for Global Inclusion **www.centreforglobal inclusion.org**	A free guidebook with a supporting suite of tools to assess the current state of your organization or department on each of four primary processes and 15 concrete actions.
Racial Equity Action Plans and Toolkit	Government Alliance for Racial Equity (GARE) **www.racialequityalliance .org/resources/**	Racial Equity Action Plans and Tools can put a theory of change into action to achieve a collective vision of racial equity.
Equitable Analytics™ with Precision Modeling	Peter York, principal and chief data scientist, BCT Partners **www.equitableanalytics .com**	A disruptive approach that uses Precision Modeling and machine learning to more precisely identify what types of DEI programming, treatments, and/or interventions are most likely to work and for whom.
The Equitable Impact Platform™ (EquIP™)	Peter York, principal and chief data scientist, BCT Partners **www.equitableimpact.com**	A big data platform built to assess, evaluate, and study the interrelationship between diversity, inclusiveness, community well-being, and equity in communities (see Figure 5.17 for a map generated by EquIP™).
Supplier Diversity Benchmark Framework	supplier.io, MSDUK, and Accenture **www.supplier.io**	A useful framework for evaluating and benchmarking a supplier diversity program.

STEP 4

DEI Initiatives—Take Action

The DEI journey is the destination.

If you fail to develop a strategy, your strategy is to fail.

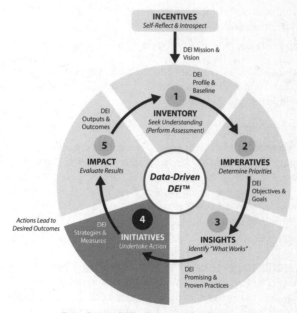

Data-Driven DEI—Step 4: DEI Initiatives

A DEI Initiative is any strategy, activity, or action you and/or your organization undertake to improve DEI. **Step 3: DEI Insights** answers the reflective question, "What could you do?," while **Step 4: DEI Initiatives** answers the resolute question, "What will you do?" Here, you decide the DEI initiatives you will pursue to fulfill your DEI objectives and achieve your DEI goals. This step is also where the complete picture of your personal and/or organizational DEI strategic plan will finally crystallize.

DEI Strategies and Measures

You will recall from **Step 2: DEI Imperatives** that our framework for DEI strategic planning is OGSM (previously shown in Figure 2.1). OGSM is an acronym that stands for objectives, goals, strategies, and measures. The OGSM Strategic Planning Framework is a method that guides people and organizations through the strategic planning process:

- Each objective should have one or more goals to evaluate results and determine impact.
- Each goal should be evaluated against one or more metrics or key performance indicators (KPIs).
- Each objective should have one or more strategies to fulfill the objective and achieve the corresponding goals.
- Each strategy should be evaluated against one or more measures.

At BCT, we use this method to connect broader aspirations to concrete and actionable steps that can be integrated into daily behaviors. We frequently apply the OGSM framework to DEI strategic planning.

If you go to **www.datadrivendei.com**, you will find a downloadable template for developing a personal DEI strategic plan, called the Crawl-Walk-Run Personal Action Plan, and an organizational DEI strategic plan. You can enter your objectives, goals, strategies, and measures directly into these templates. You will also find an extensive and comprehensive list, or menu, of DEI measures, metrics, and key performance indicators (KPIs).

In **Step 2: DEI Imperatives**, you built out the first half of a personal and/or organizational DEI strategic plan by establishing DEI objectives and setting DEI goals. Here in **Step 4: DEI Initiatives**, with the benefit of **Step 3: DEI Insights** to inform you, you will now build out the second half of your personal and/or organizational DEI strategic plan by defining **DEI strategies** and determining **DEI measures**.

This step begins by introducing a personal DEI strategy framework and an organizational DEI strategy framework. These frameworks will guide you in cascading your DEI objectives and goals down to specific DEI strategies. This step continues by outlining how to craft DEI strategy statements, how to craft specific DEI measures statements, and how to select specific DEI measures to gauge progress against each strategy. This step concludes by presenting examples of a personal DEI strategic plan and an organizational DEI strategic plan.

Personal DEI Strategy Framework

A **Personal DEI Strategy Framework** is depicted in Figure 4.1. This framework is simply an extension of the personal DEI assessment framework from **Step 1: DEI Inventory for People**, previously shown in Figure 1.1. It takes the prior assessment framework, which endeavored to assess your preferences and competences, and makes it actionable based on two basic premises for improving your DEI: *expand your preferences* and *build your competences*.

As we learned in **Step 1: DEI Inventory**, when it comes to preferences they are placed along scale or situated within a map. There is no good or bad, better or worse, right or wrong, when it comes to preferences. Your overarching strategy for preferences is to expand, stretch, or flex into areas outside of your preferences. This is about personal awareness of core preferences such as your biases, communication style, conflict style, and more. For example, you may have a direct conflict style (i.e., face-to-face resolution of disputes), which tends to be utilized in North America and Europe. Therefore, if you are in North America or Europe that preference may serve you well. However, if you are in Asia, where an indirect conflict style tends to be utilized (i.e., use of third parties to resolve disputes), you may choose to adapt your conflict style accordingly to improve conflict resolution.

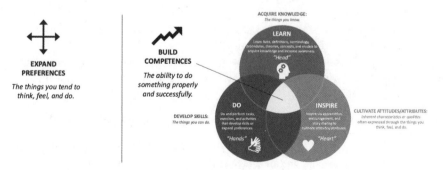

FIGURE 4.1   Personal DEI Strategy Framework

Another overarching strategy is to adapt your preferences to others by understanding their preferences and shifting your perspective and behavior accordingly. This is about increasing your awareness of the biases, communication styles, conflict styles, and so forth, of others. Continuing the previous example, if you prefer a direct conflict style but are managing a dispute with someone you know prefers an indirect conflict style, you may choose to adapt your conflict style to theirs to improve conflict resolution.

Competences are measured along a continuum. They are comprised of knowledge, skills, and attitudes/attributes (KSAs). Your overarching strategy for competences is to acquire knowledge, develop skills, and cultivate empowering attitudes and attributes. This is about personal development of core competences such as courage, cultural competence, mitigating bias, and more, that can benefit you and others. For example, you can build the competence of mitigating bias by researching different definitions and types of bias such as attribution bias, conformity bias, and affinity bias (i.e., knowledge), learning and applying techniques to mitigate bias such as source monitoring, structured free recall (SFR), and other ways to structure your decision making (i.e., skills), as well as demonstrating the initiative to learn and apply new ways of mitigating bias (i.e., attitudes/attributes). This is about personal development of core competences such as collaboration, communication, conflict resolution, and so on that can enhance your ability to engage, interact, work with, and lead other people. For example, you can build the competence of communication by researching different styles of communication such as assertive, aggressive, passive-aggressive, and aggressive (i.e., knowledge), conducting role-playing exercises to practice assertive communication (i.e., skills), and bringing a positive attitude (i.e., attitude/attribute) to the work you have undertaken to communicate with others more effectively.

Per Figure 4.1, your strategies to expand preferences and build competences should cover the following three areas, which are based on a "Head-Hands-Heart" nomenclature and the proprietary "Learn-Do-Inspire" methodology and change architecture developed by the Rali LX (Learning Transfer) platform:

Learn: Engage the Head—Learn facts, definitions, terminology, procedures, theories, concepts, and models to acquire knowledge and increase awareness.

Do: Employ the Hands—Do and perform tasks, exercises, and activities that develop skills and expand preferences.

Inspire: Enrich the Heart—Inspire yourself via appreciation, encouragement, and story sharing to cultivate positive attitudes/attributes and increase engagement.

Hereafter, I will group personal DEI strategies and measures by head-hands-heart/learn-do-inspire.

Based on this framework, naturally, the first task is to determine which preferences you want to expand and/or which competences you want to build. Now is the time to finalize the initial choices you made in **Step 1: DEI Inventory** for personal DEI core preferences or DEI core preferences and competences.

Developing a Personal DEI Preference and Competence Model

In **Step 1: DEI Inventory**, I introduced "The ABCDEs of DEI"—21 common personal DEI preferences and competences to consider as foci for your personal DEI journey (reminder: you were not limited to the items shown in the table). You made some initial choices of personal DEI core preferences or personal DEI core preferences and competences based on your personal DEI aims using the list in Table 3.4 and based on the process outlined in Table 3.5. Now, you can finalize those choices using a very similar process, only now with the benefit of the three preceding steps to do so:

- **Step 1: DEI Inventory:** You have the benefit of your completed personal DEI assessment, which generated a profile and baseline of your preferences and your level of competence in specific areas. You may decide to focus on expanding into new areas of preference and/or developing in areas of limited competence. For example, if you selected the Implicit Association Test (IAT) as one of your assessments, then you may have revealed that you have a moderate, automatic preference of men with careers and women with family (according to IAT research by Project Implicit, 32% of respondents have this implicit bias). As a result, you may choose to focus on awareness of self, awareness of others, appreciation of others, and bias awareness as core preferences.

- **Step 2: DEI Imperatives:** You also have the benefit of your personal DEI objectives and goals, which provides even clearer direction, when compared to your personal DEI aims, for exactly what it is that you hope to accomplish and how you will evaluate results and determine impact. Much as your personal DEI aims guided you during **Step 1: DEI Inventory** to identify an initial set of competences, your personal DEI objectives and goals can guide you to a final set of competences. In other words, much as Table 3.5 walked you through the process of choosing initial personal DEI core preferences and competences based on your personal DEI aims, Table 4.1 walks you through a very similar process of now choosing final personal DEI core preferences and competences based on your personal DEI objectives and goals.

- **Step 3: DEI Insights:** Finally, you have the benefit of personal DEI promising and proven practices ("What Works" models for people and organizations), which provide insights to what has been found to work for others and can therefore inform what might work for you. You may choose to adopt one of the "What Works" models identified in the previous step. In fact, Table 4.1 also walks you through a process of mapping your personal DEI objectives and goals to an appropriate "What Works." For example, if your personal DEI objective is related to being inclusive, then you could choose to adopt Intrinsic Inclusion™ as your model for personal DEI core competences based on its competences blueprint of four inclusion accelerators—Shared Trust, Significant Emotional Event/Relationship, Connected Understanding, and Respectful Empathy—to

TABLE 4.1 Mapping Personal DEI Objectives and Goals to Personal DEI Preferences and Competences and "What Works" Models for People

If your personal DEI objectives and goals relate to . . .	You must expand and/or build your . . .	Select 3–5 preferences or 5–7 preferences and competences to comprise your personal DEI preference and competence model ("The ABCDEs of DEI") . . .	Or select one of these "What Works" models for people and organizations to define or inform your personal DEI preference and competence model . . .
Diversity: The Range of Human Differences (*A Fact*)			
1. Appreciate differences	Preferences	Awareness of Self, Awareness of Others, Appreciation of Others, Cultural Awareness, Cultural Humility, Emotional Intelligence	The Whole Brain® Thinking Model; IDI Guided Development® for Building Intercultural Competence; Emotional Intelligence
2. Recognize own biases	Preferences	Awareness of Self, Appreciation of Others, Bias Awareness, Cultural Awareness, Cultural Humility, Emotional Intelligence	Intrinsic Inclusion™; The Inclusion Habit™; The Bias Progress Model; Emotional Intelligence
Inclusion: Involvement and Empowerment (*An Action*)			
3. Mitigate own biases	Preferences	Awareness of Self, Appreciation of Others, Affirmation of Others, Bias Awareness, Bias Mitigation, Communication Style Awareness, Cultural Awareness, Cultural Humility, Emotional Intelligence	Intrinsic Inclusion™; The Inclusion Habit™; The Bias Progress Model; Emotional Intelligence
	Competences	Adaptation, Communication, Cultural Competence, Cultural Humility, Emotional Intelligence	

TABLE 4.1 (Continued)

4. Navigate and bridge differences	Preferences	Awareness of Self, Awareness of Others, Appreciation of Others, Affirmation of Others, Bias Awareness, Bias Mitigation, Communication Style Awareness, Cultural Awareness, Cultural Humility, Emotional Intelligence	IDI Guided Development® for Building Intercultural Competence Emotional Intelligence
	Competences	Adaptation, Communication, Courage, Cultural Competence, Cultural Humility, Dialogue, Emotional Intelligence	
5. Be inclusive	Preferences	Awareness of Others, Appreciation of Others, Affirmation of Others, Bias Awareness, Bias Mitigation, Communication Style Awareness, Cultural Awareness, Cultural Humility, Emotional Intelligence	Intrinsic Inclusion™ The Inclusion Habit™ The Six Signature Traits of an Inclusive Leader Emotional Intelligence
	Competences	Adaptation, Advocacy, Collaboration, Communication, Courage, Cultural Competence, Cultural Humility, Dialogue, Emotional Intelligence	
6. Resolve conflict	Preferences	Collaboration, Conflict Style Awareness, Emotional Intelligence	Intercultural Conflict Style Inventory® (ICS®) Model Emotional Intelligence
	Competences	Conflict Resolution, Dialogue, Emotional Intelligence	
Equity: Fairness and Equality in Outcomes (*A Choice*)			
7. Be a mentor 8. Be a sponsor	Preferences	Awareness of Others, Appreciation of Others, Affirmation of Others, Communication Style Awareness, Cultural Awareness, Cultural Humility, Emotional Intelligence	Coaching Emotional Intelligence
	Competences	Advocacy, Coaching, Mentoring and Sponsoring, Collaboration, Communication, Cultural Competence, Cultural Humility, Dialogue, Emotional Intelligence	

(Continued)

TABLE 4.1 (Continued)

If your personal DEI objectives and goals relate to . . .	You must expand and/or build your . . .	Select 3–5 preferences or 5–7 preferences and competences to comprise your personal DEI preference and competence model ("The ABCDEs of DEI") . . .	Or select one of these "What Works" models for people and organizations to define or inform your personal DEI preference and competence model . . .
9. Be an ally 10. Be an antiracist	Preferences	Awareness of Others, Appreciation of Others, Affirmation of Others, Allyship, Antiracism, Bias Awareness, Bias Mitigation, Communication Style Awareness, Cultural Awareness, Cultural Humility, Emotional Intelligence	The Ally Conversation Toolkit (ACT) and RACE Method for Antiracism *Are You Ready to Talk?* Toolkit for Courageous Conversations about Differences
	Competences	Advocacy, Collaboration, Communication, Courage, Cultural Competence, Cultural Humility, Dialogue, Emotional Intelligence	
11. Improve performance 12. Increase compensation	Preferences	Awareness of Self, Awareness of Others, Appreciation of Others, Bias Awareness, Communication Style Awareness, Cultural Awareness, Cultural Humility, Emotional Intelligence	Intrinsic Inclusion™ The Inclusion Habit™ The Six Signature Traits of an Inclusive Leader Emotional Intelligence
	Competences	Adaptation, Affirmation of Others, Bias Mitigation, Coaching, Mentoring and Sponsoring, Collaboration, Communication, Cultural Competence, Cultural Humility, Emotional Intelligence	

behave more inclusively, or you could adopt the Six Signature Traits of an Inclusive Leader, which identifies cognizance of bias, curiosity, cultural intelligence, collaboration, commitment, and courage as the necessary competences to be an inclusive leader.

By analyzing the results of your personal DEI assessment, reflecting on your personal DEI objectives and goals, and reviewing personal DEI promising and proven practices, you should have more than sufficient information from the preceding steps to arrive at final choices for your personal DEI core preferences and competences. This will comprise your **personal DEI preference model** or **personal DEI preference and competence model**.

Table 4.1 walks you through the entire process of how to arrive at your personal DEI preference model or personal DEI preference and competence model. If your personal DEI objectives only relate to preferences, you should select a total of three to five preferences for your personal DEI preference mode or select one "What Works" model for people (i.e., a personal DEI promising or proven practice) to define or inform your model. If your personal DEI objectives relate to preferences and competences, you should select a total of five to seven personal DEI preferences and competences for your personal DEI preference and competence model or select one "What Works" model for people and organizations to define or inform your model.

This completes the first task stemming from the personal DEI strategy framework, which is to determine the preferences you want to expand and/or the competences you want to build. The second and final task is to orchestrate exactly what knowledge you will acquire ("Learn: Engage the Head"), determine exactly what actions you will take to expand the personal DEI core preferences and build the personal DEI core competences you have selected ("Do: Employ the Hands"), and decide exactly how you will cultivate positive attitudes/attributes and increase engagement ("Inspire: Enrich the Heart"). This will all be accomplished by designing a personal DEI learning journey.

Designing a Personal DEI Learning Journey

Oftentimes, people rely on training to foster behavioral change in support of a strategic objective. However, most training constitutes an "event" and does not engage you in a meaningful and effective behavioral change process. As you develop your personal DEI strategies, I recommend a **Personal DEI Learning Journey (PDLJ)** as an approach to create lasting behavioral change, learning transfer, and performance improvement along your personal DEI journey. As the name implies, a *Personal DEI Learning Journey* is a series of activities and experiences designed to achieve behavioral change, learning, and performance outcomes specifically related to DEI. A personal DEI learning journey may include training, but it embraces an even wider range of personal DEI strategies. This approach is centered on the pioneering work of Professor Robert Brinkerhoff under the banner of "High Performance Learning Journeys® (HPLJs)," which was cited as a "What Works" model for organizations in

Step 3: DEI Insights. While a Personal DEI Learning Journey doesn't fully meet the criteria of an HPLJ, which is a more comprehensive approach to designing learning journeys, it does invoke the underlying principles of an HPLJ. To delve deeper into HPLJs, I encourage you to learn more about Professor Brinkerhoff's work.

In *Improving Performance Through Learning: A Practical Guide for Designing High Performance Learning Journeys*, Brinkerhoff, Anne Apking, and Edward Boon identify five dimensions that must be "stretched" (suggesting flexibility, agility, and expansion) or fully leveraged to design an HPLJ. In the next section, I introduce and slightly reframe their five dimensions of a High Performance Learning Journey in the context of a Personal DEI Learning Journey. This will establish the foundation for designing your own PDLJs that embrace the spirit of HPLJs.

The Five Dimensions of a Personal DEI Learning Journey

As you have now selected the personal DEI core preferences and competences you will focus on for your personal DEI journey, the following five dimensions are instructive as you contemplate how you should design your own PDLJ to expand those preferences and/or build those competences:

1. **Focus**—While Brinkerhoff, Apking, and Boon officially refer to this dimension as "Business Linkage," in their words, "Stretching on this dimension [of business linkage] is really one of *focus* . . . this linkage occurs when participants define and expand, over time, the performance tasks that they own." Your focus could be on your needs, or the needs of your organization, or a combination of both. The key here is "being explicit in the alignment between the Learning and Performance Outcomes the learning will yield, and how those outcomes will have a positive impact" on you and/or your organization. In the context of *Data-Driven DEI*, this translates into making certain you have alignment between your personal DEI objectives, goals, strategies, and measures. We began to explore this topic in **Step 0: DEI Incentives** and we will complete that exploration here in **Step 4: DEI Initiatives**.

2. **Time**—Consider the duration and the pace of your PDLJ. Establish a period of time sufficient for personal growth and create a cadence of activities and experiences that are suitable to your schedule.

   As it relates to the time it takes for personal change and transformation, an article by *Healthline* entitled, "How Long Does It Take for a New Behavior to Become Automatic," which references a study published in the *European Journal of Social Psychology* in 2009 states, "It can take anywhere from 18 to 254 days for a person to form a new habit and an average of 66 days for a new behavior to become automatic. There's no one-size-fits-all figure, which is why this time frame is so broad; some habits are easier to form than others, and some people may find it easier to develop new behaviors. There's no right or wrong timeline. The only timeline that matters is the one that works best for you."

3. **Spaces**—Consider the various locations where your PDLJ can take place beyond a classroom such as your home, work, gym, car, library, movie theater, and beyond. In 2018, *Training Industry* published a report that found the following:[1]

   - *Fifty-five percent of learning take places on the job*, including job assignments, special assignments, rotational assignment, stretch assignments, and job supports such as standard operating procedures, protocols, templates, and checklists.

   - *Twenty-five percent of learning is social* via shadowing, coaching, mentoring, collaboration, observation (i.e., of experts), giving and receiving feedback, and teamwork.

   - *Twenty percent of learning is formal* such as training seminars, assignments, activities, exercises, and the like.

4. **Relationships**—Consider how you can align with or involve others in your PDLJ including family members, friends, supervisor, leaders, peers, direct reports, coaches, mentors, sponsors, subject matter experts, and customers. According to the Vanderbilt University Center for Teaching, several studies have confirmed that people learn better in groups, leading to better problem solving, more positive experiences, higher quiz and test scores, and more.[2]

5. **Tools and Structure**—Consider the tools or resources that can enhance your personal DEI learning journey including assessments, books, articles, research papers, case studies, examples/counter-examples, podcasts, videos, blogs, quizzes, tests, examinations, guides, templates, checklists, games, job aids, eLearning, virtual reality (VR), and so on. Also consider the structure or how you frame your personal DEI learning journey with respect to at-home vs. on-the-job vs. social vs. formal learning; individual vs. team vs. group learning; and in-person vs. virtual vs. eLearning.

Once you have considered the dimensions of focus, time, spaces, relationships, and tools and structure, you are ready to design your Personal DEI Learning Journey. The next section provides a menu of choices to choose from.

Examples of Personal DEI Strategies

Table 4.2 provides a list of personal DEI strategies for you to consider as a part of your Personal DEI Learning Journey to expand your preferences and build your competences (broken down into learn-do-inspire/head-hands-heart to address all three modes of engagement).

The final construct needed to finalize your PDLJ is the Crawl-Walk-Run approach, which will help you organize the journey into three distinct and successively more challenging stages.

TABLE 4.2 List of Personal DEI Strategies for Learning Journeys

Category	Description
LEARN: Engage the Head	
Training Programs	Participate in live, virtual, web-based, or eLearning training programs that present information and teach skills on DEI.
Educational Classes	Register for courses either for a fee or for free on topics related to DEI.
Books, Magazines, Articles, and Blogs	Read books, magazines, research, academic papers, white papers, articles, and blogs on topics related to DEI.
TV Shows, Videos, and Podcasts	View television shows, watch videos, and listen to podcasts on topics related to DEI.
DO: Employ the Hands	
Theater, Film, and Arts	Attend plays, movies, museums, and other cultural exhibits and events.
Travel, Site Visits, and Excursions	Explore and experience different cultures via travel, site visits, tours, and excursions. This is not limited to physical exploration but also online and virtual reality (VR).
Experiential Learning and Development Programs	Participate in live, virtual, web-based experiential learning and development programs that require practice and application of DEI skills.
Workplace Activities	Engage in activities in the workplace including cultural celebrations, employee resource groups (ERGs), DEI councils, DEI champions, international assignments, mentoring programs (especially cross-cultural and cross-gender), and the like.
INSPIRE: Enrich the Heart	
Journaling	Maintain a journal, diary, or notes that share your thoughts and feelings along your DEI journey.
Storytelling	Share your DEI experiences, challenges, opportunities, and successes with others.
ALL: LEARN (Engage the Head), DO (Employ the Hands), and INSPIRE (Enrich the Heart)	
Personal Interactions	Interact with people of a different identity, culture, and/or belief system from you.
Courageous Conversations	Participate and/or facilitate topical dialogues on sensitive or difficult topics with people or groups of people to promote greater understanding across differences.
Coaching	Seek the assistance of a life and/or career coach who can offer personalized advice, guidance, learning, and development.

TABLE 4.2   (Continued)

Category	Description
Mentoring	Seek personal, career, and psychosocial development and support from someone with more experience.
Reverse Mentoring	Provide personal, career, and psychosocial support to someone with more experience.
Sponsoring	Seek advocacy and advancement support from someone with power or influence.
Communities of Learning	Organize, join, and/or facilitate group learning via book clubs, reading groups, mastermind groups, or other communities of learning/practice on topics related to DEI.
Microcommitments	Make commitments to small actions that can make a big difference by changing your behaviors and habits to be more inclusive.

Source: Adapted from Intercultural Development Inventory® (IDI®), Intercultural Development Plan (IDP): "Key Intercultural Opportunities."

The Crawl, Walk, Run Approach to a Personal DEI Learning Journey

The Rev. Dr. Martin Luther King, Jr. once said, "If you can't fly then run, if you can't run then walk, if you can't walk then crawl, but whatever you do you have to keep moving forward." This inspired the "Crawl, Walk, Run" approach to a learning journey. According to Brinkerhoff, Apking, and Boon, "the Crawl, Walk, Run approach can be an invaluable framework," especially when undertaking an ambitious learning journey. "The premise of this approach is that crawling precedes the ability to walk, and walking must be mastered before beginning to run," and for the PDLJ to meet you where you are. The approach includes the following (with each step broken down into learn-do-inspire / head-hands-heart and each example drawing from the categories listed in Table 4.1):

> **Crawl**—Begin your PDLJ with "low-hanging fruit." Focus on acquiring entry-level knowledge, performing easy and introductory tasks, exercises, and activities to build skills, and pursuing basic appreciation, encouragement, and storytelling opportunities to cultivate your attitudes/attributes. For example, a PDLJ centered on the four personal DEI core competences (i.e., inclusion accelerators) of Intrinsic Inclusion™—Shared Trust, Significant Emotional Event/Relationship, Connected Understanding, and Respectful Empathy—could begin with the following:

Learn—**Books, Magazines, Articles, and Blogs:** Read the book, *Intrinsic Inclusion: Rebooting Your Biased Brain* by Reid and Brown.

Do—**Travel, Site Visits, and Excursions:** Shadow an inclusive leader for a day to observe their behavior and/or interview an inclusive leader to gain insight.

Inspire—**Journaling:** Maintain a journal and **Personal Interactions:** Share the objectives, goals, strategies, and measures for the overall PDLJ with a friend or family member to provide motivation and accountability.

Walk—Continue your PDLJ with intermediate-level knowledge, tasks, exercises, activities, and opportunities. The prior personal DEI learning journey could continue with the following:

Learn—**Books, Magazines, Articles, and Blogs:** Read articles on Intrinsic Inclusion™ by Janet B. Reid, PhD, and Vincent Brown in *Psychology Today*.[3]

Do—**Workplace Activities:** Participate in a workplace event or celebration sponsored by the Black employee resource group (ERG).

Inspire—**Journaling:** Maintain a journal and **Storytelling:** Share the key takeaways and lessons learned from experiences thus far with a colleague.

Run—The final phase of your PDLJ should be the more difficult and advanced-level assignments. For example, the previous PDLJ could conclude with the following:

Learn—**Training Programs:** Attend a facilitated learning experience by a certified instructor that teaches Intrinsic Inclusion™ and provides various expertly facilitated tasks, exercises, and activities for applying the inclusion accelerators.

Do—**Experiential Learning and Development Programs and Workplace Activities:** Apply the MODE model ("**m**otivation and **o**pportunity and be **d**eterminants of spontaneous behavior") after the facilitated learning experience at work while seeking feedback from colleagues who are Black and/or women ("Field Testing" chapter, "Building MODE into the Routine" section).

Inspire—**Journaling:** Maintain a journal and **Communities of Learning:** Join a virtual peer learning group from the facilitated learning experience that meets regularly to share stories, offer encouragement, and hold each another accountable to meet learning and development commitments.

The Learn-Do-Inspire/Head-Hands-Heart methodology helps ensure that your PDLJ is comprehensive in how it will expand your preferences and build your competences via knowledge acquisition, skill development, and attitude/attribute cultivation. The five dimensions of focus, time, spaces, relationships, and tools and structure help guide the design of your PDLJ to fully leverage different modes of engagement. The Crawl-Walk-Run approach helps structure the stages of your PDLJ in a way that gradually becomes more challenging.

Organizational DEI Strategy Framework

At various points along your organizational DEI journey, you have leveraged a DEI Council/Committee/Task Force/Steering Committee—a diverse and inclusive body representing different functions, levels, roles, identities, and responsibilities throughout the organization. In **Step 0: DEI Incentives**, the DEI Council developed an organizational DEI framework or charter. In **Step 1: DEI Inventory for Organizations**, the DEI Council helped review and interpret the results of your organizational DEI assessment. In **Step 2: DEI Imperatives**, the DEI Council began the organizational DEI strategic planning process by establishing organizational DEI objectives and setting organizational DEI goals. Leveraging the "What Works" models from **Step 3: DEI Insights**, here in **Step 4: DEI Initiatives**, the DEI Council will complete the organizational DEI strategic plan by determining organizational DEI strategies and defining organizational DEI measures. Based on Appreciative Inquiry (AI), a strengths-based, positive approach to organizational change and strategic innovation, the DEI Council should work intensively to develop a draft of this three- to five-year organizational DEI strategic plan. This could be accomplished at a retreat or during meetings that are spaced out over several months.

You will recall in **Step 1: DEI Inventory for Organizations** that we previously used the four groups—foundation, internal, bridging, and external—and 15 categories of the GDEIB model (see Figure 2.2 and Table 5.1) as the basis for reporting organizational DEI assessment results. In **Step 2: DEI Imperatives** you will also recall that we used the four groups and 15 categories of the GDEIB as a framework for establishing organizational DEI objectives and goals. The same framework applies here in **Step 4: DEI Initiative** for defining organizational DEI strategies and measures. Inasmuch as each objective should have one or more strategies to fulfill the objective and achieve its corresponding goals, and each strategy should have one or more measures to gauge progress against the strategy, it stands to reason that the same framework that applied to assessment findings, objectives and goals naturally flows down as a framework for the associated strategies and measures. In other words, the four groups and 15 categories of the GDEIB remain relevant as an organizing principle for organizational DEI strategies and measures, just as they were relevant for reporting organizational DEI assessment findings and establishing organizational DEI objectives, and goals. For example, as a part of the organizational DEI strategic planning process, we have sometimes divided the DEI Council into four committees that are focused on developing organizational DEI objectives, goals, strategies, and measures for each of the four GEDIB groups—foundation, internal, bridging, and external—respectively. Each of the four committees then presents its recommendations to the full DEI Council for feedback, revisions, and refinement until a draft organizational DEI strategic plan is produced.

Once the DEI Council has produced a draft of the organizational DEI strategic plan, a broader range of stakeholders, including leadership and other colleagues, should have opportunities to review, provide input, and offer feedback on the draft. This

TABLE 4.3	Mapping GDEIB Groups to "What Works" Models for Organizations
GDEIB Group	**"What Works" Model for Organizations**
THE FOUNDATION GROUP: Drive the Strategy	• Global Diversity, Equity, and Inclusion Benchmarks (GDEIB) • Racial Equity Action Plan
THE INTERNAL GROUP: Attract & Retain People	• Inclusive Recruiting and Hiring • Employee Resource Groups (ERGs)
THE BRIDGING GROUP: Align & Connect	• Human-Centered Behavior Change Experience: The Rali Platform and Learn-Do-Inspire Methodology • Scenario-Based Microlearning Journeys • High Performance Learning Journeys® and Promote • Equitable Analytics™
EXTERNAL GROUP: Listen to & Serve Society	• The Equitable Impact Platform™ (EquIP™) • Supplier Diversity Benchmark Framework

could be in the form of joint meetings between DEI Council members and leadership, organization-wide town hall meetings, and/or consultation with subject matter experts (SMEs). While the engagement of a broad set of stakeholders and the iterative nature of the process can all take time, we have found it to be time well spent to engage others and engender buy-in, both of which are critical to the success of an organizational DEI strategic plan. Through these processes of engagement and buy-in, the organizational DEI strategic plan is iteratively revised and refined until a final version is produced.

With the GDEIB as the basis for reporting your **Step 1: DEI Inventory for Organizations** results—your organizational DEI assessment broken down into findings, evidence, implications and recommendations—and with the GDEIB as the framework for your **Step 2: DEI Imperatives**—your organizational DEI objectives and goals—and with the GDEIB as the framework for your **Step 4: DEI Initiatives**—your organizational DEI strategies and measures—it is relatively straightforward to determine your organizational DEI strategies as long as you have a menu of eligible strategies to choose from. Here, you can look to the "What Works" models for organizations that were identified in **Step 3: DEI Insights** and beyond. Table 4.3 provides a mapping between the four GDEIB groups and these organizational DEI promising and proven practices.

In addition to these "What Works" models for organizations, you can also look to the menu of organizational DEI strategies provided in the next section and beyond.

Examples of Organizational DEI Strategies

Table 4.4 provides a representative, but not exhaustive, list of organizational DEI strategies to consider as a part of your DEI journey. They are broken down into the four groups and 15 categories of the GDEIB model. While each strategy is assigned to a primary category, many of them easily apply and support other categories.

TABLE 4.4 List of Organizational DEI Strategies

Group / Category	Organizational DEI Strategy	Description and Approach
THE FOUNDATION GROUP: Drive the Strategy		
Category 1: Vision, Strategy, and Business Impact	DEI Charter/Framework	Develop the governing ideas for a DEI program, which may include DEI mission, vision, values, statement of commitment, and definitions.
	DEI Business Case/ Organizational Case	Articulate the value of DEI specifically to your organization. It may be based on the research concerning the business case for DEI, but it is also tailored to your organization and expressed by your organization, from the perspective of your organization.
	Board DEI Statement	Develop a statement of commitment and/or bylaws approved by your board of directors or other governing body.
	DEI Strategic Plan	Craft a DEI-specific strategic plan with objectives, goals, strategies, and measures.
Category 2: Leadership and Accountability	DEI Scorecard	A static, focused, snapshot report that displays DEI metrics and key performance indicators (KPIs) against performance targets. A scorecard is good for *measuring progress over time.* Scorecards are static reports. Data is not updated in real time, but rather, at certain intervals such as weekly, monthly, or quarterly.
	DEI Dashboard	A dynamic, comprehensive, and interactive tool that displays multiple reports, which may include DEI Scorecard information, and provides access to multiple datasets. A dashboard is good for tracking DEI metrics and key performance indicators (KPIs) and *measuring performance in real time.* Dashboards are dynamic and updated in real time. They provide an up-to-date, big-picture, and holistic view.
	DEI Performance Management	Incorporate DEI metrics and KPIs into the human resources (HR) performance management process. *More about DEI metrics and KPIs below under "Category 8: Assessment, Measurement, and Research."*
	DEI Objectives and Goals Tied to Compensation	Tie compensation for executives, managers, and supervisors to achieving DEI objectives and goals.

(Continued)

TABLE 4.4 (Continued)

Group / Category	Organizational DEI Strategy	Description and Approach
Category 3: DEI Structure and Implementation	DEI Council/Committee/ Task Force/Steering Committee DEI Governance	Form a diverse, representative, and inclusive body to provide oversight and/or decision making for DEI efforts. There are three guiding principles for members of a DEI Council. Participants should be: (1) diverse with respect to the range of human differences; (2) representative of different functions, levels, roles, identities, and responsibilities throughout the organization; and (3) good role models and ambassadors for the work (i.e., can "talk the talk" and "walk the walk").
	DEI Champions	Identify voluntary or paid employees who serve as DEI ambassadors and whose objective is to improve DEI for the organization. The DEI Council may be comprised of DEI Champions, and/or DEI Champions may receive additional training as DEI catalysts for change.
THE INTERNAL GROUP: Attract & Retain People		
Category 4: Recruitment	Diversity Recruiting	Cast a wider net to identify more diverse talent. This may include partnering with a diversity recruiting firm and/or colleges and universities representing specific communities such as Historically Black Colleges and Universities (HBCIs), Hispanic-Serving Institutions (HSIs), Tribal Colleges and Universities (TCUs), Native Hawaiian-Serving Institutions (NHIs), and the like.
	Diverse Interview Panels	Mandate representation on interview panels (i.e., there must be at least one person of color or woman conducting interviews for the position). This could be confined to panels interviewing for only certain levels and above.
	Diverse Interview Slates	Mandate representation on interview slates (i.e., there must be at least one person of color or woman that is interviewed for the position). This could be confined to slates interviewing for only certain levels and above.
	Inclusive Hiring	Implement comprehensive and inclusive policies and practices for talent acquisition that include investing in pipelines for more diverse talent, bias-free job descriptions, diversity recruiting, partnership development, diverse interview panels, diverse interview slates, and more.
	Employee Resource Groups (ERGs)	Establish voluntary or paid, employee-led, inclusive groups whose objective is to improve DEI for the organization. ERGs are oftentimes open to all while centered on groups that share common lived experiences and identities with respect to race/ethnicity, nationality, gender, religion, sexual orientation, veteran status, disability status, and more.

TABLE 4.4 (Continued)

Category 5: Advancement and Retention	DEI HR Policies and Practices Evaluation (in one or more of the following areas):	Conduct an evaluation and benchmarking of human resources (HR) policies and practices against best practices for DEI and implement changes. This could take two forms:
Category 6: Job Design, Classification, and Compensation	1. Recruitment and Hiring 2. Learning and Development 3. Advancement and Promotions	A Review: A discovery process for learning how you are doing on HR functions as they relate to DEI (i.e., diagnosis). A review answers the questions: Is there a problem? What does the problem look like? Gather and analyze data and information (existing or new data) (i.e., get the evidence) to deliver fact-based findings and insights.
Category 7: Work, Life Integration, Flexibility, and Benefits	4. Performance Management and Evaluation 5. Succession Planning 6. Compensation and Rewards Management	An Audit: A consultative process that identifies problem areas and generates recommendations for HR functions as they relate to DEI (i.e., treatment). An audit answers the questions: What should we do? Who should be accountable? Apply expertise to explain problem areas and present expert conclusions and recommendations (i.e., provide a roadmap).
	7. Discipline, Terminations, and Exit Policy	
	8. Retention, Turnover, and Support	
	9. Discrimination, Harassment, and Bullying	
	10. Affirmative Action and/or Office of Federal Contract Compliance Programs (OFCCP) Regulations	
	11. Benefits and Assistance	
	12. Family Medical Leave Act (FMLA) and Americans with Disabilities Act (ADA)	
	13. Employee Attire and Grooming Standards	
	14. Protected and Unprotected Speech, Religious, and Political Expression	

(Continued)

TABLE 4.4 (Continued)

Group / Category	Organizational DEI Strategy	Description and Approach
	Regretted Loss Assessment	Conduct an assessment, typically qualitative research (i.e., interviews and focus groups), to understand why different groups of employees voluntarily left for whom the organization regrets the loss.
	Pay Equity Analysis	Conduct an analysis to determine if compensation for different groups is fair and equitable, and eliminate the gaps.
	Workplace Accommodations Assessment	Assess needed workplace accommodations and implement the recommendations.
	Mentorship Program	Establish formal or informal mentorship programs focused on equitable development of all groups. The pairings may also intentionally cross lines of difference (i.e., cross-cultural or cross-gender mentorship) to foster DEI.
	Sponsorship Program	Establish formal or informal sponsorship programs focused on equitable advancement for all groups. The pairings may also intentionally cross lines of difference (i.e., cross-cultural or cross-gender sponsorship) to foster DEI.
	Allyship Program	Establish formal or informal allyship programs focused on active, not passive, engagement to dismantle barriers that impede equitable development and advancement and promote equal outcomes for all.
	Group-Specific Diverse Leadership Development Program	Design and deliver a training program for specific demographic groups (e.g., people of color, women, LGBTQIA+, veterans, whites, men, etc.) to help navigate specific challenges and opportunities related to the group, promote leadership development, and accelerate advancement. For example, the Redefine the Game Institute, NAMIC Leadership Seminar, and White Men as Fully Diversity Partners.
THE BRIDGING GROUP: Align & Connect		
Category 8: Assessment, Measurement, and Research	DEI Assessment	Conduct a comprehensive DEI assessment, typically quantitative research (i.e., survey) and qualitative research (i.e., interviews and focus groups), to understand culture and climate through the lens of DEI and implement the recommendations.
	DEI Pulse Surveys	Conduct a quarterly or monthly DEI assessment, typically quantitative research (e.g., survey), with a subset of the total employee populations to gauge culture and climate.

TABLE 4.4 (Continued)

	DEI Benchmarking or DEI Maturity Model	Conduct a benchmarking of DEI policies and practices against best practices and implement the recommendations.
	DEI Metrics and KPIs	Identify DEI metrics and key performance indicators (KPI) for the organization and possibly for specific divisions, departments, functions, and teams.
Category 9: DEI Communications	DEI Communications Plan	Design and implement a DEI communications plan including messaging, talking points, forums, events, and outreach to ensure effective buy-in, change management, and employee engagement.
Category 10: DEI Learning and Development	DEI Learning and Development	Design and deliver DEI training, learning, and development using in-person, virtual, blended, and e-learning modalities on topics such as mitigating bias, cultural competence, intercultural conflict resolution, mentorship, sponsorship, allyship, antiracism, inclusive leadership, and the like.
	DEI Coaching	Provide coaching for individual contributors, managers, and executives on topics related to DEI.
	Virtual Reality (VR) Immersions	Implement virtual reality (VR) immersions to foster human understanding and empathy.
	Learning Journeys	Design and implement DEI learning journeys including scenario-based learning journeys, microlearning journeys, preference- and competence-based learning journeys, high-performance learning journeys, and the like.
	Courageous Conversations	Create space to facilitate topical dialogues on sensitive or difficult topics among groups of people to promote greater understanding across differences.
	Microcommitments	Disseminate and solicit ongoing Microcommitments—small actions that can make a big difference—to foster behavior change and new habits.
Category 11: Connecting DEI and Sustainability	DEI and Environmental, Social, and Governance (ESG) Plan	Develop and implement a DEI and ESG plan that champions collaboration with diverse stakeholders and alignment between DEI and ESG initiatives locally and globally.
	Social, Community, and Environmental Investment	Invest in programs, initiatives, and ventures that deliver the triple bottom line of social return on investment, environmental return on investment, and financial return on investment.

(Continued)

187

TABLE 4.4 (Continued)

Group / Category	Organizational DEI Strategy	Description and Approach
THE EXTERNAL GROUP: Listen To & Serve Society		
Category 12: Community, Government Relations, and Philanthropy	Corporate Social Responsibility and Philanthropy	Align donations and giving with DEI objectives and goals.
	Social and Community Investment	Invest in programs, initiatives, and ventures that deliver the double bottom line of social return on investment and financial return on investment.
Category 13: Services and Products Development	Equity-Centered Product and Service Development	Embrace equity-centered design principles that intentionally center marginalized groups and communities throughout the product and service design process.
Category 14: Marketing and Customer Service	Diverse Brand Audit	Evaluate your brand, reputation, and image with a diverse set of stakeholders; and implement changes to marketing, advertising, and outreach.
	Multicultural Marketing	Implement an approach to marketing that acknowledges, understands, respects, honors, and uplifts the differences in culture of a target market.
	DEI Customer Service Training	Design and deliver DEI training with customer-facing employees including customer service representatives, call center representatives, recruiters, salespeople, and the like.
Category 15: Responsible Sourcing	Supplier Diversity Program	Increase the amount of procurement dollars spent with, and promote the growth of, suppliers and strategic business partners representing diverse socioeconomic groups (e.g., small, locally owned, women-owned, Black-owned, Hispanic-owned, AAPI-owned, veteran-owned, LGBTQIA+-owned businesses, etc.) to foster innovation, create jobs, and promote inclusive community economic development.
	Group-Specific Diverse Supplier Development Program	Design and deliver a supplier training program for specific demographic groups to navigate barriers more effectively, build capacity, drive procurement spending, and grow their business.

Determining DEI Strategies

A series of *DEI strategy statements* represent the specific initiatives, activities, and actions you will undertake to fulfill your DEI objectives and achieve your DEI goals. Each DEI objective should have one or more DEI strategies. It is not uncommon to have 5 to 10 DEI strategies, or more, for a single DEI objective.

Formatting Your DEI Strategy Statements

Here is a simple format for a *DEI strategy statement*:

[Action verb] [an output].

Examples of action verbs include: "learn," "apply," "complete," "achieve," "accomplish," "attain," and "realize."

While personal and organizational DEI objectives are centered on *outcomes*, or final results that are difficult to measure or validate, personal and organizational DEI strategies are centered on *outputs*, or intermediate results that are easy to measure/report (refer back to Table 2.1 for a full summary of the difference between outputs and outcomes). As you saw in **Step 2: DEI Imperatives**, DEI objectives are defined according to outcomes such as increasing awareness of different cultures across the globe, increasing awareness of intercultural conflict styles to resolve conflicts effectively and harmoniously, being an effective sponsor and advocating for people of color, and being an ally in equal partnership with women. Here in **Step 4: DEI Initiatives**, DEI strategies are defined according to outputs such as the completion of educational classes, books, magazines and articles, travel, experiential learning and development, journaling, and personal interactions.

Examples of Personal DEI Strategies

Let's look at an example of how to arrive at **personal DEI strategies** that brings Steps 1 through 4 together.

For illustrative purposes, and continuing an example from before, let's assume that during **Step 1: DEI Inventory for People** you took three personal DEI assessments—the Gender-Science IAT, the Race IAT, and the Intrinsic Inclusion Inventory™ (I3™) for People—with the following results:

Personal DEI Assessment Results
- Your Gender-Science IAT results found a "slight preference" of associating women with science and men with liberal arts.
- Your Race IAT results found a "slight automatic preference" for white people over Black people.
- Your I3™ results placed you at the second level.

During **Step 2: DEI Imperatives**, you establish the following personal DEI objective and goals:

- **Personal DEI Objective:** Be an inclusive leader that personalizes individuals, treats people and groups fairly, and leverages the thinking of diverse groups.
- **Personal DEI Goals:**
  - Mitigate the impact of my Gender-Science IAT results being a "slight preference" of associating women with science and men with liberal arts by improving my diverse 360° assessment scores by 10% with women in science, technology, engineering, and math (STEM) over the next 12 months.
  - Mitigate the impact of my Race IAT results being a "slight automatic preference" for white people over Black people by improving my 360° assessment scores by 10% with people of color over the next 12 months.

Increase my I3™ rating from the second level to the third level by the end of the year.

During **Step 3: DEI Insights**, you decide to embrace Intrinsic Inclusion™ as a "What Works" model or personal DEI promising and proven practice that defines your personal DEI preference and competence model (i.e., personal DEI core preferences and competences):

- Personal DEI Preference and Competence Model: Intrinsic Inclusion™
- Personal DEI Core Preferences and Competences: Shared Trust, Significant Emotional Event/Relationship, Connected Understanding, and Respectful Empathy

This leads you here in **Step 4: DEI Initiatives** to arrive at the personal DEI strategy statements summarized in Table 4.5 to fulfill your personal DEI objective and achieve your personal DEI goals.

In one of the final sections of this step, "Personal DEI Strategic Plan Example," I will round out this personal DEI strategy example by assigning corresponding personal DEI measures to gauge progress against each strategy shown in Table 4.5. As you will see, this will complete your personal DEI strategic plan.

Examples of Organizational DEI Strategies

Let's now look at an example of how to arrive at **organizational DEI strategies** that also brings Steps 1 through 4 together.

For illustrative purposes, and continuing an example from **Step 1: DEI Inventory for Organizations** (see Table 1.19), let's assume your organization completed three organizational DEI assessments—BCT's DEI Workforce and Workplace Assessment™ (DWWA™), which evaluates organizational culture and climate; the Intrinsic Inclusion Inventory™ for Organizations, which measures inclusive behaviors; and the Global Diversity, Equity & Inclusion Benchmarks (GDEIB), which provides a global benchmark of DEI capability and maturity—with the following findings, evidence, implications, and recommendations in "The Bridging Group: Align and Connect" category of the GDEIB (excerpted directly from Table 1.19):

TABLE 4.5 Personal DEI Strategy Example

Personal DEI Learning Journey

Focus: *Complete an Intrinsic Inclusion™ learning journey focused on the four inclusion accelerators of Shared Trust, Significant Emotional Event/Relationship, Connected Understanding, and Respectful Empathy.*

	Crawl	*Walk*	*Run*
	Time: 4 months	Time: 4 months	Time: 4 months
Learn: *Engage the Head*			
Strategies to Learn: *Knowledge and Awareness*	(1) Books, Magazines, Articles, and Blogs: Read the book, *Intrinsic Inclusion™: Rebooting Your Biased Brain.* (2) Books, Magazines, Articles, and Blogs: Visit the Intrinsic Inclusion™ website to learn more about the four inclusion accelerators.	(6) Books, Magazines, Articles, and Blogs: Read articles on Intrinsic Inclusion™ by Janet B. Reid, PhD, and Vincent Brown in *Psychology Today.* (7) TV Shows, Videos, and Podcasts: Watch lecture or seminar by the authors, Janet B. Reid, PhD and Vincent Brown, on YouTube.	(11) Books, Magazines, Articles, and Blogs: Read the book, *The Phoenix Principles: Leveraging Inclusion to Transform Your Company* and complete *The Phoenix Principles Work Book.* (12) Training Programs: Attend a facilitated learning experience by an Intrinsic Inclusion™ certified instructor to learn the methodology and participate in expertly facilitated tasks, exercises, and activities for applying the inclusion accelerators.
Do: *Employ the Hands*			
Strategies to Do: *Tasks, Exercises, and Activities*	(3) Travel, Site Visits, and Excursions: Shadow an inclusive leader for a day to observe their behavior and/or interview an inclusive leader to gain insight.	(8) Workplace Activity: Participate in a workplace event or celebration sponsored by the organization's Black employee resource group (ERG).	(13) Experiential Learning and Development Programs and Workplace Activities: Apply the MODE model after the facilitated learning experience at work while seeking feedback from Black and women colleagues ("Field Testing" chapter, "Building MODE into the Routine" section).
Inspire: *Enrich the Heart*			
Strategies to Inspire: *Appreciation, Encouragement, and Storytelling*	(4) Journaling: Maintain a journal. (5) Personal Interactions: Share the objectives, goals, strategies, and measures for the overall learning journey with friends or family members to provide motivation and accountability.	(9) Journaling: Maintain a journal. (10) Storytelling: Share the key takeaways and lessons learned from these experiences with a colleague.	(14) Journaling: Maintain a journal. (15) Communities of Learning: Join a diverse peer learning group from the facilitated learning experience that meets regularly to share stories, offer encouragement, and hold each other accountable to meet learning and development objectives.

THE BRIDGING GROUP: *Align and Connect*			
Findings	**Evidence (Source)**	**Implications**	**Recommendations**
• The organization has a welcoming culture but could improve with underrepresented groups. • Employees and managers need to increase their DEI competences.	• The DWWA™ reported a statistically significant lower commitment to DEI by managers and supervisors when compared to all people. *(DWWA™ Culture and Climate Survey)* • The average employee scored at the second level and the average manager and supervisor scored at the lowest level on the Intrinsic Inclusion Inventory™ for People. *(I3™ for Organizations)* • The Intrinsic Inclusion Inventory™ (I3™) for Organizations found that 43% of employees demonstrated intrinsically inclusive behaviors. *(I3™ for Organizations)* • "The organization has a welcoming and friendly culture but far less so for underrepresented groups." *(Focus Groups)*	• The organization needs to foster an environment of greater fairness and equity; all employees can play a role and managers must play a central role.	• Implement Intrinsic Inclusion™ training for all people. • Implement an inclusive leadership program for all managers and supervisors.
	• The organization's current training curriculum does not include any DEI-specific topics; there are no Employee Resource Groups (ERGs). *(DEI HR Policies and Practices Evaluation Audit)* • The organization scored at Level 3: Proactive on the GDEIB in the Internal Group. *(GDEIB Benchmarking)*		

During **Step 2: DEI Imperatives**, you establish the following organizational DEI objective and goals in Category 9: DEI Communication and Category 10: DEI Learning and Development:

Organizational DEI Objective:

- **Category 9: DEI Communications and Category 10: DEI Learning and Development:** Design and execute an organization-wide training and awareness program that fosters intrinsically inclusive behaviors.

Organizational DEI Goals:

- Increase the number of employees exhibiting intrinsically inclusive behaviors by 10% by the end of the next fiscal year.
- Increase the number of managers and supervisors exhibiting intrinsically inclusive behaviors by 15% by the end of the next fiscal year.

During **Step 3: DEI Insights**, your organization's leadership decides to implement the following promising and proven practices that relate to learning and development:

- Intrinsic Inclusion™ to foster inclusive behaviors for all employees.
- The Rali LX platform for scenario-based micro-learning journeys for learning and development of employees, managers, and supervisors.
- *Through My Eyes*™ Virtual Reality (VR) to provide experiential learning for managers and supervisors.

This leads your organization here in **Step 4: DEI Initiatives** to arrive at the organizational DEI strategy shown in Table 4.6 to fulfill your organizational DEI objective and achieve your organizational DEI goals.

TABLE 4.6   **Organizational DEI Strategy Example**

THE BRIDGING GROUP: *Align and Connect*	
Category 9: DEI Communications	(1) Develop a DEI communications plan that includes managers and supervisors as a segment.
Category 10: DEI Learning and Development	(2) Deliver scenario-based microlearning journeys for all employees, focused on Intrinsic Inclusion™ (using the Rali LX platform).
	(3) Implement an inclusive management program for all managers and leaders (using the Rali LX platform and leveraging *Through My Eyes*™ Virtual Reality (VR)).

In the next section, I will explain how to define DEI measures to gauge progress against a given strategy. Then, in one of the final sections of this step, "Organizational DEI Strategic Plan Example," I will round out this organizational DEI strategy example by assigning corresponding organizational DEI measures to each strategy shown in Table 4.6 and more. As you will see, this will complete your organizational DEI strategic plan.

Defining DEI Measures

As mentioned in **Step 2: DEI Imperatives**, a *DEI measure* is a number or value related to a DEI process, activity, program, effort, or initiative that can be summed and/or averaged according to a particular category. A measure is unit specific such as the preference score on the IAT or HBDI® competence score on the I3™ or IDI®; and peer ratings in a specific category of a diverse 360° assessment. The metrics and KPIs used in **Step 2: DEI Imperatives** for your DEI goals were built upon the fundamental building block of measures.

The way you gauge progress against a strategy is by tracking the appropriate measures. Because strategies are centered on outputs, measures gauge progress toward outputs (i.e., intermediate results) that ultimately lead to outcomes (i.e., final results). Each strategy should have one or more measures. For people and organizations, we typically recommend one to three measures for each strategy. For organizations, it is at this juncture that your DEI Council will make these selections.

> To aid in your process, go to **www.datarivendei.com** to find an extensive and comprehensive list, or menu, of personal DEI measures for each of the personal DEI strategies previously identified in Table 4.2 and organizational DEI measures for each of the organizational DEI strategies previously identified in Table 4.4.

Formatting Your DEI Measures Statements

Here is a simple format for a *DEI measures statement*:

[Action verb] [a measure] *to* [target] *within/by* [timeframe].

Once you have determined your measures, undertake these steps to finalize your measures statement:

1. Choose an appropriate *action verb* for your measures statement such as "achieve," "increase/decrease," "improve/mitigate/eliminate," "reduce/close," or simply "change."

2. Determine a *target*—a mark you hope to achieve—for each measure.

3. Select a *timeframe*—a time period—within which you plan to reach the target.

4. Identify the *data source* to confirm that you have the necessary data to track your measures. For people, the data can often be collected manually by simply tracking your activities. For organizations, the data may be obtained from a human resources information system (HRIS), learning management system (LMS), enterprise resource planning (ERP) system, customer relationship management (CRM) system, or other DEI-related data system. Be mindful that you can only measure that for which you have the requisite data.

5. Decide on the *frequency* upon which the data can/will be collected and analyzed. For most measures, the frequency is often driven by the strategy. For example, if a pay equity initiative must be completed within six months, or a DEI council meets quarterly, or a training takes place monthly, then the frequency is self-evident.

6. Identify the *owner* of the strategy, that is, the person(s) accountable for making certain the strategy is executed.

If you go to **www.datadrivendei.com**, you will find an extensive and comprehensive list, or menu, of DEI measures organized by learn-do-inspire / head-hands-heart for people and organized by the four groups and 15 categories of the GDEIB model for organizations.

Personal DEI Strategic Plan Example

An example of a full and complete **personal DEI strategic plan** is shown in Table 4.4. Leveraging prior examples, it is replete with personal DEI objectives, goals, strategies, and measures per the OGSM strategic planning framework; learn-do-inspire / head-hands-heart methodology; and Crawl-Walk-Run approach. As you can see from Table 4.7, defining measures for strategies is relatively straightforward and a much easier endeavor than choosing goals for objectives.

TABLE 4.7 Sample Personal DEI Strategic Plan

Objectives:	Inclusion: Be an inclusive leader who personalizes individuals, treats people and groups fairly, and leverages the thinking of diverse groups.		
Goals:	1. Improve my diverse 360° assessment scores by 10% with women in science, technology, engineering, and math (STEM) over the next 12 months (to mitigate the impact of my Gender-Science IAT results being a "slight preference" of associating women with science and men with liberal arts). 2. Improve my 360° assessment scores by 10% with people of color over the next 12 months (to mitigate the impact of my Race IAT results being a "slight automatic preference" for white people over Black people). 3. Increase my I3™ rating from the second level to the third level by the end of the year.		
	Personal DEI Learning Journey		
	Focus: *Complete an Intrinsic Inclusion™ learning journey focused on the four inclusion accelerators of Shared Trust, Significant Emotional Event/Relationship, Connected Understanding, and Respectful Empathy.*		
	Crawl	*Walk*	*Run*
	Time: 4 months	Time: 4 months	Time: 4 months
	Learn: *Engage the Head*		
Strategies to Learn: *Knowledge and Awareness*	(1) Books, Magazines, Articles, and Blogs: Read the book, *Intrinsic Inclusion: Rebooting Your Biased Brain.* (2) Books, Magazines, Articles, and Blogs: Visit the Intrinsic Inclusion™ website to learn more about the four inclusion accelerators.	(6) Books, Magazines, Articles, and Blogs: Read articles on Intrinsic Inclusion™ by Janet B. Reid, PhD, and Vincent Brown in *Psychology Today.* (7) TV Shows, Videos and Podcasts: Watch lecture or seminar by the authors, Janet B. Reid, PhD and Vincent Brown, on YouTube.	(11) Books, Magazines, Articles, and Blogs: Read the book, *The Phoenix Principles: Leveraging Inclusion to Transform Your Company* and complete *The Phoenix Principles Work Book.* (12) Training Programs: Attend a facilitated learning experience by an Intrinsic Inclusion™ certified instructor to learn the methodology and participate in expertly facilitated tasks, exercises, and activities for applying the inclusion accelerators.

TABLE 4.7 (Continued)

Measures:	Complete one (1) book within four (4) months.	Complete three (3) articles within four (4) months.	Complete one (1) book within four (4) months.
	Complete one (1) full review of the website within four (4) months.	Complete one (1) video within four (4) months.	Complete one (1) training program within four (4) months.
Do: *Employ the Hands*			
Strategies to Do: *Tasks, Exercises, and Activities*	(3) Travel, Site Visits, and Excursions: Shadow an inclusive leader for a day to observe their behavior and/or interview an inclusive leader to gain insight.	(8) Workplace Activities: Participate in a workplace event or celebration sponsored by the Black employee resource group (ERG).	(13) Experiential Learning and Development Programs and Workplace Activities: Apply the MODE model after the facilitated learning experience at work while seeking feedback from Black and women colleagues ("Field Testing" chapter, "Building MODE into the Routine" section).
Measures:	Shadow and/or interview one (1) inclusive leader within four (4) months.	Participate in one (1) event or celebration within four (4) months.	Complete four (4) exercises applying the MODE model at work within four (4) months.
Inspire: *Enrich the Heart*			
Strategies to Inspire: *Appreciation, Encouragement, and Storytelling*	(15) Journaling: Maintain a journal. (5) Personal Interactions: Share the objectives, goals, strategies, and measures for the overall learning journey with friends or family members to provide motivation and accountability.	(9) Journaling: Maintain a journal. (10) Storytelling: Share the key takeaways and lessons learned from experiences thus far with a colleague.	(14) Journaling: Maintain a journal. (15) Communities of Learning: Join a diverse peer learning group from the facilitated learning experience that meets regularly to share stories, offer encouragement, and hold each another accountable to meet learning and development objectives.

(Continued)

TABLE 4.7 (Continued)

Objectives:	Inclusion: Be an inclusive leader who personalizes individuals, treats people and groups fairly, and leverages the thinking of diverse groups.		
Measures:	Complete one (1) journal entry each week for four (4) months (16 weeks).	Complete one (1) journal entry each week for four (4) months (16 weeks).	Complete one (1) journal entry each week for four (4) months (16 weeks).
	Share four (4) key takeaways and lessons learned with friends or family members within 4 months.	Share four (4) key takeaways and lessons learned with a colleague within 4 months.	Complete one (1) peer learning group meeting each month for four (4) months.
	Spaces: • Home • Work • Intrinsic Inclusion™ website	Spaces: • Home • Work • Movies and/or streaming video	Spaces: • Home • Work • Meeting space
	Relationships: • Friends • Family members	Relationships: • Inclusive leader • Colleague	Relationships: • Colleagues • Peer learning group
	Tools and Structures: • Journal • Intrinsic Inclusion™ book	Tools and Structures: • Journal • Intrinsic Inclusion™ articles	Tools and Structures: • Journal • Intrinsic Inclusion™ materials

Organizational DEI Strategic Plan Example

An example of a full and complete **organizational DEI strategic plan** is shown in Table 4.8. Leveraging prior examples, it is replete with organizational DEI objectives, goals, strategies, and measures, and is organized according to the 4 groups and a subset of the 15 categories of the GDEIB model. As you can see from Table 4.8, defining measures for strategies is relatively straightforward and a much easier endeavor than choosing goals for objectives.

TABLE 4.8 Sample Organizational DEI Strategic Plan

THE FOUNDATION GROUP: *Drive the Strategy*		
Objective #1:	**Category 1: Vision, Strategy, and Business Impact and Category 3: DEI Structure and Implementation:** Cultivate an inclusive workplace culture by creating and sustaining an atmosphere of psychological safety and trust that fully leverages unique perspectives and empowers all voices.	
Goals:	1.1 Eliminate statistically significant differences in commitment to diversity by managers/supervisors when compared to all employees.	
	1.2 Increase our GDEIB overall benchmark from Level 2 ("Reactive") to Level 3 ("Proactive") within three (3) years.	
Strategies:	**Measures:**	**Owner:**
(1) Establish a DEI council.	Establish DEI council within twelve (12) months.	Jacqueline Doe
(2) Create a DEI charter.	Create DEI charter within twelve (12) months.	Jermaine Doe
(3) Tie compensation for executives, managers, and supervisors to achieving DEI objectives and goals.	Allocate 10% of bonus pool as an incentive for achieving 90% of DEI objectives and goals.	Jessica Doe

(Continued)

TABLE 4.8 (Continued)

Strategies:	Measures:	Owner:
THE INTERNAL GROUP: Attract and Retain People		
Objective #2:	**Category 4: Recruitment and Category 5: Advancement and Retention:** Renew a diverse, representative, and high-performing workforce that draws from all segments of society by achieving diverse representation at every level throughout the organization.	
Goals:	2.1 Increase representation of people of color (e.g., Black/African American, Hispanic, and Native American) employees by 10%.	
	2.2 Increase representation of people of color (e.g., Black/African American, Hispanic, and Native American) supervisors and executives by 5% within three (3) years.	
	2.3 Increase representation of women supervisors and executives by 5% within three (3) years.	
	2.4 Increase representation of persons with disabilities employees by 10% within two (2) years.	
Strategies:	**Measures:**	**Owner:**
(4) Create five employee resource groups (ERGs) for African American or Black employees, Hispanic employees, Asian American and Pacific Islander employees, women employees, and LGBTQIA+ employees.	• Establish ERGs within six (6) months.	Jennifer Doe
(5) Conduct a Regretted Loss Assessment to understand underlying reasons for talent attrition.	• Complete Regretted Loss Assessment within six (6) months.	Jacqueline Doe
(6) Implement inclusive recruiting program that expands the range of partner colleges and universities representing people with disabilities and Indigenous people.	• Complete design and begin execution of inclusive recruiting program by nine (9) months.	Jermaine Doe
(7) Revise hiring policies and procedures to include inclusive language for position descriptions, diverse interview panels, and diverse interview slates.	• Complete revision of hiring policies and procedures within twelve (12) months.	Jessica Doe

TABLE 4.8   **(Continued)**

(8) Design and deliver a mentorship, sponsorship, and allyship training program for managers and leaders using the Ally Conversation Toolkit (ACT).	• Complete mentorship, sponsorship, and ACT allyship training program for managers and leaders within six (6) months. ○ Achieve 100% attendance of participants. ○ Achieve 4.5/5.0 or higher reaction score to content from participants. ○ Achieve 4.5/5.0 of higher reaction score to facilitation from participants.	Jennifer Doe
(9) Design and deliver a leadership development program for mid-level women managers employees. (10) Design and deliver a leadership development program for Black, Hispanic, and Native American employees.	• Complete leadership development programs within six (6) months. ○ Achieve 100% completion of participants ○ Achieve 4.5/5.0 of higher reaction score to content from participants ○ Achieve 4.5/5.0 of higher reaction score to facilitation from participants ○ Achieve 80% of higher test scores from participants	Jason Doe

THE BRIDGING GROUP: *Align and Connect*

Objective #3:	**Category 9: DEI Communications and Category 10: DEI Learning and Development:** Design and execute an organization-wide training and awareness program that fosters intrinsically inclusive behaviors.
Goals:	3.1 Increase the number of employees exhibiting intrinsically inclusive behaviors by 10% by the end of the next fiscal year.

Strategies:	**Measures:**	**Owner:**
(11) Develop a DEI communications plan that includes managers and supervisors as a segment.	• Complete the DEI communications plan within six (6) months. • Establish three DEI-specific internal communications channels that are leveraged quarterly, at minimum.	Jason Doe

(Continued)

TABLE 4.8 (Continued)

Strategies:	Measures:	Owner:
(12) Deliver scenario-based microlearning journeys for all employees focused on Intrinsic Inclusion™ (using the Rali LX platform).	• Complete scenario-based microlearning for all employees within twelve (12) months. ○ Achieve 95% attendance of participants. ○ Achieve 4.5/5.0 of higher reaction score to content from participants. ○ Achieve 4.5/5.0 of higher reaction score to facilitation from participants. • Achieve 80% of higher test scores from participants.	Jennifer Doe
(13) Implement an inclusive leadership program for all managers and leaders (using the Rali LX platform and leveraging *Through My Eyes*™ Virtual Reality (VR)).	• Complete inclusive leadership program for managers and leaders within six (6) months. ○ Achieve 95% attendance of participants ○ Achieve 4.5/5.0 of higher reaction score to content from participants. ○ Achieve 4.5/5.0 of higher reaction score to facilitation from participants. • Achieve 80% of higher test scores from participants.	Jack Doe
(14) Host quarterly "Courageous Conversations."	• Conduct one (1) per quarter for a total of four (4) sessions.	Jessica Doe

THE EXTERNAL GROUP: *Listen To and Serve Society*

Objective #4:	**Category 12: Community, Government Relations, and Philanthropy and Category 15: Responsible Sourcing:** Increase diverse supplier spend to foster supply chain innovation and promote community economic development.
Goals:	3.2 Increase procurement spend with diverse suppliers, including minority-, women-, veteran-, and LGBTQIA+-owned to 30% within twelve (12) months. 3.3 Grow the revenues of minority-owned, women-, veteran-, and LGBTQIA+-owned suppliers by 25%.

Strategies:	Measures:	Owner:
(15) Conduct a Diverse Supplier Spend Analysis, which analyzes Tier 1 and Tier 2 procurement spend with diverse suppliers by category.	• Complete Diverse Supplier Spend Analysis within six (6) months.	Jacqueline Doe
(16) Establish partnerships with organizations representing minority-owned, women-owned, veteran-owned, and LGBTQIA+-owned suppliers	• Formalize partnerships within six (6) months.	Jermaine Doe
(17) Implement a diverse supplier development program	• Launch the diverse supplier development program within twelve (12) months.	Jessica Doe
(18) Establish a supplier diversity program.	• Hire a director of supplier diversity within nine (9) months. • Launch supplier diversity program within twelve (12) months.	Jennifer Doe

STEP 5

DEI Impact—
Evaluate Results

Data is a mirror. . . of our biases and our realities.

DEI is a never-ending journey.

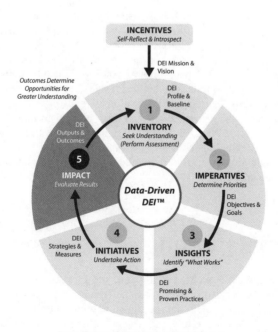

Data-Driven DEI—Step 5: DEI Impact

There has been a pattern throughout this book of combining quantitative and qualitative tenets:

- In **Step 1: DEI Inventory**, we saw how a good DEI assessment combines quantitative research methods (i.e., surveys) with qualitative research methods (i.e., interviews and focus groups).

- In **Step 2: DEI Imperatives,** we combined qualitative objectives with quantitative goals.

- In **Step 3: DEI Insights** and **Step 4: DEI Initiatives**, we leveraged promising and proven practices, to determine qualitative strategies and quantitative measures.

Here in **Step 5: DEI Impact**, we continue this pattern by presenting two important pathways to determine and demonstrate DEI impact. First, we dive into DEI data reporting, which leans more heavily on quantitative traditions and science. Most commonly in the form of DEI scorecards and dashboards, DEI data reporting is about gauging progress, determining impact, and engendering accountability for DEI performance. We round out this discussion with a focus on evaluating results and generating findings to comprehensively demonstrate DEI outputs and outcomes. As you will see, this discussion makes clear how re-administering the same DEI assessment you identified in **Step 1: DEI Inventory** (or something comparable) can be a key component of evaluating results and generating findings here in final **Step 5: DEI Impact.** You will recall that the DEI assessment established a baseline or starting data point for your *Data-Driven DEI* journey. By conducting re-assessments, you can compare results and essentially establish new baselines or reference data points for the *Data-Driven DEI* cycle to iterate from Step 1 through Step 5 over and over again.

We conclude this step by delving into the power of DEI storytelling, which leans more heavily on qualitative traditions and art. Data storytelling is about humanization, communication, motivation, and inspiration by uplifting voices and sharing narratives of DEI success and lessons learned. It integrates results and findings to craft and communicate compelling DEI stories using narrative, data, and visuals. As you will see, DEI data storytelling enables you to personalize the DEI journey, contextualize data, chronicle progress, synthesize findings, integrate results, and comprehensively demonstrate impact.

DEI Data Reporting

Data reporting is the process of collecting data and formatting it in a way that it is easily understood, interpreted, and analyzed. *DEI data reporting* enables you to understand, interpret, and analyze DEI data to gauge progress, determine impact, evaluate results, and engender accountability with you and others for DEI performance. More specifically, DEI data reporting offers three value propositions:

1. **Gauge Progress**—In **Step 4: DEI Initiatives**, we introduced "outputs" as intermediate results that are linked to the completion of strategies. DEI data reporting

enables you to gauge progress by tracking and monitoring the DEI measures associated with outputs—the various processes, activities, programs, efforts, and initiatives you have undertaken to achieve your DEI objectives and goals.

2. **Determine Impact**—In **Step 2: DEI Imperatives**, we introduced "outcomes" as final results that are linked to the achievement of objectives. DEI data reporting enables you to track and monitor the DEI metrics and KPIs that determine your and your organization's impact and effectiveness in accomplishing outcomes— the goals associated with your objectives.

3. **Engender Accountability**—DEI data reporting helps in holding you and others accountable for achieving DEI objectives and goals by clearly capturing and communicating expectations and performance. DEI data reporting provides constant reinforcement and reminders to "do the right things" and constant feedback of whether you and your organization are "doing things right." In a growing set of circumstances, rewards, compensation, and bonuses are tied to performance against DEI objectives and goals to foster greater accountability.

Two of the primary ways that DEI data can be reported effectively are a DEI scorecard and a DEI dashboard. Next, I will define scorecards and dashboards, provide examples, and help you decide which one is the best for you and/or your organization.

DEI Scorecards

A *scorecard* is a snapshot of the current and target values for measures, metrics, and KPIs (i.e., goals that quantify objectives and measures that quantify strategies) along with a trend analysis (i.e., increasing, decreasing, or unchanged relative to the target) over a period. Scorecards are static reports generated at a specific point in time and then updated at specific intervals such as weekly or monthly. Scorecards are useful for tracking and monitoring progress toward achieving targets for measures, metrics, and KPIs at a strategic and high level, and are related to a specific topic such as DEI. Strategic decisions can be made by examining the gap between current and target values for measures, metrics, and KPIs, identifying the highest-priority and/or largest gaps, and focusing efforts and resources accordingly.

You can easily and manually create your own personal DEI scorecard (examples and templates are provided in the next section). There are also personal goal-tracking, habit-tracking, task-tracking, and planning apps, tools, and platforms that can technology-enable a personal DEI scorecard. Similarly, organizations can manually or automatically create an **organizational DEI scorecard** (examples and mockups are provided in the section entitled "An Organizational DEI Scorecard"), albeit with varying degrees of effort based on the extent to which data is available, accessible, integrated, and centralized. The format and structure for an organizational DEI scorecard can also be cascaded down to generate divisional, departmental, and other team-specific DEI scorecards. You and others, including executives, managers, and supervisors, can then be held accountable for your performance, as a scorecard paints a clear and ongoing picture of what is expected and how you are performing against those expectations.

Continuing an example from the previous step, if your personal DEI objective is to "Be an inclusive leader . . ." and one of your associated goals is to "Improve my 360° assessment scores by 10% . . ." and one of your associated strategies is to "Read articles about Intrinsic Inclusion™" and one of your associated measures is to "Complete three (3) articles within four (4) months," then a personal DEI scorecard could allow you to easily track and monitor your progress toward achieving the 10% increase and completing the three articles and the extent to which your performance has increased, decreased, or remained unchanged relative to these targets, say, over the past month.

Continuing another example from the previous step, if your organizational DEI objective is to "Renew a diverse, representative, and high-performing workforce . . ." and one of your associated goals is to "Increase representation of supervisors and executives of color by 5% within three years . . ." and one of your associated strategies is to "Design and deliver a leadership development program for Black, Hispanic, and Native American employees . . ." and one of your associated measures is to "Achieve 100% completion of participants in a leadership development program . . ." then a scorecard can allow you to easily track and monitor your progress toward achieving the 5% increase and the 100% completion rate and the extent to which your performance has increased, decreased, or remained unchanged relative to these targets, say, over the past quarter.

Scorecards can be presented in a variety of ways as tables, charts, and graphics using office software (i.e., documents, slides, spreadsheets), within an intranet or portal, or as a part of a dashboard.

A Personal DEI Scorecard

An example of a **personal DEI scorecard** is shown in Table 5.1 using the same elements as the personal DEI strategic plan in the previous step. In addition to capturing objectives, goals, strategies, and measures, it also tracks the baseline from **Step 1: Inventory** (assessment), the target from **Step 2: Imperatives**, and the actual results you have achieved after you leveraged **Step 3: Insights** to inform and implement the strategies from **Step 4: Initiatives**. The score is a measure of your performance ranging from 0 (poor performance) to 100 (excellent performance) in achieving your target. It is simply calculated as follows:

$$Score = \left(Actual \, / \, Target\right) * 100$$

The *total score* represents the average across all scores.

If you go to **www.datadrivendei.com**, you will find a downloadable template for developing a personal DEI scorecard.

TABLE 5.1   A Personal DEI Scorecard

OBJECTIVES AND GOALS					
Objective:	Inclusion: Be an inclusive leader who personalizes individuals, treats people and groups fairly, and leverages the thinking of diverse groups.				
No.	**Goal**	**Baseline**	**Target**	**Actual**	**Score**
1.	Improve my diverse 360° assessment scores by 10% with women in science, technology, engineering, and math (STEM) over the next 12 months (to mitigate the impact of my Gender-Science IAT results being a "slight preference" of associating women with science and men with liberal arts).	4.17	4.54	4.43	98
2.	Improve my 360° assessment scores by 10% with people of color over the next 12 months (to mitigate the impact of my Race IAT results being a "slight automatic preference" for white people over Black people).	4.05	4.45	4.32	97
3.	Increase my I3™ rating from the second level to the third level by the end of the year.	Level 2	Level 3	Level 3	100
				TOTAL	**98**

STRATEGIES AND MEASURES					
No.	**Strategy**	**Measure**	**Target**	**Actual**	**Score**
Crawl (Time: 4 months)					
(1)	**Books, Magazines, Articles, and Blogs:** Read the book, *Intrinsic Inclusion: Rebooting Your Biased Brain.*	Complete one (1) book within four (4) months.	1	1	100
(2)	**TV Shows, Videos, and Podcasts:** Visit the Intrinsic Inclusion™ website to learn more about the four inclusion accelerators.	Complete one (1) full review of the website within four (4) months.	1	1	100
(3)	**Travel, Site Visits, and Excursions:** Shadow an inclusive leader for a day to observe their behavior and/or interview an inclusive leader to gain insight.	Shadow and/or interview one (1) inclusive leader within four (4) months.	1	1	100

(Continued)

TABLE 5.1   (Continued)

No.	Strategy	Measure	Target	Actual	Score
(4)	**Journaling:** Maintain a journal.	Complete one (1) journal entry each week for four (4) months or sixteen (16) weeks.	16	14	88
(5)	**Personal Interactions:** Share the objectives, goals, strategies, and measures for the overall learning journey with friends or family members to provide motivation and accountability.	Share four (4) key takeaways and lessons learned with friends or family members within four (4) months.	4	3	75
				SCORE	87

Walk (Time: 4 months)

No.	Strategy	Measure	Target	Actual	Score
(6)	**Books, Magazines, Articles, and Blogs:** Read articles on Intrinsic Inclusion™ by Janet B. Reid, PhD, and Vincent Brown in *Psychology Today*.	Complete three (3) articles within four (4) months.	3	4	133
(7)	**TV Shows, Videos, and Podcasts:** Watch lecture or seminar by the authors, Janet B. Reid, PhD, and Vincent Brown, on YouTube.	Complete one (1) video within four (4) months.	1	1	100
(8)	**Workplace Activity:** Participate in a workplace event or celebration sponsored by the organization's Black employee resource group (ERG).	Participate in one (1) event or celebration within four (4) months.	4	3	75
(9)	**Journaling:** Maintain a journal.	Complete one (1) journal entry each week for four (4) months or sixteen (16) weeks.	16	12	75
(10)	**Storytelling:** Share the key takeaways and lessons learned from these experiences with a colleague.	Share four (4) key takeaways and lessons learned with a colleague within four (4) months	4	4	100
				SCORE	86

TABLE 5.1 (Continued)

No.	Strategy	Measure	Target	Actual	Score
Run (Time: 4 months)					
(11)	**Books, Magazines, Articles, and Blogs:** Read the book, *The Phoenix Principles: Leveraging Inclusion to Transform Your Company* and complete *The Phoenix Principles Work Book*.	Complete one (1) book within four (4) months.	1	1	100
(12)	**Training Programs:** Attend a facilitated learning experience (FLE) by an Intrinsic Inclusion™ certified instructor to learn the methodology and participate in expertly facilitated tasks, exercises, and activities for applying the inclusion accelerators.	Complete one (1) training program within four (4) months.	1	1	100
(13)	**Experiential Learning and Development Programs and Workplace Activities:** Apply the MODE model after the FLE at work while seeking feedback from Black and women colleagues ("Field Testing" chapter, "Building MODE into the Routine" section).	Complete four (4) exercises applying the MODE model at work within four (4) months.	4	5	125
(14)	**Journaling:** Maintain a journal.	Complete one (1) journal entry each week for four (4) months or sixteen (16) weeks.	16	17	106
(15)	**Communities of Learning:** Join a diverse peer learning group from the FLE that meets regularly to share stories, offer encouragement, and hold each other accountable to meet learning and development objectives.	Complete one (1) peer learning group meeting each month for four (4) months.	1	1	100
				SCORE	109
				Total Score	93

An Organizational DEI Scorecard

An example of an **organizational DEI scorecard** can be found in Table 5.2 using the same elements as a portion of the organizational DEI strategic plan in the previous step. In identical fashion to the personal DEI scorecard, it captures objectives, goals, strategies, and measures; baseline, target, and actual figures; a score and a total score.

> If you go to **www.datadrivendei.com**, you will find a downloadable template for developing an organizational DEI scorecard.

TABLE 5.2 An Organizational DEI Scorecard

OBJECTIVES AND GOALS

Objective #2:	Category 4: Recruitment and Category 5: Advancement and Retention: Renew a diverse, representative, and high-performing workforce that draws from all segments of society by achieving diverse representation at every level throughout the organization.				
No.	**Goal**	**Baseline**	**Target**	**Actual**	**Score**
2.1	Increase representation of people of color by 50%.	6.0%	9.0%	10.0%	111
2.2	Increase representation of supervisors and executives of color by 25% within three years.	3.0%	3.75%	3.5%	93
2.3	Increase representation of women supervisors and executives by 10% within three years.	30.0%	33.0%	32.5%	98
2.4	Increase representation of persons with disabilities employees by 40% within two years.	2.0%	2.8%	2.5%	89
				Total Score	**98**

STRATEGIES AND MEASURES

No.	Strategy	Measure	Target	Actual	Score
(1)	Conduct a Regretted Loss Assessment to understand underlying reasons for talent attrition.	Complete Regretted Loss Assessment within six (6) months.	1	1	100

TABLE 5.2 (Continued)

No.	Strategy	Measure	Target	Actual	Score
(2)	Implement inclusive recruiting program that expands the range of partner colleges and universities representing people with disabilities and Indigenous people.	Complete design and begin execution of inclusive recruiting program within nine (9) months.	1	1	100
(3)	Revise hiring policies and procedures to include inclusive language for position descriptions, diverse interview panels, and diverse interview slates.	Complete revision of hiring policies and procedures within twelve (12) months.	1	1	100
(4)	Design and deliver a mentorship, sponsorship, and allyship training program for managers and leaders using the Ally Conversation Toolkit (ACT).	Complete mentorship, sponsorship, and ACT allyship training program for managers and leaders within six (6) months.	1	1	100
		• Achieve 100% attendance of participants	100	95	95
		• Achieve 4.5/5.0 of higher reaction score to content from participants	4.5	4.6	102
		• Achieve 4.5/5.0 of higher reaction score to facilitation from participants	4.5	4.8	107
(5)	Design and deliver a leadership development program for mid-level women managers employees. Design and deliver a leadership development program for Black, Hispanic, and Native American employees.	Complete leadership development programs within six (6) months.	1	1	75
		• Achieve 100% completion of participants	100	98	98
		• Achieve 4.5/5.0 of higher reaction score to content from participants	4.5	4.4	98
		• Achieve 4.5/5.0 of higher reaction score to facilitation from participants	4.5	4.5	100
		• Achieve 80% of higher test scores from participants	80	90	113
				Total Score	**99**

DEI Dashboards

A *dashboard* is a dynamic platform that provides access to current, target, and historical values for measures, metrics, and KPIs (i.e., goals that quantify objectives and measures that quantify strategies) with the ability to interactively apply different filters and run various analyses. Dashboards can include all the features of scorecards along with an even wider array of features, functionalities, and options. Dashboards are real-time reports that are updated continuously based on direct connections to source data. Dashboards therefore offer the ability to interactively drill down deeper to underlying, related, and historical data, filter the data according to certain variables and criteria, and perform a range of analysis by generating standard and customized reports and visualizations. Dashboards are not only useful for tracking and monitoring progress toward achieving targets for measures, metrics, and KPIs at a strategic and high level, but also for going much deeper to an operational and low level to understand more precisely what is feeding various numbers and driving various trends. Moreover, because dashboards can be related to multiple topics such as DEI, human resources, operations, finance, accounting, and more, by aggregating and integrating data from other systems, dashboards are excellent tools for exploring the interrelationships between and across several categories and data sets.

A personal goal-tracking, habit-tracking, task-tracking, or planning app, tool, or platform would be required to create a personal DEI dashboard. Continuing the personal example above, a personal DEI dashboard would not only allow you to track your goals, such as a 10% increase in your 360° assessment scores, and monitor progress against your measures, such as completing three articles, but also allow you to set deadlines with automatic reminders for your goals, update your status, view weekly and monthly trends, chart progress, and more, to help make certain you are accomplishing your goals in a timely manner.

Continuing the organizational example above, an organizational DEI dashboard would not only allow you to track your goals, such as a 5% increase in representation of supervisors and executives of color within three years, and monitor your progress against your measures, such as a 100% completion rate for participants in a leadership development program, but also allow each person, team, department, and division to go deeper, see the level of detail they desire, and customize their experience to make the most valuable and useful information readily available.

Creating an organizational DEI dashboard requires a business intelligence software tool, application, or platform. These tools enable the creation of tables, charts, graphics, infographics, and visualizations through a mobile app, desktop application, intranet, portal, or browser. They also support various customizations and personalizations including the ability to integrate with third-party applications and databases, generate standardized or tailored scorecards and dashboards for specific divisions, departments, and teams, and control who has permission to access certain data based on roles.

A Personal DEI Dashboard

An example of a **personal DEI dashboard** is shown in Figures 5.1 through 5.8. There are several mobile apps that allow you to track activities that could be used to develop a personal DEI dashboard including nTask, Strides, Coach.me, Way of Life, ATracker,

Habitica, Toodledo, Timelines, and Goals on Track.[1] The examples provided herein were developed using Strides based on the personal DEI strategic plan previously shown in Table 4.7. As you can see from the figures, the app allows you to enter your DEI strategies and measures as daily goals (Figure 5.1), maintain daily journal entries of progress toward goals (Figure 5.2) with associated notes (Figure 5.3), track and visualize your progress for tasks (Figure 5.4), break tasks into subtasks (Figure 5.5) with associated notes (Figure 5.6), track and visualize your progress for subtasks (Figure 5.7), and receive positive encouragement (Figure 5.8).

FIGURE 5.1   Personal DEI Dashboard (Part 1 of 8)

An Organizational DEI Dashboard

Examples of an **organizational DEI dashboard** can be found in Figures 5.9 through 5.11. These dashboards are meant to be illustrative, not exhaustive, and depict *DEI minimum viable metrics (MVMs) and KPIs*—a core set of essential DEI metrics that every organization should consider tracking (with organizational and/or industry comparators, if available):

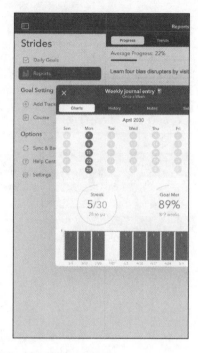

FIGURE 5.2 Personal DEI Dashboard (Part 2 of 8)

FIGURE 5.3 Personal DEI Dashboard (Part 3 of 8)

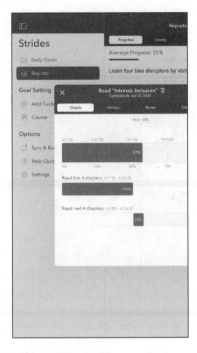

FIGURE 5.4 Personal DEI Dashboard (Part 4 of 8)

FIGURE 5.5 Personal DEI Dashboard (Part 5 of 8)

FIGURE 5.6   Personal DEI Dashboard (Part 6 of 8)

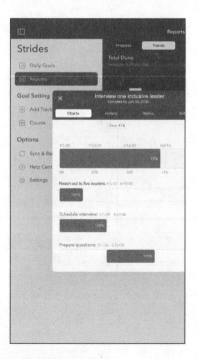

FIGURE 5.7   Personal DEI Dashboard (Part 7 of 8)

FIGURE 5.8 Personal DEI Dashboard (Part 8 of 8)

- **DEI Strategic Plan Scorecard**—A scorecard representing the current status of the DEI strategic plan's objectives, goals, strategies, and measures with the ability to drill down. By tracking this data, you can effectively gauge progress, determine impact, engender accountability, evaluate results, and generate findings to comprehensively demonstrate DEI outputs and outcomes. The scorecard is depicted on the left-hand side of Figure 5.9, while the drill-down for Objective #2 is depicted on the right-hand side of Figure 5.9.

- **Workforce: Diversity (Representation)**—Disaggregated representation data by demographics and management status. By tracking diversity data, you can effectively monitor how representative your workforce is overall and benchmark it against the general population, your industry, departments and divisions, and the geographies where you have offices, do business, and/or deliver products/programs/services. This representation is depicted in the upper left-hand corner of Figure 5.10 while the benchmarking is depicted in the lower left-hand corner of Figure 5.10.

- **Workplace: Inclusion Index**—A composite index or measure of inclusion and/or belonging or some related measure disaggregated by demographics. By tracking an inclusion and/or belonging index, you can effectively monitor how people are experiencing your organizational culture and climate as a leading indicator. This is depicted in the lower right-hand corner of Figure 5.10.

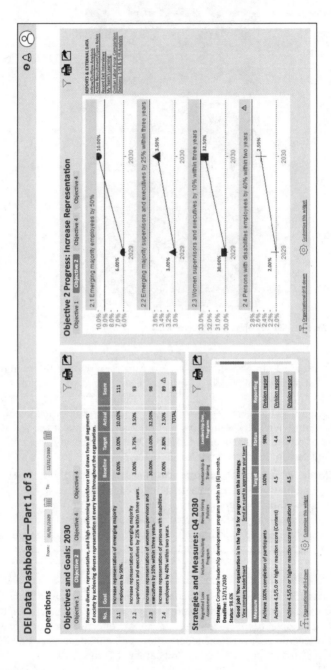

FIGURE 5.9 Organizational DEI Dashboard (Part 1 of 3)

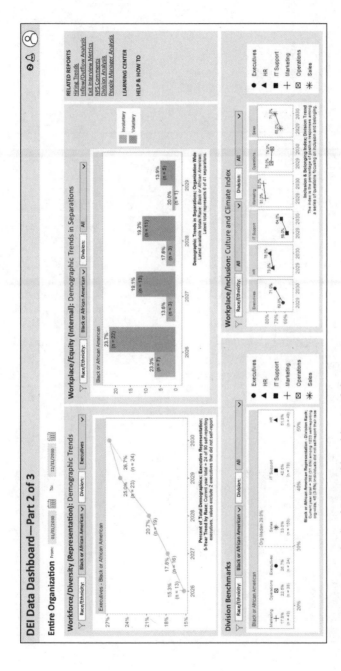

FIGURE 5.10 Organizational DEI Dashboard (Part 2 of 3)

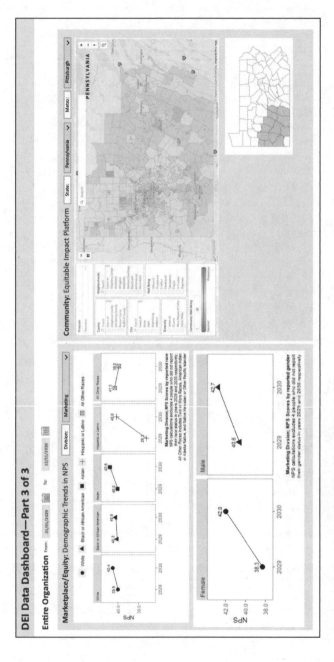

FIGURE 5.11 Organizational DEI Dashboard (Part 3 of 3)

- **Workplace: Equity (Internal)**—Rates of change across hiring, promotions, retention/separations (including voluntary and involuntary losses), and complaints disaggregated by demographics. By tracking these rates of change you can effectively monitor equity or inequity across the entire human resources (HR) lifecycle as a leading indicator. This is depicted in the upper right-hand corner of Figure 5.10.

- **Marketplace: Equity (External)**—A composite index or measure of customer or stakeholder satisfaction and/or outcomes disaggregated by demographics. One popular and simple measure is the Net Promoter Score (NPS), which asks respondents to rate their answer to the question, "On a scale of 0 to 10, how likely are you to recommend our organization/product/service to a friend or colleague?" By tracking NPS, or something comparable, you can effectively monitor how equitably you are meeting the needs of your customers or stakeholders as a leading indicator. This is depicted on the left-hand side of Figure 5.11.

- **Community**—A measure of community diversity, inclusiveness, well-being, and equity for office locations and other geographies of particular interest including partner communities for social and economic investment including recruiting, hiring, philanthropy, corporate social responsibility (CSR), environmental sustainability, supplier diversity, and the like. By tracking these indicators, you can pinpoint areas that can most benefit from social and economic investment. This is depicted on the right-hand side of Figure 5.11, which also represents an image from BCT's Equitable Impact Platform™ (EquIP™), which was previously cited as a "What Works" model for organizations and is highlighted again in the conclusion.

Creating a DEI Scorecard or Dashboard

While this topic is useful for people, it is of paramount importance for organizations as they are responsible for a diverse set of stakeholders and managing a broader array of data. A core and basic principle for creating a DEI scorecard or dashboard for organizations is *data disaggregation* (mentioned previously in **Step 1: DEI Inventory for Organizations**) or stratifying data by salient subgroups according to the following layers of "The Four Layers of Diversity" (previously shown in Figure 1.20):

- **Internal Dimensions:** The internal dimensions or "primary layer" of diversity includes age, gender, sexual orientation, physical ability, ethnicity, and race.

- **External Dimensions:** The external dimensions or "secondary layer" of diversity includes geographic location, income, personal habits, recreational habits, religion, educational background, work experience, appearance, parental status, and marital status.

- **Organizational Dimensions:** The organizational dimensions or "organizational layer" of diversity include functional level, work-content field, division/department/unit/group, seniority, work location, union affiliation, and management status.

It is imperative that this information be captured in the data system(s) producing your organizational DEI scorecard or dashboard. Whether it is a human resources information system (HRIS), learning management system (LMS), enterprise resource planning (ERP) system, customer relationship management (CRM) system, or other DEI-related data system, your ability to produce disaggregated reports will be defined (or delimited) by the data that is captured (or not) in the system. Similarly, by expanding the range of subgroups you captured (or not) in your organizational DEI assessment survey, you set the stage (or close it) to generate disaggregated organizational DEI assessment reports according to these groups. Stated simply, disaggregated data in leads to disaggregated data out.

Visualizing Data

The following are tips—adapted from the National Equity Atlas, produced by PolicyLink and the University of Southern California (USC) Equity Research Institute (ERI)—for visualizing data and creating effective scorecards and dashboards with deeply disaggregated data to power your DEI reporting.[2]

Steps to creating a scorecard or dashboard:

1. Decide what story you are trying to tell with the data and what next steps you hope the audience will take to advance the DEI journey.
2. Choose your mix of quantitative and qualitative data visualizations based on the key DEI issues of your DEI journey.
3. Create great data displays using best practices.
4. Review your data visualizations and narrative to make sure they tell a cohesive story.

Decide What Story You Are Trying to Tell with the Data

DEI scorecards and dashboards should tell a clear story about you and/or your organization, highlighting what the issues are, why they matter, and how others can take action to make meaningful progress on DEI. We will discuss DEI storytelling in great length later in this step but, in the context of scorecards and dashboards, when displaying data, you should be able to answer:

1. What does the data show?
2. Why does it matter?
3. What are the solutions?

These three basic guiding questions can also help you in designing your scorecard or dashboard. Each element of your data visual should support your articulation of those three questions, and focusing on the goal of your data visual can also help you eliminate unneeded components that may be taking up valuable space or distracting your audience.

Choose Your Mix of Quantitative and Qualitative Data Visualizations

There are a wide variety of data visual types you can choose from. Below are some of the quantitative and qualitative data visual types for displaying disaggregated data for DEI scorecards and dashboards, based on the comparisons you want to highlight in the data.

Visualizing Quantitative Data   Among options for visualizing quantitative data are bar charts, column charts, grouped bar charts, trend lines, dot plot graphics, and maps. Table 5.3 provides guidance on how to choose a chart type and examples are provided thereafter.

Comparing between a Few Groups

For example: Compare differences by race and ethnicity

Consider using: Bar Chart

As shown in Figure 5.12, *bar charts* are useful for showing categorical data, such as data by race or by gender, where you are showing comparison between groups. A horizontal bar chart makes it easy for viewers to compare between bars to recognize which bars are longer and which are shorter. Vertical gridlines provide a quick reference to estimating length and comparing differences, and labels provide exact percentages or numbers, which are particularly useful when comparing between groups with smaller differences.

Comparing between Many Groups

For example: Compare units, departments, divisions, or locations

Consider using: Column Chart

As shown in Figure 5.13, *column charts* are vertical bar charts, and are also useful for comparison between groups, particularly when there are more than

TABLE 5.3   How to Choose a Chart Type

If you'd like to:	For example:	Consider using:
Compare **between a few groups**	Compare differences by race and ethnicity	**Bar chart**
Compare **between many groups**	Compare units, departments, divisions, or locations	**Column chart**
Compare **between groups and subgroups**	Compare differences between groups by race and gender	**Grouped bar chart**
Show **gaps and change over time**	Show different rates over time by management status	**Trend line**
Show **clusters and gaps between groups over time**	Show distribution between equity scores for different years	**Dot plot graph**
Display and compare **geographically related**	Compare differences between and across office locations	**Map**

Percent of Employees Reporting Feelings of Inclusion and Belonging

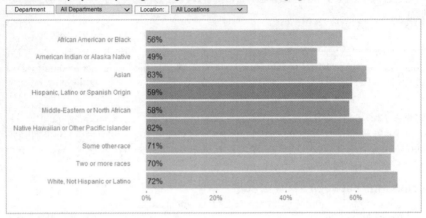

FIGURE 5.12 Bar Chart

Retention Rates for Millennials by Country

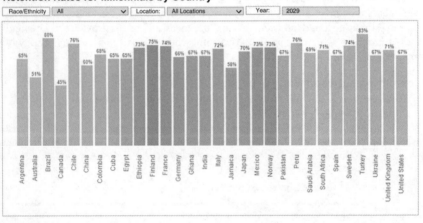

FIGURE 5.13 Column Chart

seven categories. They are also useful for illustrating ranking across many groups, such as helping users to identify how their city or state compares with other cities and states.

Note that the labels for the categories can be displayed at an angle to maximize space.

Comparing between Groups and Subgroups

For example: Compare differences between groups by race and gender

Consider using: Grouped Bar Chart

As shown in Figure 5.14, *grouped bar charts* allow you to include additional subcategories in your comparison, for example, when you are showing differences between groups by race and gender. Grouping the bars together shows rates by race/ethnicity, while using two different colors for gender allows viewers to also compare each gender across racial groups.

Show Gaps and Change Over Time

For example: Show different rates over time by management status

Consider using: Trend Lines

As shown in Figure 5.15, *trend lines* are a useful way to illustrate change over time. Using markers can help users identify key points on your chart, and using different colors for each line makes it visually clear for comparison between different groups represented.

Diversity (representation) by Race/Ethnicity and Gender

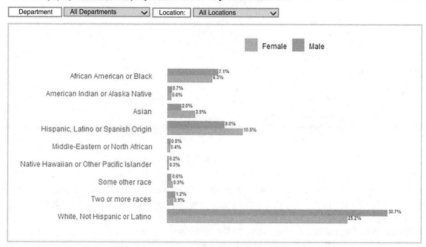

FIGURE 5.14   Grouped Bar Chart

Percentage of those who "strongly agree" or "agree" with the statement
"My organization would benefit from increased workforce diversity" **by Management Level**

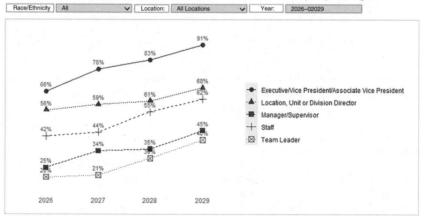

FIGURE 5.15   Trend Lines

Net Promoter Score (NPS) for Education Level BA or Higher; Black or African American Women

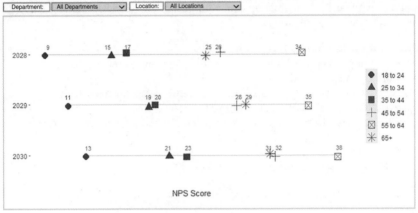

FIGURE 5.16 Dot Plot Graph

Show Clusters and Gaps between Groups over Time

For example: Show distribution between equity scores for different years

Consider using: Dot Plot Graph

As shown in Figure 5.16, *dot plots* are useful for showing distribution comparison between categories, and also show patterns of that distribution. They are efficient for when comparing between groups. One way to highlight differences between multiple groups and to bring attention to particular groups of focus is to change the shape and size of the dots.

Display and Compare Geographically Related Data

For example: Compare differences between and across office locations

Consider using: Maps

As shown in Figure 5.17, *maps* are used to illustrate differences between geographies and allow users to quickly compare across multiple geographies. Maps can help users contextualize data in a familiar frame of reference and take in multiple data points at once.

Visualizing Quantitative Data
In her article "How to Visualize Qualitative Data," Ann K. Emery of Depict Data Studio outlines several ways to bring qualitative data to life.[3] Among the options are word clouds including packed bubbles, icons beside descriptions and responses, color-coded phrases, and closed-ended data beside open-ended data. Descriptions and examples are provided below.

Word Clouds
Emery writes, "Here's the most obvious strategy for visualizing text-based data: the *word cloud*, also known as a *tag cloud*. Frequent words or phrases are shown in larger, bolder font. Less-frequent words or phrases are shown in a smaller font. Data visualization novices love to love word clouds, while data visualization experts love to hate word clouds. Word clouds are okay for visualizing one-word descriptions [and for before/after comparisons], but not for visualizing all your qualitative data. I'm

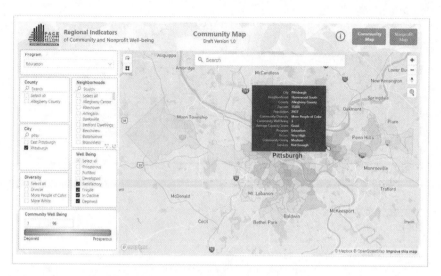

FIGURE 5.17   Map
Source: Generated by the Equitable Impact Platform™ (EquIP™).

Before   **After**

FIGURE 5.18   Before/After Word Cloud

<u>not</u> advocating for run-of-the-mill word clouds where you simply dump your interview transcripts into a word cloud and hope for the best. Simply looking at how often a word or phrase appears in your dataset is <u>not</u> a sufficient way to analyze your data! Instead, I'm talking about intentional word clouds—when you've considered other options and have purposefully chosen a word cloud as your visualization of choice."

Figure 5.18 provides an example of a before/after word cloud depicting one-word descriptions of an organization's culture before and after embarking upon a DEI journey.

Figure 5.19 shows the same data in the before/after word cloud using *packed bubbles*, which are similar to word clouds. Whereas word clouds depict word frequency via font size, packed bubbles depict word frequency via bubble size.

There are a multitude of no-cost and low-cost tools for generating word clouds. Two of my favorites are: **www.jasondavies.com/wordcloud/** and **www .freewordcloudgenerator.com**.

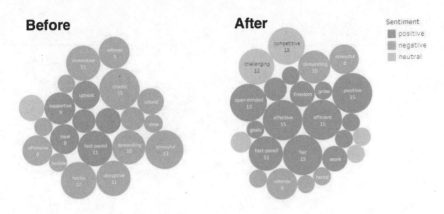

FIGURE 5.19 Before/After Packed Bubbles

Women Face Significant Barriers to Becoming Executives

👤	**Lack of Women in Leadership**	The lack of women at the executive level is a vicious cycle. It creates the perception that women cannot become executives. It creates a void of women executives to mentor and sponsor other women to become leaders. It perpetuates insular social networks that exclude women.
👥📈	**Development Opportunities for Women Are Elusive**	There is a lack of transparency and an overreliance on personal relationships when making development opportunities available. Because women are excluded from these information flows and social networks, they are often unaware that new development opportunities even exist.
👥❓	**Too Much Subjectivity in Promotion/Advancement Decisions**	The performance management process, which forms the basis for promotion and advancement decisions, is too subjective. Criteria are unclear and the ways of evaluating against those criteria are unstructured and lack consistency. Promotion and advancement decisions therefore rely on subjective measures that disadvantage women despite their qualifications.
👤	**Supervisors Are Not Effective in Developing Women Talent**	Supervisors do not have an appreciation for the barriers facing women, much less an ability to effectively mentor, develop, sponsor, and ally in equal partnership with women. In the absence of an active, rather than passive stance by supervisors, the status quo remains.

FIGURE 5.20 Icons beside Descriptions and Responses

Icons beside Descriptions and Responses
Using *icons beside descriptions and responses* is almost a no-brainer, especially to break up long sections of text and make them more visually appealing.

Figure 5.20 shows a series of icons used to visually enhance a summary of barriers facing women to becoming executives.

Color-Coded Phrases
Color-coded phrases are an easy and effective way to visually depict themes within qualitative data. It is recommended that you color-code both the words and the background/highlighting of the words for easier readability using colors with high contrast such as black letters against a green background/highlight.

Figure 5.21 shows the same focus groups transcripts that were presented previously in **Step 1: DEI Inventory** using color coding to represent challenges and opportunities for women and people of color. While you cannot discern the colors in this printed text, the responses at the top are presented with black letters against a red highlight, while responses at the bottom are presented using black letters against a green highlight.

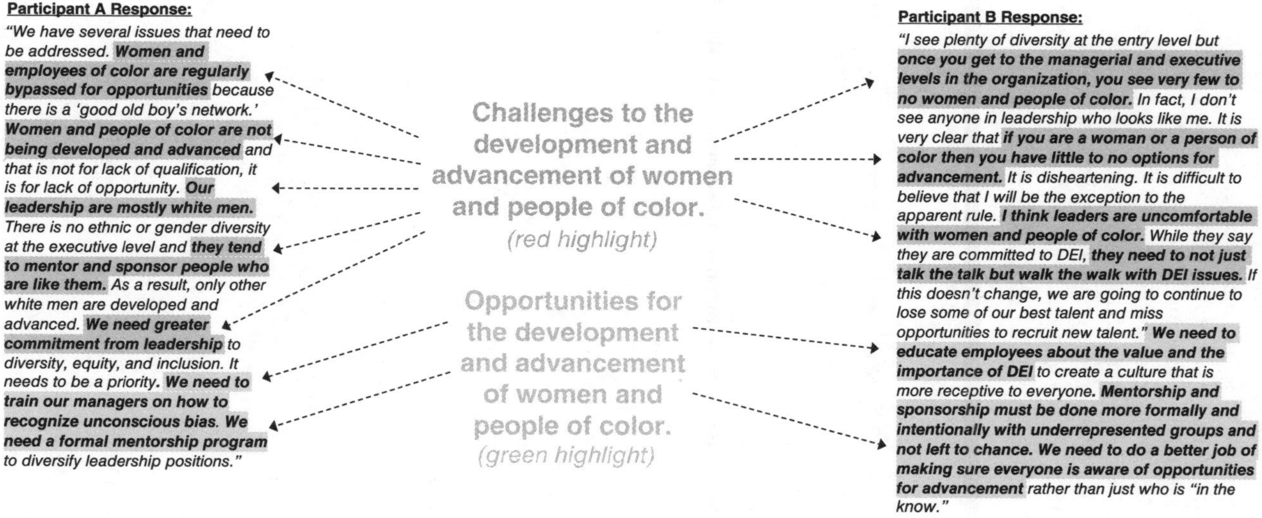

Participant A Response:

"We have several issues that need to be addressed. Women and employees of color are regularly bypassed for opportunities because there is a 'good old boy's network.' Women and people of color are not being developed and advanced and that is not for lack of qualification, it is for lack of opportunity. Our leadership are mostly white men. There is no ethnic or gender diversity at the executive level and they tend to mentor and sponsor people who are like them. As a result, only other white men are developed and advanced. We need greater commitment from leadership to diversity, equity, and inclusion. It needs to be a priority. We need to train our managers on how to recognize unconscious bias. We need a formal mentorship program to diversify leadership positions."

Challenges to the development and advancement of women and people of color.
(red highlight)

Opportunities for the development and advancement of women and people of color.
(green highlight)

Participant B Response:

"I see plenty of diversity at the entry level but once you get to the managerial and executive levels in the organization, you see very few to no women and people of color. In fact, I don't see anyone in leadership who looks like me. It is very clear that if you are a woman or a person of color then you have little to no options for advancement. It is disheartening. It is difficult to believe that I will be the exception to the apparent rule. I think leaders are uncomfortable with women and people of color. While they say they are committed to DEI, they need to not just talk the talk but walk the walk with DEI issues. If this doesn't change, we are going to continue to lose some of our best talent and miss opportunities to recruit new talent. We need to educate employees about the value and the importance of DEI to create a culture that is more receptive to everyone. Mentorship and sponsorship must be done more formally and intentionally with underrepresented groups and not left to chance. We need to do a better job of making sure everyone is aware of opportunities for advancement rather than just who is "in the know.""

FIGURE 5.21 Color-Coded Phrases

Closed-Ended Data beside Open-Ended Data Presenting *closed-ended data beside open-ended data* can be an effective way to visualize both quantitative data that captures what people think/feel and qualitative data that describes why they think/feel that way. Figure 5.22 shows closed-ended and open-ended data side by side from an unconscious bias seminar evaluation.

Word clouds, icons besides descriptions and responses, color-coded phrases, and closed-ended data beside open-ended data are all visual representations of qualitative data that can be helpful both in analyzing qualitative data and when results are being communicated. Other options to consider include flow charts, matrixes, diagrams, sketches, drawings, images, cartoons, and analogies.

Creating Great Data Displays
In summary, below are key elements of data displays that work.

Headers Headers provide short narrative explanations for the data display. Types of headers include:

- Title for the full display
- Narrative header that describes the key narrative frame for your visual
- Technical title that describes in literal terms what the data displays

Chart Elements This is the area on the chart that displays the data in the chart type chosen. Within the chart, common elements include:

- Axis titles
- Axis
- Ticks
- Gridlines
- Legends
- Markers

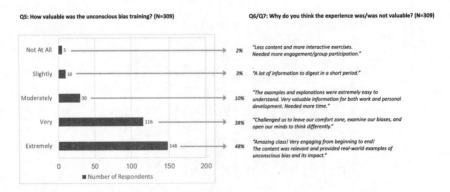

FIGURE 5.22 Closed-Ended beside Open-Ended

- Data labels
- Rollover: Many dashboard tools offer an additional feature that appears when a viewer clicks on or hovers the mouse over a data point in the visual. Rollovers can provide additional information and increase interactivity for your visualization.

Data Sources   It is important to share the original sources of the data displayed in the chart/graph/map. If you have conducted analysis of the source data, you can add "[Your name or organization] analysis of data from [source of data] . . ."

Methods   If you conducted analysis of data presented in the graphic, you should provide a description of the methods that you used to analyze the data. See Figure 5.23.

Review Your Data Visualizations and Narrative to Make Sure They Tell a Cohesive Story   Scorecards and dashboards can only tell you what is happening. Data storytelling can tell you why it is happening. Again, we will take a deep dive into DEI storytelling after we discuss developing effective DEI scorecards and dashboards and determining which one is the best fit for you and/or your organization.

Developing Effective DEI Scorecards and Dashboards

A good scorecard and dashboard should not only be easy and intuitive to interpret but should also reflect the very principles of DEI that a person and/or an organization seeks to uphold such as inclusivity, transparency, and accessibility. The following are guiding principles along these lines:

- **Focus on people first.** Descriptors, headings, legends, and other data labels should be centered on people first and not their characteristics or the demographic group to which they belong. For example, "disabled people" and "homeless people" are centered on disability and homelessness, whereas "people with disabilities" and "people experiencing homelessness," are centered on people. Similarly, phases such as "Hispanic people," "Native American employees," and "Black executives" are centered on people when compared to "Hispanic" and "Native American" and "Black," which are centered on race, ethnicity, and skin color.
- **Disclose availability of data.** When reporting data, be explicit about the availability of data according to groupings such as regions, organizational units, and demographic characteristics. For example, in their April 2021 report, "Your Voice Counts: Diversity at Reuters," Reuters disclosed that 99.9% of their employees supplied data on their gender, 17.3% on their gender identity, 16.5% on their sexual orientation, 50.0% on their race/ethnicity, and 2.1% on the disability status, which is extraordinarily helpful when interpreting the extent to which their data is, or is not, representative of these voices.[4]

Elements of an effective display

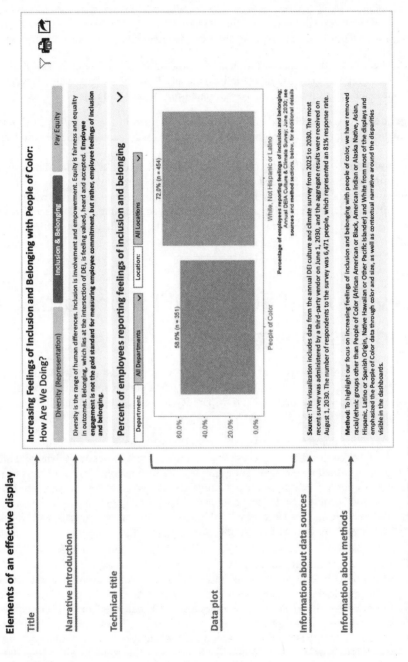

Title

Narrative introduction

Technical title

Data plot

Information about data sources

Information about methods

Increasing Feelings of Inclusion and Belonging with People of Color: How Are We Doing?

Diversity (Representation) | Inclusion & Belonging | Pay Equity

Diversity is the range of human differences. Inclusion is involvement and empowerment. Equity is fairness and equality in outcomes. Belonging, which lies at the intersection of DEI, is feeling valued, heard and accepted. **Employee engagement is not the gold standard for measuring employee commitment, but rather, employee feelings of inclusion and belonging.**

Percent of employees reporting feelings of inclusion and belonging

Department: All Departments ⌄   Location: All Locations ⌄

58.0% (n = 351)   72.0% (n = 454)

60.0%
40.0%
20.0%
0.0%

People of Color   White, Not Hispanic or Latino

Percentage of employees reporting feelings of inclusion and belonging; Annual DEIA Culture & Climate Survey; June 2030; see sources and method sections, below, for additional details

Source: This visualization includes data from the annual DEI culture and climate survey from 2025 to 2030. The most recent survey was administered by a third-party vendor on June 1, 2030, and the aggregate results were received on August 1, 2030. The number of respondents to the survey was 6,471 people, which represented an 81% response rate.

Method: To highlight our focus on increasing feelings of inclusion and belonging with people of color, we have removed racial/ethnic groups other than People of Color (African American or Black, American Indian or Alaska Native, Asian, Hispanic, Latino or Spanish Origin, Native Hawaiian or Other Pacific Islander) and White from most of the displays and emphasized the People of Color data through color and size, as well as contextual narrative around the disparities visible in the dashboards.

FIGURE 5.23   Elements of an Effective Data Display

- **Order labels and responses purposefully.** In an article entitled "Are Your Data Visualizations Racist?"[5] in the *Stanford Social Innovation Review*, Alice Feng and Jonathan Schwabish write, "Often, surveys and other data collection methods will order responses in ways that reflect historical biases. Rather than using orders that reinforce 'white' and 'male' categories as norms, consider ordering labels by sample size or magnitude of results," or alphabetically.

- **Carefully consider colors, icons, and shapes.** Scorecard and dashboard designers often employ color conventions such as red, to indicate below-target or poor performance, yellow, to indicate close-to-target or narrowly missed performance, and green, to indicate on-target or above-target performance. Be mindful that red/green color blindness is the most common, so to ensure accessibility, you should "avoid green on red and red on green," advises the Carnegie Museums of Pittsburgh Innovation Studio. "Color should not be the only indicator for interactive elements. For example, underline links on hover, or mark a required field with an asterisk"[6] and provide symbols and other visual cues to indicate rates of change such as up or down arrows to indicate increases or decreases and heat maps—data visualizations that depict variations in phenomena using variations in color—to indicate relative magnitudes. Additionally, "In many visualizations, colors can be associated with stereotypes (e.g., pink for women, blue for men) that can reinforce biased perceptions in readers. Similarly, images or icons can reinforce stereotypes (e.g., a woman as a nurse but a man as a doctor). In visualizations, images and colors can help readers connect with the data, but [people] should be mindful of their capacity to exacerbate stereotypes," also according to Feng and Schwabish.

- **Ensure accessibility.** Section 508, an amendment to the United States Workforce Rehabilitation Act of 1973, is a U.S. federal law mandating that all electronic and information technology developed, procured, maintained, or used by the federal government be accessible to people with disabilities. Technology is deemed to be *accessible* if it can be used as effectively by people with disabilities as by people without disabilities. Section 508 uses Web Content Accessibility Guidelines (WCAG) 2.0 to ensure compliance for data accessibility. Make certain data is perceivable, user interface components and navigation are operable, information is understandable, and content is robust enough that it can be interpreted reliably by a wide variety of user agents, including different browsers and assistive technologies.[7]

- **Avoid aggregating into groups that may obscure the realities of subgroups.** According to their full report, "Do No Harm: Applying Equity Awareness in Data Visualization" by the Urban Institute, ". . . a big issue when deciding which groups to include in an analysis or show in a data visualization is the underlying sample size. When there are 'too few' observations, populations may be lumped together to make analysis more convenient. Doing so, however, can have harmful effects on the communities that are lumped together. The UCLA Center for Health Policy Research conducts outreach and works with Asian American, Native Hawaiian, and Pacific Islander (NHPI) communities."[8] In the report, Ninez Ponce, MPP, PhD, a professor at the UCLA Fielding School of Public Health, says, "It's a disservice to NHPIs to aggregate to an [Asian American and Pacific Islander] group because the generally better stats of Asians hide the vulnerabilities of NHPIs. That actually could be harmful for the Native Hawaiian Pacific Islander community." For example, according to the U.S. Census Bureau's American Community Survey (ACS), the overall poverty rate for "Asian or Pacific Islander" is 9.7% but underlying this rate for several aggregated groups lies a wide range of poverty rates ranging from a low of 4.5% for those who identify as Chinese and Japanese to a high of 27.8% for those who identify as Mongolian. It is only by closely examining and disclosing these underlying numbers that the experiences of these subgroups can be properly contextualized.

As you can see, developing an effective DEI scorecard and dashboard is as much about best practices for data reporting as it as about best practices for DEI.

Choosing between DEI Scorecards and Dashboards

Table 5.4 summarizes the key differences between DEI scorecards and dashboards.

For people trying to decide between a scorecard and a dashboard, the good news is that you can have the best of both worlds. Given the range of personal goal-tracking, habit-tracking, task-tracking, and planning apps, tools, and platforms, it is relatively easy to create a personal DEI scorecard and dashboard all in one (a list of options and an example was provided earlier). These tools support the monitoring and tracking of a scorecard with the trend analysis of a dashboard. However, if you prefer to keep it simple, you can use a simple template, like the one illustrated previously, that can be found on BCT's website.

TABLE 5.4   **DEI Scorecards vs. Dashboards**

	DEI Scorecards	DEI Dashboards
Information	Current and target values for DEI measures, metrics, and KPIs along with a trend analysis.	Current, target, and historical values for DEI measures, metrics, and KPIs with the ability to interactively apply different filters and run various analyses.
Level	Executive Summary and High-Level	Executive Summary and Drill Down
Orientation	Strategic	Strategic and Operational
Interactivity	Static	Dynamic
View	Current (Snapshot)	Current (Snapshot) and Historical
Interval	Point in time	Real time
Updates	Periodic (weekly/monthly)	Constant
Topics	Single (e.g., DEI)	Multiple (e.g., DEI and more)
Technology	Optional	Required
Access	Less Control	Full Control

For organizations trying to decide between a scorecard and a dashboard, the decision is determined by what is the best fit for you and/or your organization and what arrives at the right cost/benefit, while recognizing that you can also do both.

Scorecards are relatively easier to implement and can be produced manually, again, with varying degrees of difficulty depending on the extent to which data is available, accessible, integrated, and centralized. Scorecards can be an excellent fit for organizations that are new to DEI, when the single topic of DEI is sufficient for their strategic purposes, and/or they do not have the data and technological infrastructure and capacity to support a dashboard. The downside of a scorecard is the inability to drill down and see historical trends across multiple topics. By comparison, dashboards provide these and other features and functionalities including automation, integration, customization, and personalization, across multiple topics including DEI, and can produce scorecards. While dashboards can require more effort to implement due to the organizational coordination, data integration, and technology implementation requirements, there are a growing number of tools that minimize the hurdles and streamline the process. Dashboards can be a good fit for organizations that are already along their DEI journey and have reasonably mature DEI programs. They are excellent for organizations that have multiple data sources and/or would benefit from an enterprise-level, integrated, strategic, and operational view across multiple functions including but not limited to DEI. In summary, dashboards are highly recommended but only when there is a clear and compelling cost/benefit. Otherwise, a scorecard will more than likely suffice.

Now that we have fully explored DEI scorecards and dashboards, described best practices for their deployment, and discerned how to choose between them, I will turn our attention to evaluating results and determining DEI impact.

Determining DEI Impact

DEI scorecards and dashboards provide data analyses to gauge progress (i.e., outputs) and determine impact (i.e., outcomes) based on data that has been assembled or aggregated including the data previously collected from your DEI assessment. Back in **Step 1: DEI Inventory for People**, I commented that it is often by re-administering the same assessment you identified during that step that you evaluate results. During **Step 1: DEI Inventory for Organizations**, I recommended that you evaluate your assessment instrument and develop your in-depth interview and focus group protocol on the premise that they will likely be re-administered according to a certain frequency (i.e., quarterly pulses, annually, biannually, etc.) to gauge progress, evaluate results, and demonstrate impact. The final piece of the puzzle to fully determining DEI impact is therefore to collect new data and evaluate that data against the data from your DEI assessment.

Collecting New Data

First, you must decide what portion of your assessment to re-administer. For personal DEI assessments, we recommend re-administering those that relate to competences, and perhaps adding new ones that relate to preferences and competences. With respect to competences, it is not uncommon to make progress against an assessment instrument and then regress or revert backwards, so by re-administering the same instrument for competences, you are able to monitor these and other dynamics. Moreover, depending on your results, adding new instruments for preferences and competences offers fresh insights for your DEI journey. The question of whether to re-administer a personal DEI assessment related to preferences is a nuanced one that I will answer in a moment.

You will recall that your overarching objective is to increase your level of competence in areas that are relevant to your DEI journey. It is not necessarily to change your preferences, but rather to develop an ability (i.e., a competence) to shift, stretch, flex, or expand into areas outside of your preferences and to mitigate blind spots. The immediate value of a personal DEI assessment is to know your preferences, so that you know your tendencies and your blind spots (and to understand the tendencies and blind spots of others), which only requires administering a personal DEI assessment for preferences once. Therefore, while it is useful to re-administer a personal DEI assessment for competences, it is debatable whether it is useful to re-administer one for preferences.

On this matter, the following are insights from Herrmann International based on research conducted with their HBDI® assessment for thinking preferences:[9]

> Longitudinal studies of hundreds of HBDI® participants indicate that change can take place if there is a reason for it. Change seems to take place over a long period of time with an individual's desire and willingness to change, or with a change in their life's circumstances, or as result of a significant emotional event. Profiles do not change casually; rather, a dramatic change in the person's life is required to cause a change. Profiles often change when there is an event, or series of events, that has value-shifting impact. Examples include a major change in the family (e.g., birth of a child, death, divorce), a major career change, going back to school, engaging in a completely different field of study, or maybe even going off to war. Changes to the profile in a 5% range can fairly easily occur, but usually the shape of the profile remains the same. However, if nothing has happened to the individual, and they continue to do the same things in the same way, then the profile will remain stable.

In other words, while the likelihood of preferences changing significantly is low and does not happen overnight, it does happen. Therefore, in addition to re-administering your personal DEI assessment for competences, I recommend that you re-administer your personal DEI assessment for preferences, too. This will either corroborate your prior results or illuminate changes. I also recommend combining a personal DEI assessment for preferences with a diverse 360° assessment because, as I cited in **Step 1: DEI Inventory for People**, the assessment not only reveals preferences and competences, covers a wide range of areas with depth, and seeks diverse perspectives on how well you function in diverse settings, but it also can be easily combined with other assessments. While you may not see significant changes in your personal DEI assessment for preferences within one to two years, you are almost certain to see changes in your diverse 360° assessment within one to two years, thus ensuring that you are receiving valuable feedback and data to inform your DEI journey.

At BCT, we recommend re-administering a full organizational DEI assessment including quantitative (i.e., culture and climate survey) and qualitative (i.e., IDIs and focus groups) research methods. If you are unable to re-administer a full organizational DEI assessment, for any number of reasons including cost and other circumstances, then you can explore the following alternatives, some of which were previously discussed in **Step 1: DEI Inventory for Organizations**:

- Develop a "Stratified Sampling Plan" that surveys a subset of your total employees but is representative of the population. This will reduce the number of people completing the survey.

- Deploy a "pulse survey," that is, a shorter version of the survey, based on a subset of the original questions that is administered to only a subset of the entire organization. If designed properly to focus on the questions that matter most, a pulse survey can collect valuable information in a short amount of time.

- Reduce the number of questions in your in-depth interview and focus group protocol. This will shorten the amount of time required from participants while still obtaining qualitative insights.

- Facilitate fewer IDIs and focus groups and/or only invite new voices to participate while ensuring that those voices are representative of the organization. This will reduce the number of people participating in IDIs and focus groups.

While we recommend re-administering a full organizational DEI assessment, these alternative approaches are viable especially when underrepresented and/or marginalized voices are sufficiently represented in the assessment.

Second, to determine what data should be collected, you must determine the frequency to re-administer your DEI assessment, which speaks directly to a related question: How long does it take for change to occur?

How Often Should Personal DEI Data Be Collected? How Long Does Personal Transformation Take?   According to a study referenced earlier and published in the *European Journal of Social Psychology* in 2009 entitled, "How Are Habits Formed," it takes 18 to 254 days for a new behavior to become automatic.[10] The study also found that, on average it takes 66 days (roughly two months) to form a new habit. Similarly, in the article "How to Master Skill," in the *Harvard Business Review*, Amy Gallo offers perspectives on the pace of personal transformation with insights from Heidi Grant Halvorson, a motivational psychologist and Joseph Weintraub, a professor of management and organizational behavior at Babson College:[11]

> "Too often, we approach a new skill with the attitude that we should nail it right out of the gate," says Halvorson. The reality is that it takes much longer. "It's not going to happen overnight. It usually takes six months or more to develop a new skill," says Weintraub. And it may take longer for others to see and appreciate it. "People around you will only notice 10% of every 100% change you make," he says.

This suggests that it is reasonable to re-administer a personal DEI assessment for competences at least every six months to one year, depending on the level of effort you are putting forth, as it allows for sufficient time to see measurable changes. Per the insights from Herrmann International above, I recommend re-administering a personal DEI assessment for preferences after any dramatic life changes or, at minimum, every one to two years.

Gallo also offers the following eight helpful tips for personal transformation and developing new skills:

1. Check your readiness
2. Make sure it's needed (and relevant)
3. Know how you learn best
4. Get the right help
5. Start small
6. Reflect along the way
7. Challenge yourself to teach it to others
8. Be patient

These guiding principles can help maximize your personal DEI learning journey toward achieving your personal DEI strategic plan.

How Often Should Organizational DEI Data Be Collected? How Long Does Organizational Transformation Take?

In their article "Fast Forward: A New Framework for Rapid Organization Change," in *Ivey Business Journal*, Elspeth Murray and Peter Richardson, argue that organizations should not have to wait three to five years to experience transformation. "We discovered that it was not so much *what* people did that led to success, but rather the fact that certain conditions were established during the change process," they write.[12] They proceed to identify the following 10 "winning conditions" for rapid change to be successful:

1. Correct diagnosis of the change challenge—its nature, depth, breadth, and the forces at play.
2. Early establishment of a shared understanding of the change challenge among the leadership team—a sense of vision, success measures, key programs and projects, and of the change process itself.
3. Multiple and ongoing opportunities to enrich this shared understanding—frequent progress reviews and action plan updates.
4. A sense of urgency, emphasizing speed when building an awareness and understanding of the need for change, without a crisis, and insisting on early tangible deliverables.
5. A limited and focused agenda for change, identifying two, three, or four, major priorities, at a maximum, and driving them hard and fast.
6. Rapid, strategic decision making and resource deployment; this is essential to build both speed and, subsequently, momentum.
7. A human flywheel of commitment—engaging the early adopters very rapidly, and bringing along the "fence-sitters" in a timely manner.

8. Identifying the sources of resistance and dealing with them ruthlessly—eliminating the "drag" in the process that can prevent the build-up of momentum, and waste valuable executive time.

9. Effective follow-through on changing key organizational enablers—ensuring that structure, communications, performance evaluation, and recognition/reward are aligned with the new direction.

10. Demonstrating strong and consistent leadership—appropriate behaviors that provide tangible, early evidence of true commitment to the change process and the relentless pursuit of the new direction.

Murray and Richardson write, "The first three create guidance for a change initiative [*direction*], the next three generate and maintain *speed*, and the remaining four provide critical *mass*. Together, these winning conditions create the momentum required for success," they write. "Thus, in terms of today's fast paced . . . environment, successful change occurs when sufficient speed and mass are generated quickly enough so that enough momentum is created to move the organization quickly, from its state of rest—the status quo—in the desired direction."[13]

At BCT, we've observed clients achieve measurable progress with DEI transformation within one to two years when they establish these kinds of conditions. We therefore recommend that our clients conduct a full organizational DEI assessment—quantitative and qualitative—along a similar time horizon of no more than every one to two years. Moreover, we've seen some organizations conduct the DEI culture and climate component of their organizational DEI assessment as a monthly or quarterly "pulse" survey (defined in the previous section). This enables them to respond more quickly to changes and engender accountability on a more frequent basis (i.e., track the performance and provide feedback to managers, supervisors, and leaders).

Table 5.5 summarizes guidelines for the frequency of conducting a personal and organizational DEI assessment.

Evaluating Results

You will recall that **Step 1: DEI Inventory** involved administering a personal and/or organizational DEI assessment that generated a profile and a baseline, or reference data point, for your DEI journey. By re-administering some or all of the prior DEI assessment, you can compare the current results to your baseline results while essentially establishing a new baseline or reference data point.

TABLE 5.5 **Personal and Organizational DEI Assessment Frequency Guidelines**

	Personal DEI Assessment	Organizational DEI Assessment
Frequency	Personal Preference: Every 1–2 years	Full Assessment: Every 1–2 years
	Personal Competence: Every 6–12 months	Partial Assessment (i.e., "pulse"): Monthly or quarterly

For example, let's assume that during Steps 1 through 4 for people you took the Antiracist Style Indicator (ASI) as a part of your personal DEI assessment, and it assessed you as an "underfunctioning" antiracist. It is likely that somewhere embedded within your personal DEI objectives and goals was something akin to this: "increase my level of antiracist competence from 'underfunctioning' to 'functioning,'" based on personal DEI strategies and measures informed by the promising and proven practices of a "What Works" model. It is only by re-administering the ASI in Step 5 that you will know whether you have fulfilled your objective and achieved your goal for antiracist behavior. The data produced by re-administering the ASI becomes your new baseline or reference data point, which takes you back to Step 1.

As another example, imagine that during Steps 1 through 4 for organizations, your organizational DEI assessment involved BCT's DEI Workforce and Workplace Assessment™ (DWWA™) survey combined with focus groups with members of the LGBTQIA+ community, whereas the DWWA™ survey revealed that they experienced statistically significant higher incidents of bullying and discrimination reports. It is reasonable to assume that among your organizational DEI objectives and goals was something similar to this: "decrease incidents of bullying and discrimination reports by 50% and increase feelings of inclusion and belonging by 25% among members of the LGBTQIA+ community," by leveraging the promising and proven practices of a "What Works" model that informs the DEI strategies and measures established by your organization. While you may be tracking discrimination reports in your HRIS, it is only by re-administering the DWWA™ and the focus groups in Step 5, or something comparable, that you will know whether you have fulfilled your objective and reached your goal for bullying, inclusion, and belonging. The data produced by re-administering the DWWA™ and the focus groups becomes a new baseline or reference data point, which takes you back to Step 1.

When you analyzed your personal and/or organizational DEI assessment data in **Step 1: DEI Inventory**, you began with a blank slate. For people, you sought to generate findings and insights to your personal DEI preferences or personal DEI preferences and competences. For organizations, you sought to find and identify insights to organizational DEI challenges and opportunities, such as statistically significant differences between subgroups (e.g., women vs. men vs. nonbinary; people who are visually impaired vs. people who are deaf and hard of hearing; employees in the domestic office vs. employees in the overseas office; etc.) and between intersections of subgroups (e.g., domestic women who are visually impaired vs. international men who are deaf and hard of hearing). Data is a mirror. What you see is a reflection of you and/or your organization. Here in **Step 5: DEI Impact**, you have the potential to generate three kinds of findings:

1. **New findings**—By using the same approach that you used to analyze your DEI assessment to analyze your DEI re-assessment, you will uncover new findings and insights reflecting changes that have occurred since you conducted the prior DEI assessment. For example, one year later your personal DEI re-assessment may reveal an unanticipated change in your personal DEI preferences due to a major change in your life's circumstances. Similarly, your organizational DEI re-assessment may reveal a statistically significant and/or observable difference in uncivil behavior at an office location, that was not a finding from the baseline DEI assessment, due to an influx of new employees who are misbehaving.

2. **Emergent findings**—By tracking and monitoring your DEI reports you will glean emergent findings and insights to your outputs, or progress relative to strategies and measures, as well as your outcomes, or impact relative to your objectives and goals. For example, at the end of your first year, you may find that you have completed 95% of your measures (i.e., outputs) and 90% of goals (i.e., outcomes).

3. **Comparative findings**—By comparing current DEI measures, metrics, and key performance indicators (KPIs) to the past, you will illuminate comparative findings and insights; that is, measurable differences and/or statistically significant differences between your baseline DEI assessment and re-assessment data. For example, one year later the comparison between the Intercultural Development Inventory® (IDI®) score of your personal DEI assessment may uncover a measurable increase from "minimization" (i.e., you de-emphasize differences) to "acceptance" (i.e., you deeply comprehend differences). Along the same lines, one year later the DEI culture and climate survey of your organizational DEI assessment may uncover a significant decrease in the incidents of bullying toward members of the LGBTQIA+ community.

While it is the combination of emergent findings and comparative findings that allow you to comprehensively evaluate results in the present, the new findings will help inform next steps for the future.

Distinguishing between Correlation and Causation

When evaluating results, tremendous care must be taken not to confuse causation with correlation. According to the Australian Bureau of Statistics, "Two or more variables [are] considered to be related, in a statistical context, if their values change so that as the value of one variable increases or decreases so does the value of the other variable (although it may be in the opposite direction):

- *Correlation* is a statistical measure that describes the size and direction of a relationship between two or more variables. A correlation between variables, however, does not automatically mean that the change in one variable is the cause of the change in the values of the other variable.

- *Causation* indicates that one event is the result of the occurrence of the other event (i.e., there is a causal relationship between the two events). This is also referred to as cause and effect.

Theoretically, the difference between the two types of relationships is easy to identify—an action or occurrence can cause another or it can correlate with another.[14] If you misinterpret correlation for causation you may erroneously conclude that a particular DEI initiative has led to a particular DEI impact when, in fact, there is no basis upon which to draw that conclusion.

For example, let's assume that your organization is executing a DEI strategic plan with the following objectives:

- **Objective #1:** Increase the number of people with disabilities who are hired
- **Strategy #1:** Train managers on reasonable accommodations for persons with disabilities

- **Objective #2:** Increase promotions and advancement of Asian Americans and Pacific Islanders (AAPI)
- **Strategy #2:** Train managers on allyship for the AAPI community.

If the AAPI allyship training coincides with an increase in the number of people with disabilities hired, then the two variables, "number of managers trained in AAPI allyship" and "number of people with disabilities hired," may have a correlational relationship with another (i.e., an increase in AAPI allyship trainings *is associated with* an increase in people with disabilities hired), but an action or occurrence of one does not likely cause another (i.e., an increase in AAPI allyship trainings *does not lead to* an increase in the people with disabilities hired, or vice versa). However, if we consider the two variables, "number of managers trained on reasonable accommodations for persons with disabilities" and "number of people with disabilities hired," it is reasonable to expect that there may be a causal relationship between them. How can this be established? It is easier to establish correlation than it is to establish causation.

To establish correlation between two variables, you can simply calculate the *r value* or *correlation coefficient* or *effect size*, which measures the strength of a linear relationship between the two variables. It ranges between −1.0 and +1.0, whereas:

- An effect size of −1.0 indicates a strong negative correlation between two variables (an increase in one variable leads to a decrease in the other variable)
- An effect size of 0 indicates no correlation between two variables
- An effect size of +1.0 indicates a strong positive correlation between two variables (an increase in one variable leads to an increase the other variable)

A good rule of thumb is:

- An effect size between ±0.50 and ±1.0 is said to be a strong correlation
- An effect size between ±0.30 and ±0.49 is said to be a medium correlation
- An effect size below ±0.29 is said to be a small correlation

Correlation is determined simply by the strength of the effect size. The approach to establish causation is more complex, and the bar is much higher.

A prominent approach to establishing causation is to conduct a *controlled experimental study* (i.e., "a randomized control trial (RCT)") that randomly assigns the intervention or "cause" to one group (i.e., the treatment group) and does not assign the intervention or "cause" to a comparable group (i.e., the control group) and then determines whether the outcome or "effect" produced by the treatment group represents a statistically significant improvement when compared to the control group. Continuing with the previous example, the intervention (cause) is training managers on reasonable accommodations for persons with disabilities and the outcome (effect) is the number of people with disabilities hired. A controlled experimental study would randomly select a group of managers to receive training on reasonable accommodations and randomly select a group of managers who would not receive the training, and then determine whether the proportion of people with disabilities hired by interview panels with managers who received the training represented a statistically significant increase when compared to the proportion of people with disabilities hired by interview panels with managers who did not receive the training. Conducting a controlled experimental study is often not ethical, practical, or appropriate in a real-world setting. For example, most organizations would wisely prefer to train all of their managers as opposed to randomly training certain managers. In these instances, you can explore two options.

The first option you can explore is a *quasi-experimental study*. For example, if you're able to track the interview panels with managers that happen to have been trained on reasonable accommodations (treatment group or Group A) and compare their results to interview panels with managers that happen to not have been trained on reasonable accommodations (control group or Group B), you can compare the outputs of the two groups—the proportion of people with disabilities hired—to determine if there is a statistically significant difference between them. While the determination of which managers would be trained on reasonable accommodations for people with disabilities was not randomly assigned, Group A and Group B represent a "naturally occurring experiment" nonetheless because they manifested organically by virtue of the fact that some managers happened to have been trained and some managers happened to have not been trained thus far. This approach can enable you to paint a picture of causation as long as you incorporate one final and important technique: blocking.

Blocking is the arrangement of experimental units in groups (blocks) that are similar to one another. Blocking stems from a determination of the variables considered salient for comparison (also known as the variables you want to "control for"). Stated simply, blocking allows you to compare apples to apples and oranges to oranges. Continuing with the previous example, let's assume you want to arrange your experimental units (i.e., the people interviewed) according to years of experience and level of education. In other words, when examining the number of people interviewed, you only want to compare people with the same years of experience and the same level of education, so you are comparing apples to apples. You could reasonably select people interviewed with three to five years of experience and a bachelor's degree as your block for comparison. This will allow you to control for years of experience and level of education when you test for statistical significance to determine causality.

Table 5.6 depicts this scenario based on 400 people interviewed in Group A and 500 people interviewed in Group B. After blocking (controlling) for experience and education, these numbers drop to 200 and 300, respectively, leading to a proportion of people with disabilities hired of 25% for interview panels with a trained manager and 10% for interview panels without a trained manager, respectively. A test of statistical significance results in a p-value of 0.002, which indicates statistical significance at the $p \leq 0.01$ level and an effect size of 0.6, which indicates a strong correlation. This would suggest that the reasonable accommodations training did indeed have a causal relationship with the hiring and should be expanded to continue making progress in hiring people with disabilities.

As mentioned in **Step 1: DEI Inventory for Organizations**, there are several software applications that can automate calculations of effect size (correlation) and tests of statistical significance such as SAS, SPSS, Stata, SUDAAN, and WesVar. Moreover, if you leverage a standardized DEI culture and climate survey from a vendor, it is very likely that they have also automated these calculations and tests into their analysis and reporting. At BCT, we have been developing an algorithmic approach to quasi-experimental studies that leverages data analytics and machine learning called Equitable Analytics™. Equitable Analytics™ was identified as a "What Works" model for organizations in **Step 3: DEI Insights** and will be highlighted again in the conclusion.

TABLE 5.6	Quasi-Experimental Study of Training and Hiring Persons with Disabilities				
GROUP	Number of People Interviewed	Number of People Interviewed with 3–5 Years of Experience and a Bachelor's Degree	Number of People with Disabilities Interviewed	Number of People with Disabilities Hired	Proportion of People with Disabilities Hired
Group A (Panels with a Trained Manager)	400	200	30	8	25.0%
Group B (Panels without a Trained Manager)	500	300	45	5	10.0%
				p-value	0.002
				Effect Size	0.6

The second option you could explore to establish causality is an *observational study*, which closely observes the experiences of interview panels and, using some combination or surveys, interviews, focus groups, outputs, and/or outcomes, assesses the strength of the relationship between cause and effect. For a deep dive into determining causation, I recommend *The Book of Why: The New Science of Cause and Effect* by Judea Pearl and Dana Mackenzie.

The important lesson here is to not jump to conclusions that your DEI strategies or outputs are necessarily the cause of, versus correlated with, your DEI results and outcomes when interpreting findings and evaluating results.

Generating Findings

Generating findings represents the final piece of the puzzle to fully determining impact. This necessitates a close examination of the following results to paint a comprehensive picture of impact:

- **For People:**
  - Based on your personal DEI assessment and re-assessment data, you should examine:
    - The extent to which your *preferences*—the things you tend to think, feel, and do—have changed or remained the same and the extent to which you have greater awareness and/or appreciation of your preferences and those of others.

o The extent to which you have increased your level of *competence*—the ability to do something properly and successfully—and improved your knowledge, skills, and attitudes/attributes (KSAs) in the areas you have designated.

o Depending on the personal DEI assessment tool(s) you selected, this may include examining the extent to which you are able to shift, stretch, flex, or expand into areas outside of your preferences and mitigate blind spots in the areas you have designated.

- **For Organizations:**

  o Based on your organizational DEI assessment and re-assessment data (with disaggregated data), you should examine:

  o The extent to which the comparative results show significant and/or observable differences in the areas you have designated, as evidenced by *quantitative data*, which captures what people think/feel about a topic, and *qualitative data*, which captures why or how people think/feel that way.

- **For People and Organizations:**

  o Based on your DEI results data and reports (with disaggregated data)—scorecard and/or dashboard—including *leading indicators*, often related to equity and inclusion, that look forward at future outcomes and events, and *lagging indicators*, often related to diversity, that look back at whether the intended result was realized, you should examine:

  o The extent to which progress has been made because *strategies* have been executed and evaluated against *measures* (i.e., *outputs*).

  o The extent to which an impact has been achieved because *objectives* and *goals* have been accomplished and appraised against *metrics* and *key performance indicators (KPIs)* (i.e., *outcomes*).

The totality of the results and findings—new, emergent, and comparative—from your DEI reports and DEI re-assessment (**Step 1: DEI Inventory**) will likely reshape, refine, or redefine the DEI objectives and goals you embrace (**Step 2: DEI Imperatives**), the DEI promising and proven practices or "What Works" model you adopt (**Step 3: DEI Insights**), and the DEI strategies and measures you pursue (**Step 4: DEI Initiatives**) thereafter, particularly given that certain objectives will likely be achieved, certain strategies will no longer be tenable, and certain promising and proven practices will no longer be relevant, while others will likely remain. In this regard, **Step 5: DEI Impact** does not signify the culmination, but rather, the continuation of your DEI journey and the cornerstone for a cycle of continuous learning, development, and improvement. The final part of **Step 5: DEI Impact** is DEI data storytelling or integrating the results and findings to craft and communicate compelling DEI stories.

The Power of DEI Storytelling

In her TED Talk "The Danger of a Single Story," Nigerian writer and feminist Chimamanda Ngozi Adichie speaks to the power of storytelling.[15,16] She explains that when we tell a single story about others—stereotype them, place them into groups, and no longer see them as individuals: "It robs people of dignity. It makes our recognition of our equal humanity difficult. It emphasizes how we are different rather than how we are similar." She poignantly explains the interrelationship between stories and power:

> It is impossible to talk about the single story without talking about power. There is a word, an Igbo word, that I think about whenever I think about the power structures of the world, and it is "nkali." It's a noun that loosely translates to "to be greater than another." Like our economic and political worlds, stories too are defined by the principle of nkali: How they are told, who tells them, when they're told, how many stories are told, are really dependent on power.

> Power is the ability not just to tell the story of another person, but to make it the definitive story of that person. The Palestinian poet Mourid Barghouti writes that if you want to dispossess a people, the simplest way to do it is to tell their story and to start with, "secondly." Start the story with the arrows of the Native Americans, and not with the arrival of the British, and you have an entirely different story. Start the story with the failure of the African state, and not with the colonial creation of the African state, and you have an entirely different story.

Adichie's words are reminiscent of two popular quotes: The African Proverb, "Until the lion learns how to write, every story will glorify the hunter" and "History will be kind to me, for I intend to write it," as stated by former prime minister of the United Kingdom, Winston Churchill. Stories have power so there is power in storytelling. There is power in your sharing your story and the stories of others, which speaks to the power of DEI data storytelling or data storytelling through the lens of DEI.

DEI Data Storytelling

Data storytelling is the process of crafting a compelling narrative and sharing insights based on data using visuals. *DEI data storytelling* enables you to personalize the DEI journey, contextualize data, chronicle progress, synthesize findings, integrate results, and comprehensively demonstrate impact. When done effectively, DEI data storytelling can also inspire and motivate you and others to build momentum and take action. More specifically, DEI data storytelling offers three value propositions:

1. **Humanize data and empower**—Personal stories can get lost in any data-driven approach. People are the "what" and the "why" for DEI. Personal stories must remain front and center. DEI data storytelling can help ensure that a diverse set of voices are uplifted representing a diverse range of lived experiences. In doing so, we humanize data by "putting a face" on it. Ngozi Adichie states, "Many stories matter. Stories have been used to dispossess and to malign. But stories can also be used to empower, and to humanise."

2. **Communicate lasting and emotional messages**—Storytelling is among the most effective ways to communicate a lasting message. Research has found that

stories are more memorable, more persuasive, and more engaging.[17] For example, according to a study by Chip Heath at Stanford University, 63% of people can recall based on stories, while only 5% of people can recall based on statistics.[18] In his article "The Neuroscience of Storytelling," Erik Larson explains how stories engage more of the brain than data and facts. "When packaged into a story, your fact set has a bridge to the emotional part of the brain. What neuroscientists observed is that factual information only engages two parts of the brain, Broca's and Wernicke's area. This is in stark contrast to the spectrum of other parts of the brain engaged by a story, including movement, smell and emotion. *People hear statistics, but people feel stories*,"[18] writes Larson. DEI storytelling enables people to feel the experiences of those who are different from them.

3. **Inspire and motivate action**—DEI storytelling can paint a clear and compelling picture of what has happened and why it has happened. When people can relate to these stories and see reflections of their lived experience, it can inspire them to see greater possibilities for themselves and others. In doing so, the lasting impression left by a well-crafted DEI story can also represent a call to action. By seeing what is possible, and how to make it possible, DEI stories can motivate people to pursue new paths or recommit to existing ones. Interestingly, this hearkens back to the very beginning of our DEI journey in **Step 0: DEI Incentives** where we discussed intrinsic and extrinsic motivation. DEI storytelling can lead to intrinsic motivations such as self-interest or internal desires, or extrinsic motivations by demonstrating benefits or rewards. In his article, "Storytelling for Action," Peter Minimum, a market researcher, concludes, "The movement captured in a complete story is the best way to engage an audience and communicate an idea that results in action."[19]

I will now explain the elements of DEI data storytelling.

The Three Elements of DEI Data Storytelling   The three elements of DEI data storytelling are:

1. **Data**—A complete and integrated analysis of the relevant quantitative and qualitative data, including data from your assessment, measures, metrics, and KPIs, to paint a full picture and set the stage for the narrative.
2. **Narrative**—An oral or written storyline reflecting insights from the data analysis, context surrounding the data, messages being communicated, ideas sought to convey, and call to action.
3. **Visuals**—A visual representation of the data according to the narrative in the form of tables, charts, pictures, diagrams, graphics, infographics, videos, and the like.

These elements should combine to produce clear and compelling stories that are lasting and lead to desired change. Along these lines, in his *Forbes* article "Data Storytelling: The Essential Data Science Skill Everyone Needs," Brent Dykes explains how these different elements work together to produce associated outcomes (see Figure 5.24):[20]

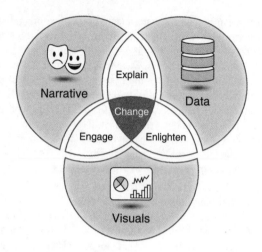

FIGURE 5.24   The Three Elements of Data Storytelling
Source: https://www.forbes.com/sites/brentdykes/2016/03/31/data-storytelling-the-essential-data-science-skill-everyone-needs/?sh=61ac6e8152ad.

When narrative is coupled with data, it helps to **explain** to your audience what's happening in the data and why a particular insight is important. Ample context and commentary are often needed to fully appreciate an insight. When visuals are applied to data, they can **enlighten** the audience to insights that they wouldn't see without charts or graphs. Many interesting patterns and outliers in the data would remain hidden in the rows and columns of data tables without the help of data visualizations. Finally, when narrative and visuals are merged together, they can **engage** or even entertain an audience. It's no surprise we collectively spend billions of dollars each year at the movies to immerse ourselves in different lives, worlds, and adventures. When you combine the right visuals and narrative with the right data, you have a data story that can influence and drive **change**.

A key takeaway is that while DEI data collection, data analysis, and data reporting are all distinct and important capabilities, DEI data storytelling is equally distinct and important. In fact, ineffective data storytelling can completely negate and undermine all its predecessor steps no matter have effectively they have been executed. It is therefore of paramount importance that DEI stories be crafted and communicated with care to honor the DEI journey and maximize impact.

The Eight Components of Crafting and Communicating a Compelling DEI Story

Crafting and communicating a compelling DEI story is made up of the same components of crafting and communicating a compelling story, only data, narrative, and visuals play a central role. These components are summarized according to the following eight "P's" of population, premise, people, problem, plot, principles, packaging, and platform. As you will see, they artfully weave together the three elements of data storytelling of data, narrative, and visuals.

Population (Audience)   Question: *Who is the intended audience for the DEI story?*

The first and foremost "P" is to identify the target population, audience, or recipients of your DEI story. For example, from a personal perspective, you may target friends, family, or colleagues to share your experiences. From an organizational perspective, you may target the entire organization, or people in certain divisions, departments, locations, or roles, to share accomplishments. Moreover, your intended audience may be internal and allow greater disclosure of confidential data, or external and place certain restrictions on disclosure of confidential data. Making the determination of audience can significantly impact what story you tell and how you tell it.

Premise (Scene and Setting)   Question: *What is the scene or site for the DEI story?*

For the second "P" of premise you should define the locus or locale for your DEI story whether it is your personal journey, that of someone else, a specific team or group, or the entire organization. The premise sets up the remaining components.

Question: *What is the setting or the internal and external environmental conditions that relate to the DEI story?*

As a part of defining the premise, you should also determine what background information is important to consider or disclose to provide sufficient context for your audience. For example, from a personal perspective, you may have just moved to a different city with greater diversity and desired to diversify your friendships, or your DEI journey may be part of an even broader journey of personal transformation. Moreover, you may have recently joined an organization with a strong commitment to DEI, or you were just promoted to a leadership position with DEI responsibilities, or your performance appraisal may now include DEI performance measures. Alternatively, your organization may have recently made a public commitment to DEI, or your organization may have experienced a precipitous decrease in the representation of people of color in the managerial and supervisory ranks, or your organization may have recently hired a new CEO or Chief DEI Officer who has ushered in a new strategic agenda for DEI. These are important contextual matters that help people to better understand and appreciate the DEI story.

People (Characters)   Question: *Who are the primary characters in the DEI story?*

The third "P" is identifying the people who will be highlighted within the DEI story. To the greatest extent possible, include diverse characters in the story. Also consider which characters are the best representatives for the DEI story and which characters can best relate to the intended audience for the DEI story. If the story relates to addressing the challenges faced by people of color, then you will necessarily need to include Black, Hispanic, and/or Native American characters. At the same time, if your intended audience includes white men then it may also be beneficial to include a white male character, say, who served as an ally with people of color, with whom they can relate. Quantitative and qualitative data from your DEI assessment or DEI results can help pinpoint groups that are experiencing particular challenges or demonstrating noteworthy success. Permission should always be obtained to retell someone's experiences. Use pseudonyms when it is necessary or desired to protect their confidentiality, maintain their privacy, or ensure their anonymity.

Problem (Conflict)   Question: *What is the problem, conflict, or issue in the DEI story?*

DEI stories are often about solving the root causes of problems, resolving conflicts between people and groups, dismantling barriers, mitigating or eliminating inequities, and achieving equitable outcomes for all. The fourth "P," problem, prompts you to make clear the underlying issues that were sought to be addressed in the DEI story. These matters are often revealed from the quantitative and qualitative data found in your DEI assessment. For example, your personal DEI assessment results may have revealed a bias in favor of young people over the elderly, or your organizational DEI assessment results may have found a higher proportion of harassment toward women in the accounting department. Direct quotes, testimonials, and visuals are often especially helpful in clearly and effectively depicting challenges and opportunities.

Plot (Storyline) Question: *What are the main elements of the DEI story (i.e., the storyline)?*

Principles (Themes) Question: *What are the key themes and ideas you want the audience to take away from the DEI story (i.e., principles)?*

The storyline represents the essence of the DEI story. It outlines the premise, introduces the people, and explains the challenge or opportunity, eventually leading to purposeful resolution and/or insights that portray specific principles. The storyline artfully weaves together narrative and data to explain to the audience what happened including the premise, the challenge or opportunity, and resolution; the visuals and data to enlighten the audience to key insights (e.g., successes, failures, lessons learned, etc.); and narrative and visuals to engage the audience by presenting data displays.

The fifth "P," plot, and sixth "P," principles, are about crafting a compelling storyline that brings valuable principles to life. Principles are woven into the tapestry of the storyline. They represent the larger takeaways you hope the audience draws from the storyline that can inspire and motivate action and influence and drive change.

For example, a personal DEI storyline could chronicle your yearlong efforts to successfully increase your intercultural competence. The storyline could explain to your audience of family, friends, and colleagues how relocating to a new city with greater diversity presented new opportunities to explore cultural differences and motivated you to become more effective in navigating cultural differences as well as the number and nature of the books, articles, plays, travel, excursions, journal entries, and coaching sessions you completed (narrative and data). The storyline could engage your audience with reflections and visuals from your travel and excursions and your personal testimonial of the impact increased intercultural competence has had on you personally and professionally (narrative and visuals). The storyline could enlighten your audience by sharing the Intercultural Development Continuum™ (IDC™) and visually depicting the increase in your Intercultural Development Inventory® (IDI®) score from a developmental orientation score of 102 to 120 on the IDC®, which represents an improvement from "minimization" (i.e., you de-emphasize differences) to "acceptance" (i.e., you deeply comprehend differences) (visuals and data). Principles such as persistence, the benefits of stepping outside of one's comfort zone into their growth zone, and the value of deeply comprehending differences could be woven into the storyline, thus inspiring and motivating you to continue your journey and others to do the same.

For example, an organizational DEI storyline could explain to your audience of managers and supervisors throughout your organization how the organizational DEI assessment data revealed that people of color were underrepresented within the managerial and supervisory ranks with statistically significant differences in discrimination and a lack of mentorship, sponsorship, and visibility to new opportunities (narrative and data). It could further explain the purpose and number of participants in a formal mentoring program and an allyship training program to address these issues (narrative and data). The storyline could engage your audience with the personal stories and testimonials, including direct quotes, of both people of color and their mentors and allies that describe their experiences as participants in these various initiatives, as well as pictures from training sessions and an awards ceremony where certain participants were recognized as "DEI Champions" for their exemplary contributions (narrative and visuals). The storyline could enlighten your audience with charts and graphs showing increased representation of managers and supervisors of color and decreased incidents of discrimination over time (visuals and data). Embedded within the storyline could be principles such as fairness, the importance of creating a culture of inclusion and belonging, and equitable outcomes for all that could influence and drive greater change.

Packaging (Format)   Question: *How will you package the DEI story?*

Platform (Channels)   Question: *What are the most effective communications channels to distribute the DEI story?*

The seventh "P" of packaging determines the format for your DEI story and the eighth "P" determines the appropriate platforms to communicate it. There is a plethora of options along both lines. Format options include videos, newsletters, press releases, blogs, reports including annual reports, articles, marketing materials, talking points, speeches, advertisements, and more. Potential communications channels include direct e-mails, mass e-mails, social media, news media (wires, radio, television, print, digital), text messages, chat, intranets, websites, conferences, events, one-on-one or group meetings, in-person or virtual meetings, lunch-and-learns, retreats, and more. Of course, the key is to match the format to the channel and the channel to the audience. For example, a video posted on social media may be effective in reaching tech-savvy colleagues while a newsletter delivered via mass e-mails or an intranet may be effective in reaching others. Talking points and speeches delivered via meetings and town halls may be effective in reaching an internal audience of employees while a press release distributed through a website or newswire may be effective in reaching an external audience of stakeholders. Consider which format and channel are most likely to be effective in reaching your target audience.

Continuing the Five-Step Cycle of *Data-Driven DEI*

In conclusion, be mindful that you can tell your DEI story at every step along your DEI journey: after you've completed your assessment (**Step 1: DEI Inventory**), once you've established your objectives and goals (**Step 2: DEI Imperatives**), at the point when you have identified promising and proven practices (**Step 3: DEI Insights**) and arrived at strategies and measures (**Step 4: DEI Initiatives**) and, of course, when you have results to be shared (**Step 5: DEI Impact**). Whether you are sharing your DEI story in a 280-character post on social media among friends and family, or in an 80-page annual report that is widely distributed and released to the public, DEI is a never-ending journey, so DEI storytelling is a never-ending endeavor.

Visit **www.datadrivendei.com** to read several case studies—real-world DEI stories and examples of pioneering people and organizations that have embraced a data-driven approach to DEI and achieved measurable results.

Conclusion:
The Future of
Data-Driven DEI

Innovation is the introduction of something new . . .
   after you were born.

Nothing about us, without us.

Any book highlighting innovations runs the risk of quickly becoming outdated. In fact, the moment this book hits bookshelves the clock is already ticking that there will be a new concept, tool, technique, technology, model, methodology, program, platform, or approach that redefines the game for data-driven DEI. While I'm reasonably confident that the five-step cycle of *Data-Driven DEI* is sufficiently durable to stand a test of time, I humbly accept that certain innovations I have profiled will inevitably become obsolete (and therein lies the opportunity to write future editions of this book!).

Nonetheless, I conclude this edition by offering my thoughts on the future of *Data-Driven DEI* and, more specifically, a few thematic areas that will likely transform the landscape of *Data-Driven DEI*. While I highlight specific innovations, I also emphasize guiding principles to help you navigate whatever future lies ahead.

> Join the *Data-Driven DEI* movement by sharing your tools, metrics, promising and proven practices, and stories with others at **www.datadrivendei.com**.

DEI and Equitable Analytics™

At various points throughout this book, I have referenced Equitable Analytics™ and the Equitable Impact Platform™ (EquIP™), which is powered by geospatial Equitable Analytics™. Pioneered by Peter York, BCT's principal and chief data scientist, Equitable Analytics™ points to the future of *Data-Driven DEI* both methodologically and ideologically.

As a methodology, Equitable Analytics™ is an equitable solution for figuring out what works for whom or, stated differently, what "causes" a result or outcome for whom. Equitable Analytics™ is a part of what Judea Pearl, in his book *The Book of Why: The New Science of Cause and Effect*, refers to as the "the Causal Revolution," because the underlying concept of "what works" is cause and effect. Referring to our discussions in **Step 3: DEI Insights** about "What Works" models and in **Step 5: DEI Impact** about correlation vs. causation, "what works" does not equate to what is associated or correlated with a desired result or outcome, but rather, what *causes* a desired result or outcome. "Nowadays, thanks to carefully crafted causal models, contemporary scientists can address problems that would have once been considered unsolvable or even beyond the bale of scientific inquiry. . . . The mere mention of 'cause' or 'effect' would create a storm of objections in any reputable statistical journal," writes Pearl. Even two decades ago, asking a statistician questions like, "Does DEI training mitigate unconscious bias?" or "Do ERGs increase feelings of inclusion and belonging?" would have been like asking if she believed in voodoo, according to Pearl. He continues, "But today [we can] pose such questions routinely and answer them with mathematical precision. To me, this change is nothing short of a revolution. I dare to call it the Causal Revolution, a scientific shakeup that embraces rather than denies our innate cognitive gift of understanding cause and effect."[1]

Equitable Analytics™ uses BCT's Precision Modeling to build *causal models* that understand cause and effect for specific populations and accomplish this at a level of granularity that is more nuanced and more insightful than simply disaggregating data by demographics. While disaggregating data by demographics is a recommended and useful practice, we also know that our ability to understand what works for whom is insufficient when examined solely through a demographic lens. Equitable Analytics™ can provide deeper insights and will increasingly supplant disaggregating data by demographics alone (see Figure 6.1). According to Peter during a one-on-one conversation, "With the tools we now have available, we can make tailored and precise recommendations that predict a desired DEI outcome in the same way Netflix and Amazon can make a tailored and precise recommendation that predicts enjoyment from watching a specific movie or reading a specific book. This is revolutionizing DEI, social and community programs." Understanding the Equitable Analytics™ process helps you to fully understand its power.

FIGURE 6.1   The Equitable Analytics™ Process

Step 1: Determine the Focus of Analysis

The first step in the Equitable Analytics™ process is to determine the *focus of analysis* or the unit of the analysis. This breaks down to either *cases*, which includes people and groups of people, or *places*, which includes various geographic locations. More specifically, there are three choices for the unit of analysis:

1. **Individuals (Cases)**—Defined as individual contributors, managers, supervisors, executives, etc.
2. **Groups (Cases)**—Defined by departments, divisions, office locations, etc.
3. **Geographies (Places)**—A variation of Cases: Groups, defined as geographic locations including neighborhoods, communities, Census Tracts, ZIP codes, counties, and regions.

The focus of analysis determines the entity you desire to say something about. When Equitable Analytics™ is applied to cases, it helps determine and recommend the optimal mix of initiatives and strategies for individuals to improve personal DEI and for groups to improve organizational DEI. When Equitable Analytics™ is applied to places via EquIP™, it helps determine whether a community is receiving the locally accessible government support, philanthropic support, public contributions, social services programming, and volunteerism it needs to improve diversity, inclusiveness, and well-being, equitably, along with recommendations of the optimal mix.

Step 2: Build a Causal Logic Model

The second step in the Equitable Analytics™ process is to build a *causal logic model* for the desired outcome with stakeholder engagement. A logic model is a visual diagram depicting the causal assumptions. It uses directional arrows to represent the relationship between contextual factors and resources that best support the workplace experiences that lead to the greatest level of equitable outcomes for all employees. Think of your logic model as a visual diagram of your organization's hypotheses as to what it takes for every employee to succeed. This framework will guide the next steps of Precision Modeling.

For example, let's assume that a desired outcome for your organization is that every employee have an equitable opportunity to advance and be promoted to the management level. However, your organization has experienced challenges with equitably advancing and promoting Black women to the management level. To begin the Equitable Analytics™ process, a team comprised of DEI experts, HR professionals, and diverse colleagues who have had positive and negative experiences reaching the management level, would be engaged in building a causal logic model for advancement and promotion to the management level within your organization. The logic model could include variables such as the number and type of learning and development courses, number and location of departmental rotations, existence of mentorship and sponsorship relationships, and number and type of leadership development programs (see Figure 6.2).

FIGURE 6.2 Equitable Analytics™ Causal Logic Model

When it comes to diversity, equity, and inclusion, it is critically important *not* to assume that an employee's race, gender, sexual orientation, or other identity characteristics should causally affect their workforce experience. That would be antithetical to valuing DEI. So, your causal logic model should not include workplace context variables reflecting demographic characteristics such as race/ethnicity, gender, age, sexual orientation, disability status, and so forth, with arrows connecting them to one's workplace experience. For example, being a Black woman should not "cause" a different workplace experience, and therefore, demographic and identity variables (e.g., race/ethnicity, gender, age, disability status, etc.) should not be represented in your causal logic model with arrows that affect the workplace experience. In doing so, and recognizing that, unfortunately, it is often the case that demographic and identity variables are sometimes the reason people are selected (and not selected) for certain workplace experiences, such as mentorship and sponsorship, Equitable Analytics™ mitigates this selection bias by excluding these variables from the causal logic modeling (and subsequent Precision Modeling) process.

Instead, your causal logic model should incorporate identity into the outcome of promotion and advancement. Specifically, demographic and identity variables should be represented in your causal logic model as a part of the end result or outcome. For example, demographic and identity variables should be in your causal logic model as the effect of a positive workplace experience at the end of an arrow where your outcome statement states something like "Advancement and promotion of more Black women to management level."

Step 3: Develop an Analytical Framework

The third step in the Equitable Analytics™ process is to build an *analytical framework* that will serve as the instructions for conducting the data modeling. The key step in developing the analytical framework is to determine which variables in your administrative data (i.e., existing data in an HRIS, LMS, ERP, CRM, or other DEI-related data system) align with each of your workplace logic model components (i.e., context factors, experiences, and outcomes). For example, your workplace logic model will likely include contextual factors like employee educational background, position, and level. Your analytical framework will need to identify the specific variables in your administrative data that align with these logic model elements.

Step 4: Conduct Precision Modeling

The fourth step in the Equitable Analytics™ process is to conduct *Precision Modeling*, which includes the following two tasks:

1. Train machine learning algorithms to find *matched comparison groups* of employees based on sharing similar workplace contexts, like title, educational background, and level of authority/accountability. We all know that the pathways to promotion and advancement are different for different jobs and job contexts. Finding matched comparison groups based on these differences is the foundation of an equitable analytical framework. As noted previously, it is vital that these contextual factors *not* include demographic or identity variables as these should never be determinants of an employee receiving the ideal workplace experience.

   Continuing with the previous example, Equitable Analytics™ could find that there are nine matched comparison groups (refer to Figure 6.3) based on the workplace contextual factors that will affect their likelihood to experience what it takes to advance. Let's assume that matched comparison Group #2 is "project managers in the operations department with 3+ years of experience and a bachelor's degree." As you can see in Figure 6.3, the current success rate with advancing and promoting members of Group #2 to the management level is 55%, whereas the overall success rate across all groups is 61%.

2. Train machine learning algorithms to find and evaluate natural experiments within each matched comparison group. Organizational leaders, managers, and supervisors of similarly positioned employees don't make the same decisions regarding their promotion and advancement. These differences are like natural experiments, where some of the same types of employees get treated differently. The Equitable Analytics™ process applies machine learning algorithms to evaluate these natural experiments to determine what types of workplace experiences cause the greatest gains in promotion and advancement for each matched comparison group of employees.

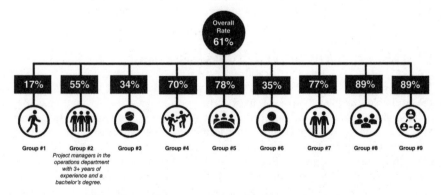

FIGURE 6.3 Equitable Analytics™ Matched Comparison Groups

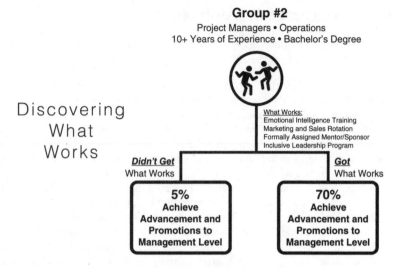

Group #2
Project Managers • Operations
10+ Years of Experience • Bachelor's Degree

Discovering
What
Works

What Works:
Emotional Intelligence Training
Marketing and Sales Rotation
Formally Assigned Mentor/Sponsor
Inclusive Leadership Program

Didn't Get
What Works

Got
What Works

| 5%
Achieve
Advancement and
Promotions to
Management Level | 70%
Achieve
Advancement and
Promotions to
Management Level |

FIGURE 6.4   Equitable Analytics™ Discovering What Works

Continuing the previous example, Equitable Analytics™ would determine the optimal mix of strategies—including learning and development courses, departmental rotations, mentorship/sponsorship relationships, leadership development programs, and the like—that maximize the likelihood of everyone in Group #2 advancing and being promoted to the management level. The analysis could reveal that an emotional intelligence course, a departmental rotation into marketing and sales, a formally assigned mentor/sponsor, and an inclusive leadership development program represent the most effective mix of strategies (i.e., what causes or "what works") for members of Group #2 to advance and be promoted to the management level. In fact, when people in this group receive what works, their success rate is 70%, and when people in this group do not receive what works, their success rate is only 5%, as shown in Figure 6.4.

Step 5: Perform an Equity Assessment

Once these determinations have been made of what works for whom, the fifth step in the Equitable Analytics™ process is to perform an *equity assessment* by putting demographic characteristics such as race/ethnicity, gender, age, disability status, and so forth, back into the algorithmic model to determine whether what works for a matched comparison group has been equitably administered, as shown in Figure 6.5. Continuing with the previous example, Equitable Analytics™ could look at all project managers in the operations department with 3+ years of experience and a bachelor's degree to determine if Black women have been equally as likely as white men to receive what works. As you can see in Figure 6.6, 65% of white men got what works while only 45% of Black women got what works within the same Group #2. Additionally, Equitable Analytics™ could identify which mentors/sponsors have been the most effective (and ineffective) in helping Black women to be promoted and advance to the

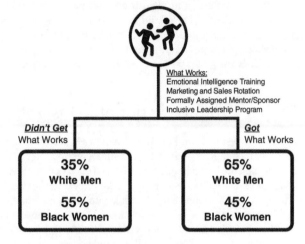

Group #2

Project Managers • Operations
10+ Years of Experience • Bachelor's Degree

Assessing
Equitable
Treatment

What Works:
Emotional Intelligence Training
Marketing and Sales Rotation
Formally Assigned Mentor/Sponsor
Inclusive Leadership Program

Didn't Get
What Works

Got
What Works

35% **White Men** **55%** **Black Women**	**65%** **White Men** **45%** **Black Women**

FIGURE 6.5   Equitable Analytics™ Assessing Equitable Treatment

management level. This offers very nuanced and powerful insights regarding exactly by whom and where inclusivity and allyship are enabling people to advance and exactly by whom and where bias or discrimination may be impeding advancement, which could lead to very targeted actions such as unconscious bias and conscious inclusion training.

Mitigating Algorithmic Bias   In addition to mitigating selection bias, Equitable Analytics™ also mitigates *algorithmic bias*. All too often, data scientists uphold predictive accuracy as the measuring stick for an effective algorithm, but it is not an equitable criterion. For example, an algorithm designed to predict who is the most ideal candidate to become the next CEO of a corporation, nonprofit organization, or private foundation will increase its accuracy by including race/ethnicity as a variable in the model. However, because the majority of CEOs are white men,[2] doing so would translate a race/ethnicity bias into an algorithmic bias that advantages certain groups and disadvantages other groups. Hypothetically speaking, based on historical data, the algorithm could predict with 99% accuracy that whites are the most probable selection to become CEOs. However, this would be due to the fact that prior successful CEOs were much more likely to be white as a result of historical racial biases. Once again, race/ethnicity should not be a factor in making this determination. If this hypothetical algorithm were then used to select candidates deemed to be most likely to become CEOs for a leadership development program, it would advantage whites and disadvantage people of color, much like the prior example of how Amazon's computer models translated a gender bias into an algorithmic bias that advantaged men and disadvantaged women seeking jobs. An algorithmic model that removes race/ethnicity would be less accurate; however, it would better reflect the *unbiased truth*, or representation of what is fair and equitable, that race/ethnicity should not predict who becomes a

CEO. By removing demographic variables as predictors of experiencing what it takes to succeed, the Equitable Analytics™ methodology mitigates the algorithmic biases that can result when demographic variables are included in the algorithmic modeling process, thus resulting in algorithms that prioritize the unbiased truth over predictive accuracy. Cathy O'Neil, author of *Weapons of Math Destruction: How Big Data Increases Inequality and Threatens Democracy*, advocates for such an approach when she writes, "But wait, many would say. Are we going to sacrifice the accuracy of the model for fairness? Do we have to dumb down our algorithms? In some cases, yes."[3]

Step 6: Produce Actionable Insights

Finally, the results from Equitable Analytics™ produce summaries of both the current success rate that is attributable to the strategies and interventions each person currently receives and the best possible success rate if each person received the strategies and interventions that work for their group. Put another way, the results present "counterfactual" findings of what happened when a group was and was not appropriately supported to experience what it takes to advance. Once you and your organization determine which strategies and interventions are feasible from among those recommended for each group, such as an emotional intelligence course and a formally assigned mentor/sponsor only for Group #2, Equitable Analytics™ offers a prediction of the success rate you can now anticipate for that group, as shown in Figure 6.6. The solid bar depicts the attributable success rate; the line marked with "X" depicts the best possible success rate if everyone received what works for their group; the gap between the two lines is a performance gap, or a gap between our current performance and our best possible performance given the strategies and interventions currently being offered and tracked. As you can see, if everyone in Group #2 received what works for their group, their

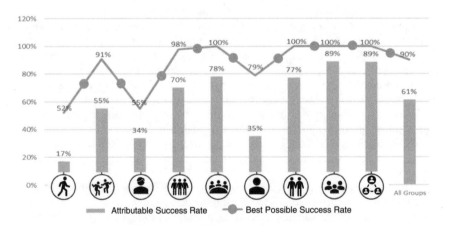

FIGURE 6.6   Equitable Analytics™ Results

success rate would increase from 55% to 91%. Equitable Analytics™ can automatically generate these and other actionable insights in reports and dashboards.

Methodologically, Equitable Analytics™ can be applied to any number of desired outcomes including identifying the mix of strategies to maximize inclusion and belonging, increase intercultural competence, and achieve equity for every employee to advance and be promoted to the executive level, and much more. Ideologically, as you can clearly see from the preceding description, Equitable Analytics™ also embraces and espouses several tenets that should guide the responsible use of data analytics in DEI including machine learning, NLP, and other branches of AI. They include:[4]

- **Causality: Understand What Causes, Not What is Correlated with a Desired Result or Outcome**—Determine the root cause and effect for specific people and not the "average" person.

- **Community: Ensure Diverse and Representative Stakeholder Engagement**—Engage diverse and representative stakeholders directly in the process of developing logic models, theories of change, analytical frameworks, and algorithmic models. This helps to ensure that efforts reflect the lived experiences and are centered on the voices of those stakeholders who are likely to be impacted and what they consider to be beneficial to their needs.

- **Equity: Remember, One Size Does Not Fit All**—Use data analytics to disaggregate overall populations into matched comparison groups based on unique backgrounds, histories, and contexts. Exclude variables that should not be a factor in determining whether someone receives a strategy or intervention. Build models that produce tailored recommendations to each group's needs, maximizing each person's probability of success.

- **Transparency: Choose Transparency over "Black Box" Opacity**—Do not build algorithmic models whose inner workings or underlying assumptions cannot be explained, examined, or interrogated. For example, avoid the use of "black box" algorithms such as neural networks and deep learning algorithms (discussed further in the next section) that learn from data without being able to show how their conclusions were derived.

- **Veracity: Seek the Unbiased Truth over Predictive Accuracy**—When developing algorithms, prioritize the unbiased truth—a representation of what is fair and equitable—over predictive accuracy, that can advantage certain groups and disadvantage other groups.

Based on these principles and its seven-step process, Equitable Analytics™ offers both an ideological and methodological vision for *a more precise* future of *Data-Driven DEI.*

DEI and Deep Learning

The term *neural networks* refers to a branch of machine learning that loosely mimics the biological neurons and learning processes of the human brain. Neural networks are comprised of a series of algorithms that learn by endeavoring to recognize patterns in data. Artificial neurons represent levels of abstraction or layers in the neural network that perform basic to increasingly more complex pattern recognition. For example, a neural network to identify the numbers 0 through 9 might begin with a layer that identifies pixels as black or white, and then pass this information on to a subsequent layer that identifies different lines and curves, and then pass this information on to a final layer that identifies each number by its unique combination of lines and curves.

Deep learning refers to a process by which a neural network seeks to identify patterns or solve a problem through a never-ending cycle of trial and error called "training" that strengthens its understanding of certain underlying relationships in data and weakens others leading to more complex understandings. The deeper the layers of the neural network, the deeper the learning. Deep learning has deep implications for the future of *Data-Driven DEI*. Before I share these implications, I will provide brief background on a specific and growing genre of deep learning programs, large language models (LLMs), that have the deepest implications.

Large Language Models

Large language models (LLMs) are trained on massive data sets using natural language processing (NLP) and natural language understanding (NLU) to strive toward *artificial general intelligence*, or the ability of machines to learn or understand general tasks performed by human beings (which is yet to be achieved). NLP is a branch of AI that deals with the structure of human language. NLU analyzes the syntactic and semantic elements of text to derive meaning. Combining the use NLP and NLU can help identify patterns and meaning in unstructured data (i.e., raw text and narratives), such as the internet and its vast library of content, including articles, blogs, and social media posts, that would be difficult for a human to find. Unstructured data often contains powerful patterns within nuanced context, but these patterns go unnoticed because it is difficult for humans to process and make meaning from large amounts of text data. This is where LLMs, NLP, and NLU can offer mind-blowing assistance.

Arguably, the most recognized LLM program is the Generative Pre-Trained Transformer (GPT)[5], and its associated chatbot, ChatGPT, by OpenAI, an AI research laboratory consisting of a for-profit and parent nonprofit, whose mission is to ensure that artificial general intelligence benefits all of humanity. GPT is currently the largest LLM program, trained on 45 TB of text, but there is a growing list of others including GPT-J, GPT-NeoX, DeepMind, Google's BERT (Bidirectional Encoder Representations from Transformers), Facebook's BART (Bidirectional Auto-Regressive Transformers), and DistilBERT, to name a few.

These programs have trained on content as vast as the internet (filtered), collections of digitized books, the entirety of Wikipedia, and more, to solve a single problem: predicting the next word in a text (you've experienced something comparable if your phone, computer, or search engine has offered suggestions to help complete a sentence while you are typing). The results are impressive to say the least.

LLM programs are able to produce original, coherent, often thoughtful, and well-written paragraphs of prose in response to simple prompts. For example, here is what GPT produced in response to my prompt, "Write an essay that compares and contrasts diversity, equity and inclusion with racial equity":

There are many ways to think about the relationship between diversity, equity and inclusion (DEI) and racial equity. Both DEI and racial equity are about ensuring that everyone has an opportunity to participate in and benefit from society. However, there are some important distinctions between the two.

DEI is about creating a society in which everyone can participate and feel included, regardless of their background. This includes things like making sure that people of all races, ethnicities, genders, sexual orientations, abilities and socioeconomic backgrounds have an equal opportunity to succeed.

Racial equity, on the other hand, is specifically about ensuring that people of all races have an equal opportunity to succeed. This includes things like addressing historical and current inequities that have put people of color at a disadvantage, as well as making sure that people of color have an equal voice in decisions that affect them.

Both DEI and racial equity are important for creating a just and fair society. However, racial equity is specifically focused on addressing the disparities that exist for people of color, while DEI is about creating an inclusive society for everyone.

I thought this was pretty good! Not only can GPT and other LLM programs create an essay in a fraction of a second, but they can produce an unlimited number of original essays in response to the same prompt (they can also produce poems, stories, computer code, and more), and the prompt can include more nuanced instructions such as a particular style or voice (i.e., "Write an essay . . . like a hip-hop song").

Large Language Models and DEI

LLMs will revolutionize DEI in several ways such as automatically, quickly, and accurately:

- Extracting key topics from large corpuses of documents via Automated Topic Modeling (ATM) based on Latent Dirichlet Allocation (LDA), a generative and statistical model of a collection of documents. This will aid significantly in extracting the key insights from libraries of DEI content such as articles, books, and reports.
- Coding and summarizing the themes from raw qualitative data such as IDI and focus group transcripts. This will make it considerably easier to incorporate qualitative data analysis into DEI assessment and evaluation.
- Converting text to different reading levels, styles, and tones. This will make DEI communications more broadly accessible to readers of various literacy abilities and preferences.
- Translating text in surveys, questionnaires, presentations, and reports into multiple languages, while capturing cultural nuances. This will make all DEI efforts more inclusive of different cultures.

- Generating reports, briefs, and executive summaries from DEI assessments and evaluations and tailoring them to different audiences. This will help amplify DEI storytelling.

With all of their power, potential, and promise, LLM programs, like all computer programs, must be governed and used in a proper ethical context that benefits humanity. This raises the question: What constitutes a benefit to humanity? In the *New York Times Magazine* article "A.I. is Mastering Language. Should We Trust What It Says?," Steven Johnson asks related and important questions such as, "How do we train them to be good citizens? How do we make them 'benefit humanity as a whole' when humanity itself can't agree on basic facts, much less core ethics and civic values?"[6] In the article, Tulsee Doshi of Google says that one of its principles is "making sure we're bringing in diversity of perspectives—so it's not just computer scientists sitting down and saying, 'This is our set of values.' How do we bring in sociology expertise? How do we bring in human rights and civil rights expertise? How do we bring in different cultural expertise, not just a Western perspective? And what we're trying to think through is how do we bring in expertise from outside the company. What would it look like to bring in community involvement? What would it look like to bring in other types of advisers?" While these are the right questions, the answers are yet to be found and must be vigorously sought after to safeguard the future of *Data-Driven DEI*.

Under Peter York's leadership, we have an ever-expanding range of experiences at BCT with deep learning including fine-tuning LLM programs and developing and training NLP and NLU models to accomplish the kinds of tasks described earlier. Perhaps more importantly, we fully understand the importance and obligation to include safeguards against the improper use of any machine learning techniques, including NLP and NLU. When analyzing text using LLM programs, it is important to be aware of potential biases that may be present in the data. We therefore espouse several guiding principles to monitor for bias when using these models:

- Ensure diverse and representative stakeholder engagement including *lived experience experts* who have personal, authentic, and first-hand experience within the context being modeled. This includes exposure to certain acts, experience with certain interventions (or lack thereof), and dealing with certain behaviors. As a result of these lived experiences, they are likely to produce richer insights and be more attuned to particular issues. For example, Listen4Good (listen4good.org) promotes high-quality listening and equity-driven feedback practices.

- Responsibly curate training data such that biased language and prejudiced views are not replicated.

- Examine the training/fine-tuning data for any patterns or trends that could indicate bias. This includes looking at the distribution of data points, as well as the values of any features that could be used to identify a particular group of people (e.g., gender, race, etc.).

- Pay close attention to the results of the model to look for any patterns or trends that could indicate bias.

- Compare the results of the model to other models that have been trained on similar data. This can help to identify any potential biases that may be present in the data.

- Use human evaluation (such as subject matter and lived experience expertise) to examine the results of the model. This can be done by having people manually label a subset of the data, and then comparing the results of the model to the human labels. This can help to identify any potential biases that may be present in the data.
- Conduct a traditional *algorithmic audit*, to confirm that the model is doing what it is intended to do scientifically using test cases, and what Dr. Joy Buolamwini, founder of the Algorithmic Justice League, defines as an *evocative audit*, to examine the impact of the model on people emotionally based on their feedback. This is "an approach to humanizing the negative impacts that can result from algorithmic systems,"[7] according to Dr. Buolamwini.

While I explicitly cautioned against the use of neural networks and deep learning algorithms in the previous section due to their lack of transparency—it is difficult to extract exactly how they do what they do—it's clear they are likely here to stay. Their proliferation must adhere to these principles. The diligence and rigor that is applied to training deep learning algorithms must be surpassed by the diligence and rigor of ensuring that myriad voices are reflected in how models are built, what is used for training data, and how the training takes place. This will signify more than just deep learning, but rather deep, *diverse, equitable, and inclusive* learning as the future of *Data-Driven DEI*.

DEI and Transparency/Ubiquity

Throughout this book, I've made repeated references to transparency as a guiding principle that engenders trust and sets the tone for an organizational DEI journey. Interestingly, a growing cadre of tools are no longer making transparency the exception but rather the norm by providing three types of insights:

1. **Personal Dynamics**—Tools such as Overtly and Atlas integrate directly with internal systems such as e-mail, calendars, chat, and other collaboration tools to examine patterns of collaboration and information sharing through a DEI lens. They can therefore leverage NLP, NLU, organizational network analysis (ONA), and interpretive visualizations to explore the nature of the interactions between people and informal networks within an organization. These tools can uncover personal dynamics such as who, how often, in what ways, and about what topics people interact with others (and who, how often, in what ways, and on what topics people do not interact with others), thus identifying personal preferences and biases at a much deeper level.

2. **Group Discussions and Decision Making**—Tools such as ThoughtExchange, Fishbowl, PopIn, and Converge enable large groups of people to have anonymous and simultaneous discussions about topics, thoughts, and ideas in a transparent and trusted place. These can also be used to crowdsource conversations on DEI initiatives such as giving, recruitment, outreach, and partnerships. They can empower voices and enable buy-in from the bottom up, thus leveraging input from hundreds and even thousands of people simultaneously. They also support some or all of the following features: peer-to-peer ratings that mitigate bias by

rating ideas on their merit and not who is sharing or endorsing them; transparent decision making, prioritization, and alignment; and organizing and ranking responses according to the most important thoughts and ideas using machine learning and other techniques.

3. **Organizational Dynamics**—Tools such as Comparably and Glassdoor are making organizational cultures, climates, and compensation visible to the public. In a similar manner to online customer ratings of products and services, these tools provide insight to organizational dynamics such as strengths, areas for improvement, institutional barriers, and inequities. In doing so, they facilitate greater transparency and can lead to greater accountability.

As these tools become more ubiquitous and it is less obvious that personal data is being collected, analyzed, publicized, and used to make decisions, it will become increasingly important that explicit prior permission (opt-in) is obtained from users for any data collection, so they can make informed decisions, and the data is collected in a safe and ethical way. For example, in Europe "consent must be freely given, specific, informed and unambiguous through a clear affirmative action, which means that pre-checked boxes or other types of implied consent is not sufficient. The recipient must also be told exactly how their data will be used. Senders must keep evidence of the consent and provide proof if challenged."[8] As another example, Streamlytics, a next-generation data ecosystem, provides "safe and ethical access to accurate consumer activity from all aspects of their lives." Data is currency. It has value. People must be fully informed about how their data is being used—how their currency is being spent—as we move toward *a more transparent* future of *Data-Driven DEI*.

DEI Integrated Platforms

At BCT, we envision and are working toward a future where a single platform can integrate all DEI functions such as assessment, planning, learning, development, reporting, evaluation, and more. The entire *Data-Driven DEI* five-step cycle will be captured:

- **Step 1: DEI Inventory**—Administer and/or upload the results of any individual and/or organizational DEI assessment, independent of the vendor.

- **Step 2: DEI Imperatives**—Capture and track the objectives and goals of any individual and/or organizational DEI program while leveraging a library of DEI metrics and KPIs.

- **Step 3: DEI Insights**—Access and library of individual and/or organizational DEI best practices and leverage Equitable Analytics™ to predict and prescribe what works for an individual, team, department, division, and so on, to optimize their desired outcomes.

- **Step 4: DEI Initiatives**—Capture and track the strategies and measures of any individual and/or organizational DEI program while leveraging a library of DEI metrics and KPIs.

- **Step 5: DEI Impact**—Manage data and generate reports, scorecards, and dashboards that gauge progress, determine impact, engender accountability, evaluate results, and generate findings for individuals and/or organizations and comprehensively demonstrate DEI outputs and outcomes.

In doing so, the DEI integrated platform will also centralize DEI data including assessment data, experience data, HR data, output data, and outcomes data, which often reside in disparate and siloed data systems such as an HRIS, ERP, CRM, and LMS. By integrating DEI functions and integrating DEI data, the platform will paint a hyper-personalized picture of DEI for people and a comprehensive picture of DEI for organizations: What is the optimal learning and development pathway for an individual to increase diversity? What are the optimal KSAs for an individual to foster inclusivity? What are the optimal activities such as mentorship, sponsorship, and allyship for an individual to foster equitable outcomes?

This vision is rooted in *the science of the individual* and the belief that, according to Todd Rose in *The End of Average: How We Succeed in a World That Values Sameness*,[9] "If we want a society where each of us has the same chance to live up to our full potential, then we must create professional, educational, and social institutions that are responsive to individuality." Rose espouses three guiding principles of individuality:

1. *The Jaggedness Principle*—Any meaningful human characteristic, including DEI preferences and competences, consists of multiple dimensions that are complex and jagged. To understand something that is jagged, we must apply multidimensional thinking.

2. *The Context Principle*—Individual behavior cannot be explained or understood apart from the context, situation, and circumstances of the individual. To understand a person, you must understand how they behave under context-specific circumstances.

3. *The Pathways Principle*—There is no single, "normal" pathway for any type of human learning and development. There are several, equally valid pathways, and individuality determines the unique and optimal pathway for any individual as well as the pace and sequence of that pathway.

As I've said before, organizations don't change. People change. These individual principles are therefore useful in guiding the future of *Data-Driven DEI* for both people and organizations. They also expand upon BCT's vision for a DEI integrated platform that will support personal and organizational transformation via a library of DEI learning journeys, Microcommitments, VR immersions, and more, that are all adaptive, personalized, and tailored to the unique preferences and competences of people and the unique people, practices, and policies of an organization.

There is a growing number of DEI integrated platforms that begin to approximate this vision including Kanarys, Mathison, Co:Census, GlobeSmart, OpenSesame, Blueprint Strategy Platform, Included.ai, MESH Diversity, and Emprising™, but none of them fully encompass all pieces of this futuristic puzzle. BCT has begun to bring this vision to reality through our Equitable Analytics™, which helps determine the optimal mix of strategies and interventions for individuals and/or organizations, our *Through My Eyes*™ VR immersions, and our partnerships with Rali's Change

Experience Platform (CxP), Intrinsic Inclusion™, and The Inclusion Habit®. Together, they provide an integrated suite of methods and features that can optimize personal and organizational impact by applying multi-dimensional thinking, context-specific understanding, and a unique pace and sequence for DEI pathways and journeys that represent the future of *individualized Data-Driven DEI*.

DEI and DNA

Throughout this book, I have tried to show how data can be used in an efficient, effective, and ethical way along with the tools and metrics to improve your personal and organizational DEI journey. In addition to five specific steps and a plethora of tools and metrics, I have outlined several principles to guide the present and safeguard the future of *Data-Driven DEI*. With this roadmap as both an anchor for grounding and a compass for guidance, I place my hope in what lies before us, and I place my faith in what lies within us.

As I stated in the introduction, our world is increasingly comprised of "communities of the like-minded." Far too often, we surround ourselves and associate with people who are like us—people who share the same values, beliefs, race/ethnicity, religion, socioeconomic status, political affiliation, and other identifiers, as ourselves. As a result, we are increasingly less likely to befriend people who are not like us, which only leads to greater division and misunderstanding. DEI represents a unique and unparalleled opportunity to break down the walls that can separate us in our personal lives, within our organizations, and throughout our society. While I firmly believe that *Data-Driven DEI* is a means to these ends, I once again acknowledge that data is not a panacea to DEI; it is simply a tool. What ultimately makes the difference is you and the intentional steps you take to move beyond your comfort zone into your growth zone; be a bridge between people that would otherwise remain separated; and get comfortable with being uncomfortable. The true solution to a better tomorrow is what lies within you today.

I have often said to people that the ultimate objective is to make DEI a part of your DNA. In other words, your overarching aim is that the five-step, never-ending, continuous cycle of *Data-Driven DEI* becomes a natural part of who you are and what you do. Inasmuch as DNA is the hereditary materials in humans, I now say to people that the ultimate objective is to also make our DNA a part of DEI. In other words, our overarching aim is that our humanity, empathy, and service to one another remain first and foremost and are fully embedded in any DEI tools and techniques, methodologies and technologies, platforms and programs, and deep learning algorithms and databases. That is, a future of DEI that is certainly driven by data, but is fundamentally centered on love, benefits all of humanity, and unites us as a people.

Notes

Introduction

1. https://deming.org/myth-if-you-cant-measure-it-you-cant-manage-it/
2. Homi Kharas, "The Emerging Middle Class in Developing Countries," OECD Development Centre, working paper no. 285 (2010), p. 27, http://www.oecd.org/dev/44457738.pdf
3. https://cis.org/Report/One-Five-US-Residents-Speaks-Foreign-Language-Home-Record-618-million
4. https://www.worldatlas.com/articles/the-fastest-growing-religions-in-the-world.html
5. Boston Consulting Group, "The Readiness Gap: Most Innovative Companies 2021" (2021), p. 1, https://www.bcg.com/publications/2021/overcoming-the-readiness-gap
6. Ibid.
7. https://www2.deloitte.com/content/dam/Deloitte/au/Documents/human-capital/deloitte-au-hc-six-signature-traits-inclusive-leadership-020516.pdf
8. https://www.glassdoor.com/employers/blog/diversity-inclusion-workplace-survey/
9. https://www.nielsen.com/us/en/press-releases/2019/african-american-spending-power-demands-that-marketers-show-more-love-and-support-for-black-culture/
10. https://www.changeboard.com/article-details/15981/keeping-diversity-and-inclusion-at-the-top-of-the-agenda/
11. https://www2.deloitte.com/us/en/insights/focus/human-capital-trends/2020/creating-a-culture-of-belonging.html
12. https://www.betterup.com/press/betterups-new-industry-leading-research-shows-companies-that-fail-at-belonging-lose-tens-of-millions-in-revenue
13. https://www.forbes.com/sites/eriklarson/2017/09/21/new-research-diversity-inclusion-better-decision-making-at-work/?sh=2fe75a294cbf
14. https://www.bcg.com/publications/2017/people-organization-leadership-talent-innovation-through-diversity-mix-that-matters
15. The Millennium Poll on Corporate Social Responsibility: Global Public Opinion on the Changing Role of Companies, Environics International Ltd.: December 1999, https://globescan.com/wp-content/uploads/2018/01/GlobeScan_MillenniumPoll_1999_FullReport.pdf
16. https://www.nielsen.com/us/en/press-releases/2019/african-american-spending-power-demands-that-marketers-show-more-love-and-support-for-black-culture/
17. https://www.mckinsey.com/featured-insights/diversity-and-inclusion/diversity-wins-how-inclusion-matters (Exhibit 1).
18. https://www.mckinsey.com/business-functions/people-and-organizational-performance/our-insights/why-diversity-matters
19. Chimamanda Ngozi Adichie, *We Should All Be Feminists* (Vintage Books, 2014), p. 46.
20. https://www2.deloitte.com/us/en/insights/topics/talent/six-signature-traits-of-inclusive-leadership.html
21. https://sph.umich.edu/pursuit/2018posts/social-relationship-diversity-important-in-aging-112118.html
22. https://inclusive.princeton.edu/sites/inclusive/files/pu-report-diversity-outcomes.pdf
23. https://www.forbes.com/sites/kourtneywhitehead/2019/06/27/why-building-diverse-friendships-improves-your-career/?sh=20084e126d21
24. https://sph.umich.edu/pursuit/2018posts/social-relationship-diversity-important-in-aging-112118.html
25. https://jbam.scholasticahq.com/api/v1/attachments/1962/download
26. http://www.orgnet.com/MCO.html

27. https://www.publiclandsalliance.org/what-we-do/jedi
28. https://www.whitehouse.gov/briefing-room/presidential-actions/2021/06/25/executive-order-on-diversity-equity-inclusion-and-accessibility-in-the-federal-workforce/

Step 0: DEI Incentives—Self-Reflect and Introspect

1. Stephen R. Covey, A. Roger Merrill, and Rebecca R. Merrill, *First Things First: To Live, to Love, to Learn, to Leave a Legacy* (Free Press, 2003), 107.
2. https://blog.ongig.com/diversity-and-inclusion/diversity-mission-statement/

Step 1: DEI Inventory for People—Seek Understanding

1. https://www.thinkherrmann.com/hubfs/CP_Site/HBDI_and_Whole_Brain_Thinking_FAQ.pdf
2. Sondra Thiederman, *3 Keys to Defeating Unconscious Bias: Watch, Think, Act* (San Diego, CA: Cross-Cultural Communications, 2015).
3. Daniel Kahneman, *Thinking, Fast and Slow* (New York: Farrar, Straus and Giroux, 2013).
4. Myriam Callegarin, "Three Things You Should Know About How the Brain Works," LinkedIn Pulse, December 4, 2015.
5. https://www.pnas.org/content/116/26/12590
6. https://implicit.harvard.edu/implicit/education.html
7. https://implicit.harvard.edu/implicit/aboutus.html
8. N. Herrmann, *The Creative Brain* (Lake Lure, NC: Ned Herrmann/Brain Books, 1989).
9. http://paei.wikidot.com/herrmann-ned-brain-dominance-instrument
10. J.B. Reid and V.R. Brown, *Intrinsic Inclusion: Rebooting Your Biased Brain* (Cincinnati, OH: New Phoenix Publishing, 2021).
11. J. B. Reid, "Neuroscience of Bias," Chrysalis Coalition (2022).
12. https://idiinventory.com/products/
13. M. R. Hammer, "The Intercultural Development Inventory® (IDI v5)" (Olney, MD: IDI, LLC, 2016).
14. M. R. Hammer, "The Intercultural Development Inventory® (IDI®) Resource Guide" (Olney, MD: IDI, LLC, 2020).
15. https://asi.dlplummer.com/understanding-your-score
16. J. N. Hook, D. E. Davis, J. Owen, E. L. Worthington Jr., and S. O. Utsey, "Cultural Humility: Measuring Openness to Culturally Diverse Clients." *Journal of Counseling Psychology* 60, no. 3 (2013), 353.
17. https://www.reuters.com/article/us-amazon-com-jobs-automation-insight/amazon-scraps-secret-ai-recruiting-tool-that-showed-bias-against-women-idUSKCN1MK08G
18. https://icsinventory.com/ics-inventory/why-using-the-ics-inventory-is-best-option
19. C. Rudolph, E. Toomey, and B. Baltes. "Considering Age Diversity in Recruitment and Selection: An Expanded Work Lifespan View of Age Management," in *The Palgrave Handbook of Age Diversity and Work*, edited by J. McCarthy and E. Parry (Palgrave-Macmillan, 2016), 626–628.

Step 1: DEI Inventory for Organizations—Seek Understanding

1. https://lattice.com/library/7-tips-for-conducting-your-next-de-i-survey
2. https://centreforglobalinclusion.org/
3. R. Krueger and M. Casey, *Focus Groups: A Practical Guide for Applied Research,* 5th ed. (Thousand Oaks, CA: Sage Publications, 2015).
4. https://www.verywellmind.com/parroting-therapeutic-use-2671631
5. https://lattice.com/library/7-tips-for-conducting-your-next-de-i-survey

Step 2: DEI Imperatives—Determine Priorities

1. https://eric.ed.gov/?id=EJ997652
2. https://www.koan.co/okr-examples/diversity-inclusion
3. https://firststartpartnerships.org/wp-content/uploads/planning-topic-1.pdf
4. https://blog.ongig.com/diversity-and-inclusion/diversity-goals/
5. https://diversity.sf.ucdavis.edu/about/strategic-plan/goals-and-objectives#Goal%204
6. https://diversity.rutgers.edu/diversity_priorities
7. https://www.managementcenter.org/resources/smart-to-smartie-embed-inclusion-equity-goals/
8. https://www.managementcenter.org/resources/smartie-goals-worksheet/
9. Marianne Bertrand and Sendhil Mullainathan, "Are Emily and Greg More Employable than Lakisha and Jamal? Field Experiment on Labor Market Discrimination," *American Economic Review* 94 (2004): 991.
10. https://www.cdc.gov/reproductivehealth/maternal-mortality/disparities-pregnancy-related-deaths/infographic.html
11. "Orchestrating Impartiality: The Impact of 'Blind' Auditions on Female Musicians," *American Economic Review* 94 (2000): 715.
12. https://www.klipfolio.com/blog/kpi-metric-measure
13. https://www.klipfolio.com/blog/kpi-metric-measure
14. https://bernardmarr.com/what-is-a-leading-and-a-lagging-indicator-and-why-you-need-to-understand-the-difference/
15. https://medium.com/aleria/diversity-is-a-lagging-measure-of-inclusion-b8dfa4d01059
16. https://blog.ongig.com/diversity-and-inclusion/diversity-goals/
17. https://corporate.mcdonalds.com/corpmcd/our-purpose-and-impact/jobs-inclusion-and-empowerment/diversity-and-inclusion.html
18. https://blogs.duanemorris.com/esg/tag/dei/
19. https://diversity.sf.ucdavis.edu/about/strategic-plan/goals-and-objectives#Goal%204
20. https://www.redcross.org/tiffany-circle-source/about-tiffany-circle/strategic-plan.html

Step 3: DEI Insights—Identify "What Works"

1. Definition from HelpGuide.org.
2. M.M Kaplan, E. Sabin, and S. Smaller-Swift, "The Catalyst Guide to Employee Resource Groups, 1-Introduction to ERGs" (2009), www.catalyst.org/knowledge/catalyst-guide-employee-resource-groups-1-introduction-ergs (accessed January 7, 2015).

Step 4: DEI Initiatives—Take Action

1. https://www2.trainingindustry.com/Deconstructing_70-20-10
2. Adapted from https://cft.vanderbilt.edu/guides-sub-pages/setting-up-and-facilitating-group-work-using-cooperative-learning-groups-effectively/
3. https://www.psychologytoday.com/us/blog/the-social-brain/201803/can-t-we-all-just-get-along-time-inclusion-diversity (March 14, 2018); https://www.psychologytoday.com/us/blog/the-social-brain/201807/the-potential-intrinsic-inclusion (July 24, 2018); https://www.psychologytoday.com/us/blog/the-social-brain/201809/new-approach-diversity-and-inclusion (September 6, 2018); and https://www.psychologytoday.com/us/blog/the-social-brain/201811/new-path-diversity-and-inclusion (November 27, 2018).

Step 5: DEI Impact—Evaluate Results

1. https://www.ntaskmanager.com/blog/goal-tracking-apps/
2. https://nationalequityatlas.org/lab/get-started-data-visualization
3. https://depictdatastudio.com/how-to-visualize-qualitative-data/
4. https://static.reuters.com/resources/media/editorial/20210405/DiversityReportApril2021.pdf
5. https://ssir.org/articles/entry/are_your_data_visualizations_racist
6. http://web-accessibility.carnegiemuseums.org/design/color/
7. https://alpine-consulting.com/blog/508-compliance-and-tableau/
8. https://www.urban.org/research/publication/do-no-harm-guide-applying-equity-awareness-data-visualization
9. https://www.thinkherrmann.com/hubfs/CP_Site/HBDI_and_Whole_Brain_Thinking_FAQ.pdf
10. Phillippa Lally, Cornelia H. M. van Jaarsveld, Henry W. W. Potts, and Jane Wardle, "How Are Habits Formed: Modelling Habit Formation in the Real World," *European Journal of Social Psychology*, July 16, 2009.
11. https://hbr.org/2012/11/how-to-master-a-new-skill
12. https://iveybusinessjournal.com/publication/fast-forward-a-new-framework-for-rapid-organizational-change/
13. https://iveybusinessjournal.com/publication/fast-forward-a-new-framework-for-rapid-organizational-change/
14. https://www.abs.gov.au/websitedbs/D3310114.nsf/home/statistical+language+-+correlation+and+causation

15. https://www.ted.com/talks/chimamanda_ngozi_adichie_the_danger_of_a_single_story?language=en
16. https://maorilandfilm.co.nz/chimamanda-ngozi-adichie-the-danger-of-a-single-story/
17. https://www.forbes.com/sites/brentdykes/2016/03/31/data-storytelling-the-essential-data-science-skill-everyone-needs/?sh=61ac6e8152ad
18. http://eimpact.report/blog/18/01/09/the-neuroscience-of-data-storytelling.html
19. https://martech.org/storytelling-action-brands-need-tell-complete-story/
20. https://www.forbes.com/sites/brentdykes/2016/03/31/data-storytelling-the-essential-data-science-skill-everyone-needs/?sh=61ac6e8152ad

Conclusion: The Future of
Data-Driven DEI

1. Judea Pearl, *The Book of Why: The New Science of Cause and Effect* (New York: Basic Books, 2018).
2. https://whorulesamerica.ucsc.edu/power/diversity_update_2020.html
3. Cathy O'Neil, *Weapons of Math Destruction: How Big Data Increases Inequality and Threatens Democracy* (New York: Broadway Books, 2016).
4. Peter York, *Unlocking Real-Time Evidence for Practitioners: How Evaluation and Data Analytics Are Generating On-Demand, Actionable Evidence for Front-Line Practitioners at First Place for Youth and Gemma Services* (Project Evident and the Bill and Melinda Gates Foundation, 2021).
5. As of this publication, the latest version is GPT-3.
6. https://www.nytimes.com/2022/04/15/magazine/ai-language.html
7. https://www.media.mit.edu/events/joy-buolamwini-defense/
8. https://www.lsoft.com/resources/optinlaws.asp
9. Todd Ross, *The End of Average: How We Succeed in a World That Values Sameness* (New York: HarperOne, 2016).

About the Author

D r. Randal Pinkett has established himself as an entrepreneur, innovator, speaker, author, media personality, scholar and DEI expert who is leading the way in business, technology, data and equity for all. A highly sought-after DEI trainer, facilitator, and global strategist for corporations, colleges and universities, government agencies, foundations, faith-based institutions, nonprofit and community organizations, he has over 30 years of experience in organizational development, leadership and management, and cultural transformation.

Dr. Pinkett is the co-founder, chairman, and CEO of his fifth venture, BCT Partners, a multimillion-dollar research, training, consulting, technology, and data analytics firm headquartered in Newark, New Jersey. BCT's mission is to harness the power of diversity, insights, and innovation to transform lives, accelerate equity, and create lasting change. BCT is a global leader in helping organizations make better decisions, improve outcomes, and amplify their impact toward a more equitable society. The company offers a full range of DEI services and solutions including DEI assessment, strategy, planning, learning and development, as well as the DEI Workforce and Workplace Assessment™ (DWWA™) which assesses organizational culture and climate through a DEI lens; *Through My Eyes*™ Virtual Reality (VR), which is a series of immersions that foster human understanding and empathy; Equitable Analytics™, a disruptive approach that uses Precision Modeling and machine learning to more precisely identify what types of programs, treatments, and/or interventions are most likely to work and for whom; the Equitable Impact Platform™ (EquIP™), a big data platform built to assess, evaluate, and study the interrelationship between diversity, inclusiveness, community well-being, and equity in communities; The Inclusion Habit™, a mobile-friendly behavior change platform replete with a library of Micro-commitments that lead to specific inclusive behaviors and create inclusive habits; and Rali, a comprehensive Change Experience Platform (CxP) built on a human-centered approach to behavior change—a comprehensive suite of communications, structured journeys, and interactive media capabilities that shape culture for initiatives that matter. BCT has been recognized by *Forbes* as one of America's Best Management Consulting Firms, Ernst & Young as EY Entrepreneur of the Year, and *Manage HR Magazine* as a Top 10 Company for Diversity & Inclusion, and has been named to the *Black Enterprise* BE100s list of the nation's largest African American–owned businesses, and the *Inc.* 5000 list of the fastest-growing private companies in America.

A former Rhodes Scholar who has been recognized by *USA TODAY* as one of the top 20 scholars in the country, Dr. Pinkett is the co-author of *Black Faces in White Places* and *Black Faces in High Places* and the author of *Campus CEO* and *No-Money Down CEO*. A regular contributor on MSNBC, CNN, and Fox Business News, he is the producer of the YouTube video "Candid Conversations with a Black Businessman: 7 Myths of Racial Equity." Dr. Pinkett is an Intercultural Development Inventory® (IDI®) Qualified Administrator, Herrmann Brain Dominance Instrument® (HBDI®) Certified Practitioner, High Performance Learning Journey® (HPLJ) Certified Champion, Intrinsic Inclusion™ Certified Facilitator, and official reference for the Global Diversity, Equity & Inclusion Benchmarks (GDEIB). Most notably, he was the first and only African American to receive the prestigious Rhodes Scholarship at Rutgers University and he was inducted into the Academic All-America Hall of Fame as a former high jumper, long jumper, sprinter, and captain of the men's track and field team. Dr. Pinkett holds five academic degrees including a BS in electrical engineering from Rutgers University, an MS in computer science from the University of Oxford in England, an MS in electrical engineering from the MIT School of Engineering, an MBA from the MIT Sloan School of Management, and a PhD from the MIT Media Laboratory.

Index

Page numbers followed by *f* and *t* refer to figures and tables, respectively.